Sydney Shoemaker is one of th
writing on philosophy of minc
lection deal with the way in w
the nature of those mental states of which we have our most direct conscious awareness.

Professor Shoemaker opposes the "inner sense" conception of introspective self-knowledge. He defends the view that perceptual and sensory states have nonrepresentational features – "qualia" – that determine what it is like to have them. Amongst the other topics covered are the unity of consciousness, and the idea that the "first-person perspective" gives a privileged route to philosophical understanding of the nature of mind.

This major collection is sure to prove invaluable to all advanced students of the philosophy of mind and cognitive science.

CAMBRIDGE STUDIES IN PHILOSOPHY

The first-person perspective and other essays

CAMBRIDGE STUDIES IN PHILOSOPHY

General editor ERNEST SOSA, Brown University

Advisory editors JONATHAN DANCY, University of Keele,
JOHN HALDANE, University of St. Andrews, GILBERT HARMAN,
Princeton University, FRANK JACKSON, Australian National University,
WILLIAM G. LYCAN, University of North Carolina at Chapel Hill,
SYDNEY SHOEMAKER, Cornell University, JUDITH THOMSON,
Massachusetts Institute of Technology

RECENT TITLES

The first-person perspective and other essays

Sydney Shoemaker

Cornell University

CAMBRIDGE
UNIVERSITY PRESS

Published by the Press Syndicate of the University of Cambridge
The Pitt Building, Trumpington Street, Cambridge CB2 1RP
40 West 20th Street, New York, NY 10011-4211, USA
10 Stamford Road, Oakleigh, Melbourne 3166, Australia

First published 1996

Printed in the United States of America

Library of Congress Cataloging-in-Publication Data

Shoemaker, Sydney.
 The first-person perspective ; and other essays / Sydney
Shoemaker.
  p.   cm. – (Cambridge studies in philosophy)
 Most essays previously published.
 ISBN 0-521-56030-6. – ISBN 0-521-56871-4 (pbk.)
 1. Philosophy of mind.   2. Self (Philosophy)   3. Consciousness.
4. Perspective (Philosophy)   I. Title.   II. Series.
BD418.3.S54   1996
128'.2—dc20   96-7931
                                                   CIP

A catalog record for this book is available from the British Library

ISBN 0-521-56030-6 hardback
ISBN 0-521-56871-4 paperback

For Norman Kretzmann

Contents

Preface

This volume brings together my recent work in the philosophy of mind. All of the essays were completed within the last ten years, although "On Knowing One's Own Mind" is a descendant of an essay I first presented in 1981. All except two have been previously published, the exceptions being "Intrasubjective/Intersubjective" and "Unity of Consciousness and Consciousness of Unity." The version of "Moore's Paradox and Self-Knowledge" included here is a substantial revision of the previously published version. Only very minor changes have been made in the other essays, although in some cases new notes have been added.

While all of the essays in the volume deal in one way or other with "the first-person perspective," the title essay, as distinct from its title, is in some ways unrepresentative of the collection as a whole. It is concerned with the idea that what we can conceive or imagine from the first-person perspective is revealing about the nature of mental phenomena in a way in which what we can conceive or imagine in other ways is not; and since it is critical of that idea, it might be seen as downplaying the philosophical importance of the first-person perspective. But as I say in that essay, I have always held that an essential part of the philosophical task is to give an account of mind that makes intelligible the perspective mental subjects have on their own mental lives. And the other essays in the collection are devoted to this task.

One part of the task is the elucidation of the distinctive sort of knowledge people have of their own mental states. And the nature of this self-knowledge, and the self-reference involved in it, is one of the two central topics discussed in these essays. Here I oppose an "inner sense" model of introspective self-knowledge, and defend the view that the mental states of which we have such self-knowledge are constitutively "self-intimating." In functionalist terms – and the essays in this volume are basically functionalist in orientation – my concern is to show that, and how, the first-person accessibility of these mental states is a consequence of the functional roles that constitute their natures. These themes are first developed in "Introspection and the Self," "On Knowing One's Own Mind," and "First-Person Access," and are further developed in the first and second Royce lectures and in "Moore's Paradox and Self-Knowledge."

The second central topic in these essays is the nature of perceptual experience and sensory states. If there is anything to which we have a distinctive first-person access, it is the "phenomenal character" of such states, or, in Nagelian terms, "what it is like" to have them. A crucial question here is whether, as held by "intentionalists" like Gilbert Harman, the introspectible features of such states are limited to intentional or representational properties (being "as of red," for example), or whether they include as well nonrepresentational features, "qualia," which bestow on them a "qualitative character" that in some way underlies or grounds their representational features. In previous writings I have defended the view that there are qualia, and have been concerned to show that their existence is compatible with functionalism. In several of the essays in the present volume – "Qualities and Qualia: What's In the Mind?", "Qualia and Consciousness," and the third Royce lecture – my concern is to show how the view that there are (and must be) qualia can accommodate the intuitions that support the intentionalist view. The issues discussed here intersect with ones about the nature of color and other secondary qualities. "Intrasubjective/Intersubjective" buttresses the case for qualia and answers objections (including one by me) to my earlier arguments for them.

"Unity of Consciousness and Consciousness of Unity" is concerned with issues about the relation between mental unity and our awareness of mental unity. Some of these issues are also addressed, from a very different direction, in "The First-Person Perspective."

There is some overlap between the essays in this collection – one argument occurs no less than three times! And, to make up for that, there are inconsistencies between them. My views on these issues have been evolving, hopefully in the right direction, and this is reflected in differences between the earlier and later essays in the collection. The main instance of this is in the treatment of our awareness of qualia; the most recent treatment, in the third Royce lecture, is rather closer to the intentionalist view than the earlier treatments – to such an extent that some "qualiaphiles" may think that I have sold out to the enemy.

Some of the work represented here was done while I was a Fellow during 1987–1988 at the National Humanities Center in North Carolina, supported by a Guggenheim fellowship, a fellowship from the Center, and a sabbatic leave from Cornell. I wish to express my warm thanks to the National Humanities Center, to the John Simon Guggenheim

Foundation, and to Cornell University for this support. "First-Person Access" was written for a conference in Moscow, Russia, sponsored by the IREX foundation; "Qualia and Consciousness" was written for a conference at Bielefeld University, Germany, and a predecessor of the second Royce Lecture was written for a conference in London sponsored by CIBA; thanks are therefore due to those institutions. I am also grateful to the many friends, colleagues, and students who have given me comments, criticisms, and advice on one or another of the essays. These include William Alston, Kent Bach, Simon Blackburn, Ned Block, Paul Boghossian, Earl Conee, Mark Crimmins, Dan Dennett, Jennifer Dworkin, Carl Ginet, Gilbert Harman, Chris Hill, Jaegwon Kim, Hilary Kornblith, Norman Kretzmann, William Lycan, Richard Miller, Richard Moran, Ulrich Neisser, Dave Robb, Susanna Siegel, Ernest Sosa, Bill Taschek, Michael Tye, David Velleman, Allen Wood, and Steve Yablo. I am especially grateful to Ernie Sosa, general editor of the Cambridge Studies in Philosophy series, for his encouragement and advice.

An earlier version of "Moore's Paradox and Self-Knowledge" was read at a colloquium in honor of Norman Kretzmann, held at Cornell University in December of 1994. Although that version was already on its way to being in print, that occasion stimulated me to rethink the essay, and to revise it into what I think is a substantial improvement on the previously published version. But that is the very least of my debt to Norman Kretzmann. I dedicate this book to him, in gratitude for his warm friendship and his wise counsel over many years.

Sources

"Introspection and the Self," *Midwest Studies in Philosophy*, X (1986), 101–120. Reprinted by permission of *Midwest Studies in Philosophy*.

"On Knowing One's Own Mind," *Philosophical Perspectives, 2, Epistemology* (1988); 183–209, ed. James E. Tomberlin (copyright by Ridgeview Publishing Co., Atascadero, Cal.). Reprinted by permission of Ridgeview Publishing Co..

"First Person Access," *Philosophical Perspectives, 4, Action Theory and Philosophy of Mind* (1990, 187–214, ed. James E. Tomberlin (copyright by Ridgeview Publishing Co., Atascadero, Cal.). Reprinted by permission of Ridgeview Publishing Co.

"Moore's Paradox and Self-Knowledge," *Philosophical Studies* 77 (1995), 211–228. Reprinted (with revisions) by permission of *Philosophical Studies*.

"Qualities and Qualia: What's in the Mind?", *Philosophy and Phenomenological Research*, 50, Supplement (1990), 109–131. Reprinted by permission of *Philosophy and Phenomenological Research*.

"Qualia and Consciousness," *Mind*, 100 (1991), 507–524. Reprinted by permission of *Mind*.

"The First-Person Perspective," *Proceedings and Addresses of the American Philosophical Association* 68 (1994), 7–22. Reprinted by permission of the American Philosophical Association.

"Self-Knowledge and 'Inner-Sense,'" *Philosophy and Phenomenological Research*, LIV (1994), 249–314. Reprinted by permission of *Philosophy and Phenomenological Research*.

The first-person perspective and other essays

PART I

Self-knowledge

1

Introspection and the self

Few passages in philosophy are better known than David Hume's denial that there is introspective awareness of a self or mental subject: "For my part, when I enter most intimately into what I call *myself*, I always stumble on some particular perception or other, of heat or cold, light or shade, love or hatred, pain or pleasure. I never can catch myself at any time without a perception, and never can observe anything but the perception."[1] Hume's denial has been repeated by philosophers as different as Kant and Wittgenstein and has commanded the assent of the majority of subsequent philosophers who have addressed the issue. And it has been widely seen as having important implications concerning the nature of the self and the nature of self-knowledge and self-reference. Some have followed Hume in concluding that a self is "no more than a bundle or collection of different perceptions," or, in more recent versions of the view, that it is a "logical construction" out of experiences and other mental particulars. Some have taken the Humean denial to support the Lichtenbergian view, which has had the endorsement of Wittgenstein and more recently of Elizabeth Anscombe, that the word "I" does not refer. And many have taken it to undermine Cartesian dualism. A recent expression of this last assessment is Saul Kripke's observation in *Naming and Necessity* that "Descartes' notion seems to me to have been rendered dubious ever since Hume's critique of a Cartesian self."[2] In a more recent work, Kripke has argued that the Humean denial is one of the things that underlies Wittgenstein's rejection of the idea that we imagine the sensations of others on the model of our own.[3]

But despite the intuitive appeal of Hume's denial, it is far from clear what its basis is, what exactly it means, or what its philosophical implications are. On the face of it, the basis is empirical; Hume looks within for a self and finds only particular perceptions. But Hume's denial that he is

My thanks to William Alston for very helpful comments.
1 Hume 1888, 252.
2 Kripke 1980, n. 77.
3 Kripke 1982.

3

aware of a self can hardly have the same basis as my present well-founded denial that I see a teakettle. The latter denial is well founded only on the assumption that I have some idea of what it would be like to see a teakettle. Hume, on the other hand, is quite emphatic on the point that he has no idea of "self" (*qua* subject of experiences) and so, presumably, no idea of what it would be like to introspect one. And while many who find Hume's denial credible would not agree with his claim that we have no idea of "self," I think that most of them would admit no more than he would to a conception of what it would be like to confront a self as an object of introspection. First appearances notwithstanding, the basis of the Humean denial can hardly be empirical.

If the basis of the Humean denial is less than clear, so also is its meaning. Sometimes it is put by saying that we are not "acquainted" with a self or that we are not, in introspection, presented with a self "as an object." But what is it to be acquainted with something in the required sense? Adapting the answer to this once suggested by Paul Grice, we might say that "I am acquainted with X," where X is a particular, means "(a) I have direct (noninferential) knowledge of some facts about X, and (b) X is not a logical construction."[4] I think this captures one meaning that might reasonably be given to talk about acquaintance with, or awareness of, objects. But it can hardly be the meaning it commonly has in the Humean denial that there is introspective acquaintance or awareness of the self. On Grice's construal of the denial that there is acquaintance with the self, this denial presupposes that the self is a logical construction, i.e., that something like the Humean bundle-theory is true – it presupposes this on the reasonable assumption (which those who make this denial are committed to) that we do have some direct knowledge of facts about ourselves. And in that case, as Grice points out, the denial cannot be offered as *grounds* for the view that the self is a logical construction. But one of the reasons why the Humean denial has been philosophically interesting and disturbing is that it has seemed to provide prima facie grounds for that view. Moreover, many philosophers who have accepted Hume's denial, or at any rate found it plausible, have believed both that persons do have direct knowledge of facts about themselves and that persons (selves) are *not* logical constructions. And unless these philosophers

4 Grice 1941. In Grice's own formulation (p. 82 in Perry 1975), (a) reads simply "I know some facts about X." On most people's intuitions about knowledge, this would force one to choose between saying (1) that I (who have never been to India) am acquainted with the Taj Mahal, and (2) that the Taj Mahal is a logical construction. My wording of (a) avoids this.

have been very confused indeed, they cannot have meant by Hume's denial what it means on Grice's construal – for on that construal they are committed to its rejection.

A natural suggestion is that what Hume and others have meant to deny is that we have in introspection anything like a *perceptual* awareness of a self; that we perceive a self by an "inner sense." Perception is in the first instance a relation to *non*factual objects; we perceive facts by perceiving objects that they are facts about – e.g., we perceive that the branch is bent by perceiving the branch.[5] The Humean denial, on this suggestion, is that in having introspective knowledge one stands in a perceptual or quasi-perceptual relation to a self. This seems to me right, but it raises the question of what it is to stand in a *perceptual* relation to something; or, more to the point, it raises the question of how those who have accepted Hume's denial, or taken it seriously, have conceived the perceptual relationship. It is initially tempting to give some such account as the following of what it is to perceive a thing: S perceives O just in case S stands to O in a relation R such that, for any x and y, x's standing in R to y is apt for the production in x of (direct) knowledge of y. Examples of the relation R would be the relation a person stands in to a tree when she is conscious, in good light, and has well-functioning eyes that are open and directed towards a tree, and the relation a person has to a cat when he is stroking it. But no one who accepts the Humean denial, or thinks that it is even possibly true, can accept this definition. For on this definition it is beyond dispute that in introspection we *do* perceive a self; here R can be the relation x has to y just in case x is a conscious subject and identical to y. So this definition of perception shares with the Gricean definition of acquaintance (which it resembles) the defect that it does not permit the Humean denial to get off the ground. On the other hand, we do not want to trivialize the Humean denial by giving an account of what it is to perceive that is tailored to fit the five senses and nothing else. Obvious though it may seem, the Humean denial is a striking and (on first hearing) startling claim, and it is certainly not the truism that introspective awareness is not by means of sight, touch, hearing, smell, or taste. The Humean denial requires a conception of perception somewhere in between the narrow conception that would trivialize it and the broad conception that would trivialize its rejection.

5 "Nonfactual" is not meant to connote "false" or "erroneous"; by nonfactual objects I simply mean objects, of which tables and chairs are examples, that are not themselves facts or factlike entities.

A philosopher who seems to accept something like the broad conception of perception just considered is David Armstrong; and Armstrong is a staunch supporter of the view that introspection is "inner sense," i.e., is to be conceived on the model of perception. He writes: "Eccentric cases apart, perception, considered as a mental event, is the acquiring of information or misinformation about our environment. It is not an 'acquaintance' with objects, or a 'searchlight' that makes contact with them, but is simply the getting of beliefs. Exactly the same must be said of introspection. It is the getting of information or misinformation about the current state of our mind."[6] Given this view, one might expect that Armstrong would hold that in introspection one perceives a self (or mind, or mental subject). But Armstrong apparently thinks of himself as accepting the Humean denial. He says that:

> we must . . . grant Hume that the existence of the mind is not something that is given to unaided introspection. All that 'inner sense' reveals is the occurrence of individual mental happenings . . . I suggest that the solution is that the notion of 'a mind' is a *theoretical* concept: something that is *postulated* to link together all the individual happenings of which introspection makes us aware. In speaking of minds, perhaps even in using the word 'I' in the course of introspective reports, we go beyond what is introspectively observed. Ordinary language here embodies a certain theory.[7]

Here it looks as though Armstrong is endorsing the view, to be considered later, that accepts a perceptual model of introspection but denies that the self is among the objects perceived by this "inner sense."[8] Of course, what Armstrong explicitly denies here is not that the self is perceived but that its existence is "given to unaided introspection." Perhaps he could hold that one perceives what is in fact a self, but that the fact that it is a self – indeed that there are such things as selves – is not something "given" but rather something one comes to believe as the result of accepting a theory (rather as one might see what is in fact a supernova and only later, after learning some astronomy, realize that there are such things). But if he did mean to deny that one perceives a self, this denial is at least in prima facie conflict with his apparent acceptance of the broad conception of perception.

6 Armstrong 1968, p. 326.
7 Armstrong 1968, p. 337. There are similar remarks in Armstrong 1981; see especially pp. 64–65.
8 As I argue in my Royce lectures [Essays 10–12], the perceptual model has many versions. Armstrong does not subscribe what I there call the "object perception model" (which goes with an act-object conception of experience), but does subscribe to what I there call the "broad perceptual model." (The latter is not the same as what in this essay I call the "broad conception of perception" – see note 27).

It might seem that the task of interpreting and evaluating the Humean denial is essentially that of giving a satisfactory account of perception – one that enables us to see whether perception, or something strongly analogous to it, is involved in our introspective awareness of our mental states. But I think that what matters here is not so much what the true nature of perception is (supposing indeed that there is something common to all of those things that are counted as modes of perception) as what is involved in the conception of it that underlies the thinking of those philosophers who have accepted, or been tempted or disturbed by, the Humean denial. It seems a good bet that there is a noncontrived conception that makes the Humean denial true; and it seems likely that we can learn something of importance about the nature of self-knowledge (and not just about philosophers' conceptions of it) by trying to see what this conception is.

I now want to begin considering the sources of the Humean denial. I will start with a consideration that I think must have been operating in the case of Hume himself and that I feel sure has been an influence on others as well. I should perhaps insert a warning here that this essay is not primarily an exercise in Humean exegesis; any sources of the Humean denial that are *peculiarly* Humean, and cannot plausibly be supposed to be at work in the thinking of many of the philosophers who have seconded Hume's denial, are of no interest to me here.

Earlier in the *Treatise*, Hume wrote: "To hate, to love, to think, to feel, to see; all this is nothing but to perceive."[9] In this passage there is no hint that Hume thinks that there is no subject that does the perceiving. And what is suggested by this passage, and consonant with much else that Hume says, is that all mental states are relational – that having a mental state always consists in having a certain relation, namely perceiving, to a perception (impression or idea) of one sort or another. This cannot have been Hume's official position in the end, given his denial that there is anything that could be the subject of such relational states. But I think that we can say that Hume took it for granted that if there were a mental subject, a self which is something over and above particular perceptions, its mental properties would all have to be relational properties of this sort. Given that mental states are the only states of which one can be introspectively aware, and given that on this conception all mental states of selves would be relational rather than intrinsic, it would follow that a self could not have any intrinsic states at all that could be accessible to intro-

9 Hume 1888, p. 67.

spective awareness. But surely it makes no sense to speak of being aware of something, by a certain kind of perception, if the thing has no intrinsic properties whatever that it could be perceived as having by that kind of perception. I suggest, then, that Hume had a conception of what a mental subject would have to be – namely, something whose mental states are all relational – which implies that such a thing could not be introspectively perceived.[10]

No doubt it is also the case the Hume was enough of a dualist to take it for granted that a *mental* subject could have no intrinsic properties that are not mental – e.g., that what we would ordinarily think of as the bodily properties of a person could not count as intrinsic properties of a self. From this, and the conception just mentioned, it would follow not only that mental subjects lack introspectable intrinsic properties but that they lack intrinsic properties altogether. And from this it is natural to conclude that no such thing could exist. On the other hand, someone who thinks that selves have some intrinsic physical properties, but agrees with the idea that all mental states are relational, could hold that a self could be perceived in virtue of its physical properties, and even that it could be so perceived by itself – as when one sees oneself in a mirror, or in foreshortened view. But it would still be ruled out that the self could be an object of *introspective* perception.

An important ingredient in this line of thought is what is sometimes called the "act-object conception" of sensations and other mental states. Feeling pain, for example, is taken to consist in standing in a certain relation to a mental particular of a certain sort, namely a pain; and visualizing a tree is taken to consist in standing in a certain relation to a mental particular of another sort, namely an image of a tree. And if we ask what the relation is, the answer is "perceiving," "apprehending," "being acquainted with," or the like. As I have already indicated, it cannot be said that Hume's official position incorporates the act-object conception, if the act is taken to require an actor, a mental subject. But I think it is fair to say that this conception is what he starts from. Humean perceptions are precisely the sorts of entities the act-object conception calls for on the object side.

The act-object conception of mental states goes naturally with, and may be said to incorporate, what I have called the perceptual model of introspection – the idea that our access to our own minds is to be con-

---

10 If this is right, Hume had some conception of what a self or mental subject would have to be, despite his denial that he had any idea of such a thing.

ceived on the model of sense-perception, differing from other sorts of perception only in being, in Kantian terminology, "inner sense" rather than "outer sense." If Humean perceptions are, as I have said, just the sort of entities the act-object conception calls for on the object side, they are also just the sort of entities the perceptual model of introspection calls for, if there are to be mental particulars other than the self to serve as objects of introspective awareness. What we have just seen is that the very conception of mental facts that provides us with a stock of mental particulars to serve as objects of introspective awareness tends to make it appear that the self, or mental subject, cannot itself be an object of introspective awareness. The more widely the act-object conception is applied, the greater is the number of mental states that are construed as relational – and if all are conceived as relational, it will make no more sense to speak of perceiving a self introspectively than it does to speak of seeing or feeling a point in empty space.

The attitude of contemporary philosophers towards the act-object conception seems to me somewhat equivocal. When they face the issue squarely, I think, most of them reject the conception as mistaken. J. J. C. Smart noted some time ago that in order to maintain that experiencing a roundish, yellow-orange afterimage is identical to a state of the brain he had to reject the idea that having this state is a matter of standing in a certain relation to a roundish, yellow-orange particular.[11] Although it is possible to be a materialist without accepting Smart's sort of identity theory, it does not appear that any version of materialism can plausibly allow that what is called having a roundish, yellow-orange afterimage involves being related to something actually roundish and yellowy orange. Materialism aside, moreover, the grounds philosophers have given for rejecting the sense-datum theory of perception are precisely grounds for rejecting the act-object conception as applied to sense experiences. I think it is widely accepted that the act-object conception ought also to be rejected in its application to sensations like pain. Yet when we are not addressing this specific issue, most of us tend to slide back into this conception in our thinking about the mental. Nothing is more natural than to speak of pains that we feel and images we see and to think of the feeling and seeing as our perceptual access to mental particulars. I think it is partly because of this that the Humean denial is so striking. If we did not take it for granted that we do perceive *something* by introspection, and that this introspective perception is the source of our introspective

11 Smart 1962.

9

knowledge, it would not be so likely to strike us as significant or disturbing that we do not introspectively perceive any self or mental subject.[12]

Suppose that the act-object conception is rejected for all mental states; will there then be any mental particulars suited for being the objects of introspective awareness, conceived as a kind of perception? Well, even if we refuse to allow that there are such things as yellowy-orange afterimages, we will allow that there are such things as experiencings of yellowy-orange afterimages or (in another idiom) states of being appeared yellowy orange to; and surely these will be mental particulars of a sort. But an experiencing is something whose existence is "adjectival on" a subject of experience. The ontological status of an experiencing, or an episode of being appeared to, is similar to that of a bending of a branch or a rising of the sun. One perceives a rising of the sun by observing the sun rising; here the primary nonfactual object of perception is the sun. Likewise, one perceives a bending of a branch by observing a branch bending; and here the primary nonfactual object of perception is a branch. It hardly makes sense to suppose that there could be a mode of perception that has as its objects bendings of branches and risings of the sun, but never branches or the sun. And it makes equally little sense to suppose that there might be a mode of perception that had as its objects experiencings but never experiencers – never subjects of experience. Experiencings and the like seem as ill-suited as sun-risings and branch-bendings for being the primary nonfactual objects of a mode of perception.[13] I am of course taking it as an obvious conceptual truth that an experiencing is necessarily an experiencing by a subject of experience, and involves that subject as intimately as a branch-bending involves a branch.

Where does this leave us? Since the time of Hume, it has been widely held that we do have introspective perception of many sorts of mental particulars, but never of a self or mental subject. But what I have just inferred from the rejection of the act-object conception is that if we have

12 As William Alston has pointed out to me, one could not say that on the act-object conception one has introspective perception of mental *states* but not of a mental subject. For a state, on the act-conception, will not be an object of the sort Hume thinks he finds when he looks within but rather a relational state of affairs consisting in a subject's being aware of such an object – and this, presumably, will not be perceivable if the subject is not. But if we characterized introspection as awareness of mental particulars of whatever kind, rather than as just awareness of mental states, then it will still be true on such a view that there is something that is an object of introspective perception, even though the self is not such an object.

13 Here sun-risings should be distinguished from sunrises. One can perhaps see a sunrise without seeing the sun – maybe seeing a glow in the east is sufficient. But this is not to see a sun-rising, i.e., is not to see the sun to rise.

introspective perception of anything, we have it of the self, and that only the self could be the primary nonfactual object of introspective perception, if such a mode of perception exists. Earlier I sketched a line of argument against the possibility of introspective perception of the self that was grounded on the act–object conception, and so on the view that there is a multitude of possible nonfactual objects for introspective perception. This was the argument that if the act–object conception is applied universally, all mental states will be relational and the self will lack the sorts of intrinsic properties it would have to have to be an object of introspective perception. Let us now see what reasons there might be for rejecting introspective perception of the self if we assume that the act–object conception is mistaken, or at least is not to be applied universally. Notice that if what I have said is right, such reasons would be, if combined with the reasons for rejecting the act–object conception, grounds for holding that there is no such thing as introspective perception at all – that is, they would be grounds for rejecting altogether the perceptual model of introspective self-knowledge.

Ordinary modes of perception admit of our perceiving, successively or simultaneously, a multiplicity of different objects, all of which are on a par as nonfactual objects of perception. There is such a thing as singling out one from a multiplicity of perceived objects, distinguishing it from the others (which may be of the same kind as it) by its perceived properties and its position in a space of perceived objects. Perceived objects are candidates for several sorts of perceptually based identification. One can identify one of them, or misidentify it, as being of this or that sort – call this sortal identification. And one can identify one of them, or misidentify it, as being a certain particular thing – call this particular identification. Where the perceived object is a continuant, it will also be a candidate for what Strawson has called "reidentification," the identification of something observed at one time with something perceived at another time. This will be on the basis of resemblances and other relationships between the observed properties manifested at different times; and, in the most favorable case, where there has been continuous observation of a thing over a period of time, it will be grounded on a sort of perceptual "tracking" that presents the observer with an observed continuity of properties of a kind that constitutes the most direct evidence of identity, for things of that sort, that perception can provide.

Now none of this seems to apply in the case of one's introspective awareness of oneself. If this is a mode of perception, then either there is for each person exactly one (nonadjectival) object, namely himself, that is

11

perceived by that person in this way (this will be so if the act-object conception is mistaken across the board and selves are the only basic objects of introspective perception); or, at least, there is exactly one self that the person can perceive in this way. In the latter case there can be no such thing as picking out a self and distinguishing it from other selves by its introspectively perceived properties; and in the former case there can be no such thing as picking out a self and distinguishing it from other perceived things, of any sort whatever, by its perceived properties. It would seem to go with this that there could be no question of one's having to identify this self as oneself by its perceived properties, or of one's having to identify selves perceived at different times as one and the same. Moreover, it seems that if such identification were possible, it ought to be possible for one to misidentify an introspected self as oneself, or to misidentify a presently introspected self as the same as one introspected previously. But in fact no such possibility of misidentification seems to exist. Similarly, if sortal identification of an introspected self were possible, it seems as if sortal misidentification ought to be possible, analogous to the case in which I misidentify a mole as a mouse. And again it seems that in fact no such possibility of misidentification exists – there is no such thing as introspective misidentification of nonselves with selves.[14]

Faced with these claims, the proponent of the perceptual model of introspection must either deny that these differences really exist or deny that they matter. If he takes the latter line, he can be expected to say that it was clear from the start that there are some differences between introspective awareness and standard sorts of perception. No one supposes, for example, that there is an *organ* of introspection – yet most philosophers have not regarded that as an insuperable obstacle to conceiving introspection on the model of sense perception. What we now find, he might say, is that there is a further difference, which we might sum up by saying that introspective perception does not play the role of providing us with "identification information" about the perceived objects, namely ourselves. But unless we can show that this role is essential to perception, this leaves his view untouched.

Rather than attempting immediately to meet this response head on, I want to go on to a different point that eventually I will link up with the point that the self is not presented in introspection as a candidate for identification and that introspection does not play the role of providing identification information. I hope that this point will help to make plau-

14 See Shoemaker 1968.

12

sible the claim that this role is essential to perception (on at least one central conception of it).

Presumably it will be pointless, at best, to suppose that there is introspective perception of a self unless this perception plays some role in explaining our introspective self-knowledge – our knowledge of our own mental states. The most straightforward account would be this: I know that I have thus and such a mental state – that I am angry, in pain, or desirous of a drink – because I introspectively observe myself having it.[15] Obviously, however, the introspective observation of a self being angry is not going to yield the knowledge that *I* am angry unless I know that that self is myself. How am I supposed to know this? If the answer is that I identify it as myself by its perceived properties, we have to point out that this requires that I already know that I have those properties. Indeed, it requires that I know that I am the unique possessor of that set of properties, because otherwise the observation that the perceived self has them would not suffice to identify it as me. So I would already have to have some self-knowledge, namely the knowledge that I have certain identifying properties, in order to acquire any self-knowledge by self-observation. If it is supposed that this self-knowledge is in turn acquired by self-observation, then still other self-knowledge is required: namely, the knowledge that one has whatever identifying properties one used to identify as oneself the self that one observed to have the first set of identifying properties. And so on. On pain of infinite regress, it must be allowed that somewhere along the line I have some self-knowledge that is not gotten by observing something to be true of myself.

It may be objected that I am overlooking the point that only one self could be the object of my introspective perception; there is no need to identify the observed self as myself by its perceived properties, since, given that I perceive it introspectively, there is no other self it could be. But this amounts to saying that I can infallibly identify the observed self as myself by the fact that it is introspectively observed by me. That requires that I know that I introspectively observe it. And that is a piece of self-knowledge I could not get by introspective observation; for unless I already know that this self is myself, observing that it perceives itself is not going to tell me that I observe it. So it remains true that if I am to get self-knowledge by introspective perception I must have some that I have not gotten by introspective perception. But if to explain our introspective self-knowledge we have to posit some self-knowledge that is not ob-

---

15 Bertrand Russell seems to have held such a view at one time; see Russell 1912.

servational, in the sense that it is not gotten by perceiving what one knows to be oneself and observing something to be true of it, why shouldn't we suppose that all of our introspective self-knowledge is of this nonobservational character? At best, the hypothesis that there is introspective self-perception seems to explain nothing that cannot be equally well explained without it.[16]

I think that the only way around this for a proponent of introspective self-perception is to hold that "I" is synonymous with "this self," where "this" functions as a logically proper name in Russell's sense.[17] Obviously, "this" could not be here the ordinary demonstrative pronoun, for the latter can be used to refer to selves (persons) other than the speaker. But if we think of it as a special sort of demonstrative pronoun that can be used to refer only to objects of introspective perception, then the proposal finesses the problem of how one is to identify an observed self as oneself. We were, in effect, imagining our introspective perceiver asking himself "Is this self me?" and attempting to answer this on the basis of facts he observes about it together with facts he knows about himself.

16 This argument was given in Shoemaker 1968, p. 563. It might be objected (and has been by William Alston) that the argument proves too much. Won't the same reasoning lead to the false conclusion that all of my knowledge of your house might be nonobservational? It will prove (and it is true, not false) that if I am to identify your house by its observed characteristics, I must have knowledge that is not observational in the sense (call it the narrow sense) that it is gotten by observing your house and observing something to be true of it. Here, of course, I might acquire knowledge of the identifying characteristics by observing other things – e.g., by hearing you describe your house. I would then be relying on knowledge of the past and background knowledge of various sorts (e.g., about the tendency of houses to retain certain sorts of characteristics) my acquisition of which was, in a broad sense, observational. But it is agreed on all sides that reports of immediate experience containing "*I*" are minimally dependent on background knowledge and knowledge of the past; total amnesia would presumably impair my knowledge to identify someone's house perceptually, but would not impair my ability to make "*I*" statements. The philosopher who is the target of my argument is someone who thinks that "*I*" statements are simply "read off" from the contents of immediate experience, and such a philosopher could not allow that anything comparable to what might enable me to know the identifying characteristics of someone's house could explain my ability to identify an introspectively perceived self as my self. Once such a philosopher sees that my knowledge of identifying characteristics of myself could not be observational in the narrow sense, I think he has no recourse but to allow that it is not observational at all. And then, I think, he has no principled way of justifying the requirement that other introspective self-knowledge be observationally (or perceptually) based.

17 I have the hazy recollection that Russell somewhere makes this suggestion, but cannot find any place where he did so. After he abandoned the view that there is acquaintance with a self, Russell did in various places advance the suggestion that "*I*" means something like "the subject of this," where "this" names some object of immediate experience – but that of course is a different view.

But on the present proposal, the question "Is this self me?" is equivalent to "Is this self this self?" – which answers itself.

Bizarre and farfetched though this suggestion may seem, there is a certain appropriateness about it, given the view that we have introspective perception of a self and that this is the source of our self-knowledge. Perception and demonstrative reference are intimately related; to perceive something is, among other things, to be in a position to refer to that thing demonstratively, and it is a necessary condition of the primary sort of demonstrative reference that the speaker perceive (or remember recently perceiving) the object referred to. It is quite natural that a view that construes self-knowledge as based on self-perception should attempt to assimilate self-reference to demonstrative reference.

But can such an assimilation be correct? If we focus only on present tense judgments, the assimilation of first-person judgments to demonstrative judgments may seem promising. It is characteristic of both sorts of judgments that they are "identification free" and "immune to error through misidentification."[18] It is not the case that I say "I am angry" because I find that someone is angry and identify that person as myself; and normally it is not the case that I say "This is red" because I find that something is red and identify that thing as "this." But when we turn to the past-tense versions of these judgments, the situation seems different. Briefly, and omitting necessary qualifications, the immunity to error through misidentification of first-person judgments is preserved in memory, whereas that of demonstrative judgments is not. If I say, pointing, "This *was* red then," meaning to express the knowledge I previously expressed with "This is red," then my judgment involves an identification that could be mistaken; it could be that the thing I see now is not the thing I remember seeing earlier. By contrast, and still omitting the qualifications, if I say "I was angry then," meaning to express the knowledge I previously expressed by saying "I am angry," then a mistake of identification is impossible. It goes with this that the past-tense demonstrative judgment rests on an observationally based reidentification of the thing referred to with "this," whereas the past-tense, first-person judgment does not rest on an observationally based reidentification of the person referred to with "*I*." "This was red" might be grounded in part on an observed similarity between the thing one sees now and the thing one remembers seeing to be red in the past, or it might be grounded in part on a series of phenomena one observed in perceptually tracking an object

18 For these notions, see Evans 1982, and Shoemaker 1968.

15

over time. "I was angry," if said on the basis of memory in the ordinary way, could not be grounded either on an introspectively observed resemblance between a past self and a present self, or on an introspective tracking of a self over time. This is the point, familiar from discussions of personal identity, that first-person memory judgments are not grounded on criteria of personal identity.[19]

The qualification I have mentioned has to do with the possibility, which I have discussed elsewhere, that one might "quasi-remember" past experiences or actions that are not one's own.[20] For example, this could happen if it were possible for someone to undergo "fission" and split into two people, both of whom remember (or quasi-remember) "from the inside" the actions and experiences of the original person. To allow that this is possible is to allow that in a certain sense, first-person memory judgments are subject to error through misidentification. But this does not really affect the point I am making. It remains true that first-person memory judgments do not involve identifications of oneself that are grounded on observed similarities between selves observed at different times, or on a perceptual tracking of a self over time. Assuming that quasi-remembering of the experiences and actions of persons other than oneself is a logical possibility, what entitles us to think that it has not occurred in our own case is not that the contents of our memories provide us with direct evidence that one and the same person was involved in the various actions and experiences we remember "from the inside" (for in general they provide us with no such evidence), but rather the fact that our general knowledge of the world supports a presumption that "fission" and the like do not in fact occur. Given the truth of this presumption, my awareness that I remember (quasi-remember) from the inside a past action is decisive evidence that I did that action – but it is not the sort of evidence that grounds observationally based identifications.

There is an additional reason for declining to assimilate self-reference to demonstrative reference, and this is that such an assimilation makes inexplicable one of the constitutive features of self-reference. As recent writers have noted, one of the distinctive features of first-person belief is the role it plays in the explanation of behavior. Having a genuine first-person belief, of the sort one expresses by saying "*I*," is not merely a matter of believing something of what is in fact oneself. To use David Ka-

19 See Shoemaker 1963, and Strawson 1966.
20 See Shoemaker 1970.

plan's example, if I merely believe of the person I in fact am that his pants are on fire (I see someone in a mirror with his pants on fire, but do not realize that it is me), this will not influence my behavior in the way that the belief I would express by saying "My pants are on fire!" would.[21] It seems reasonable to hold that part of what makes a belief a belief about the person who has it (in the way beliefs expressed by first-person sentences are about the speaker) is the fact that it plays this distinctive role in the determination of action. It is a consequence of this, I believe, that the reference of "*I*" in the idiolect of a particular speaker is determined very differently than is the reference of other expressions, including demonstratives. Roughly, whereas the reference of other expressions is determined by facts about the causal etiology of their use, the reference of "*I*," when used as first-person pronoun, is determined by the causal role of the beliefs it is used to express. To suppose that "*I*" is just a special sort of demonstrative pronoun, one used to refer to introspectively perceived selves, and that its reference is determined in the way that of demonstratives in general is determined, leaves totally unexplained the role of "*I*"-beliefs in the determination of behavior. Why should the belief that *this self's* pants are on fire, together with the desire not to be burnt, gird me into fire-dousing behavior? It will, of course, if I know that this self is myself; but given what turns on it, knowing that cannot be just a matter of knowing that this self is this self. The way in which a belief is about oneself is utterly different from the way in which a belief is about a perceived object *qua* observed object.

We have seen, I think, that introspective knowledge of ourselves cannot legitimately be assimilated to either of two paradigms of perceptual knowledge of an object – that in which the knowledge involves an observationally based identification of the object, and that in which the object is designated demonstratively. This seems to me to provide a strong reason for denying that introspective awareness should be conceived on the model of sense perception. But this plainly links up with my earlier point that in introspection we are not presented, and do not need to be presented, with "identification information" about ourselves: the sort of information we would need to have to identify a self as oneself, to reidentify a self, or to "track" a self perceptually over an interval of time. For the assimilation to either of these paradigms would require that introspection be a source of identification information in a way that in fact it is not.

21 See Lewis 1979 and Kaplan 1989. See Perry 1977 and 1979 for other examples.

It is worth asking, in connection with this, why it has been so commonly assumed that if we were aware of a self in introspection, the self would have to be something nonbodily. It is of course assumed to be obvious that in fact we are not presented with ourselves in introspection *as* bodily entities. But why is it assumed that if the self were something bodily and were perceived introspectively, it would have to be perceived *as* something bodily? What underlies this assumption, I suspect, is the idea that a way of perceiving a thing of a certain sort must be a source of identifying information about things of that sort, and so must reveal the sorts of properties by which things of that sort are individuated. Bodily entities are individuated in part by their bodily properties and by their spatial relations to other things, and for this reason perception of them ought to provide information about such properties and relationships. Given that introspection does not provide such information, either it is not perception at all or it is perception of something nonbodily. Wittgenstein says in the *Blue Book*: "We feel . . . that in cases in which '*I*' is used as subject, we don't use it because we recognize a person by his bodily characteristics; and this creates the illusion that we use this word to refer to something bodiless, which, however, has its seat in our body. In fact, *this* seems to be the real ego, the one of which it was said 'Cogito, Ergo sum'."[22] The tacit assumption underlying this diagnosis of the attractions of dualism is that we assume that we must be provided in introspective perception with identifying facts about ourselves; and therefore that since we are not presented with identifying facts of the sort appropriate to bodily entities, we are not bodily entities. I have argued that we are not presented with identifying facts of any sort and therefore that the proper conclusion is that introspection is not a mode of perception (a conclusion with which Wittgenstein would have agreed). Here it is worth quoting Kant's observation that "in what we entitle 'soul' everything is in continual flux and there is nothing abiding except (if we must so express ourselves) the '*I*,' which is simple solely because its representation has no content, and therefore no manifold [of intuitions], and for this reason seems to represent, or (to use a more correct word) denote, a simple object."[23] Patricia Kitcher glosses this by saying, "The Rational Psychologists go astray because they expect to find intuition of the self and so mistake the absence of any intuition for the intuition of something with

22 Wittgenstein 1958.
23 Kant 1953. The bracketed addition to Kemp Smith's translation is Patricia Kitcher's (see Note 24).

18

remarkable properties."[24] I suggest that the lack of content, or of a manifold of intuition, is basically the lack of introspectively provided identification information; and that this is a large part of what lies behind the denial that there is introspective perception of a self.

I now want to give what seems on the face of it to be a very different objection to the idea that there is introspective perception of a self. This will be, in fact, an objection to the idea that there is introspective perception of anything whatever. But I think this objection turns out to be closely related to the objection just given, that which rests on the claim that perception ought to be a source of identification information about the objects of perception and that introspection is not a source of such information about the self.[25]

It is characteristic of sense perception, of all of the familiar kinds, that perceiving something involves its appearing in a certain way to one, a way that may or may not correspond to the actual nature of the thing perceived. An object's appearing a certain way to someone involves that person's being in a subjective state, call it a sense impression, having a certain phenomenal character; and how the object appears will be a function of the phenomenal character of the sense impression. There is (in the phrase made current by Thomas Nagel) "something it is like" to perceive something, and we can equate what this is like on a given occasion with the phenomenal character of the sense impression. Having a sense impression with a certain phenomenal character is not just a matter of having certain beliefs, or certain inclinations to believe, about the properties of the object of perception. For one thing, one sometimes has to learn to interpret the phenomenal character of one's sense impressions; and prior to one's learning this, the phenomenal features of the sense impressions will not be associated with features of the perceived objects.[26]

Now some of the states we are aware of in introspection are themselves sensory states having a phenomenal character. And in the case of these, it is natural to say that there is "something it is like" to be aware of them. But it seems plain that this "something it is like" is just the phe-

---

24 Kitcher 1982.
25 It is perception conceived in terms of what in the Royce lectures I call the "object perception model, " which takes vision as the paradigm of perception, that ought to be a source of identification information. This does not hold of every mode of knowledge acquisition that is counted as perception – see Essay 10, Section. viii.
26 This assumes a different notion of phenomenal character than that developed in Essay 12.

nomenal character of the states themselves, and not the phenomenal character of still other states that are sense impressions of them. There is something it is like to be in pain. And because being in pain and feeling pain are one and the same thing, there is something it is like to feel pain. If one holds the act-object conception of sensation, one may be tempted to equate the introspective awareness of the pain with the feeling of the pain: adopting the perceptual model of introspection, one thinks of "feeling" as the mode of perception by which one has introspective awareness of pain. But that has to be a mistake, whether or not one adopts the act-object conception. Feeling pain and being in pain are, to repeat, the same thing; and the introspective knowledge that I am in pain is at the same time the introspective knowledge that I feel pain. And it is certainly not the case that I feel my self feeling pain; there is not a feeling of the feeling that is something over and above the feeling of pain. There is something it is like to be in pain, or to feel pain, but there is nothing additional it is like to be aware of pain, or of feeling pain; and the same goes for other sensory states. And so there is no such thing as a sense impression of a sensory state, having a phenomenal character of its own.

If being aware of being in pain does not involve having something analogous to a sense impression of the pain, it can scarcely involve having a sense impression (or quasi-sense-impression) of the self. If one perceives the self at all in introspection, one perceives it as having various states, like being in pain; so one could not have sense impressions of it without having sense impressions of its various states, which I have just denied that we have. And I think that there is not the slightest plausibility in the idea that in introspection we have quasi-sensory states that relate to the self as our sense impressions of a tree relate to the tree. The self does not appear in any way to itself in introspection. One does, of course, have beliefs about oneself in introspection. And no doubt it is possible for some of these beliefs to be mistaken. But having a mistaken introspective belief cannot be said to constitute the self's appearing to itself other than it is; for as I said earlier, something's appearing (perceptually) a certain way to one is not just a matter of one's believing, or being inclined to believe, certain things about it.

But what is the status of this denial that the self appears in a certain way to itself in introspection? Is it itself a deliverance of introspection. If it were that, or only that, then the use of this denial as a basis for the denial that there is introspective self-perception would not be much of an advance on Hume's claim that when he looks within himself he finds no self over and above his particular perceptions. But I believe that we can find another basis for this denial by reflecting on the function in ordinary sense perception of the phenomenal character of sense impressions. What I suggest is that the informational content of a sense impression is embodied in its phenomenal character and that a crucial part of this informational content consists of what I have been calling identification information. As I walk around the table, its appearance changes without there being any corresponding change in my beliefs about its intrinsic properties. What do change are my beliefs about its spatial relations to myself; and facts about these spatial relations are an important part of the identification information provided me by ordinary sense perception. If there were introspective sense impressions of the self, they could not play any such role in providing us with identification information about the self, given that introspection does not provide such information at all. The only other role they could play is that of providing information about the intrinsic features of the self, such as that it is in pain. But for there to be (quasi) sense impressions that do this would be for there to be sense impressions of such states as pain — and it seems quite obvious that there are no such things. The conclusion seems to be that there is no such thing as an introspective sense impression of the self, just as there is no such thing as a sense impression of a pain or other mental state and (assuming that sense impressions are essential to perception) that there is no such thing as introspective perception of the self, or indeed of anything else.

I expect that what I have just said will meet some resistance. Indeed, it does so even in me. It is natural to object that there is such a thing as picking out one afterimage from others, and also such a thing as introspectively tracking an afterimage over time. If so, our introspective awareness of afterimages does involve the provision of identification information. But it should be remembered that in this part of my discussion I am assuming that the act-object conception of sensation is false. To reject the act-object conception is to hold that although there is such a thing as experiencing-an-afterimage, there is no such thing as an afterimage *qua* colored patch that hovers in front of one when one closes one's eyes after looking at a bright light. Experiencing an afterimage is merely *seeming* to see such a colored patch. And just as the seeing of afterimages is only seeming-as-if-one-were-seeing, the picking out of afterimages is only seeming-as-if-one-were-picking-out and the tracking of afterimages is only seeming-as-if-one-were-tracking. It is indeed true that when one is experiencing an afterimage it is *as if* identification information about perceived objects were being provided; this is part of

21

what constitutes its being as if one were seeing something. But its being as if something is so, from the subject's point of view, is not the same thing as its actually being so.

This is not the place for an attempt to refute the act-object conception. I will only record my conviction that if I am mistaken in thinking that this conception is wrong as applied to experiencing afterimages and the like, then the whole philosophical establishment has been mistaken in its rejection of the sense-datum theory of perception. For there is this much truth in the "argument from illusion": *if* it is right to give an act-object analysis of such phenomena as "seeing afterimages," "seeing double," etc., and thus to posit sense data (images) that are seen in such cases, there is no justification for refusing to give such an analysis of the sensory experiences that occur in normal perception – i.e., there is no justification for refusing to accept the claim that in all perception, "veridical" as well as "illusory," we directly perceive sense data. Those who wish to reject the sense-datum theory, as I think nearly all philosophers nowadays do, will be well advised to deny the antecedent of this conditional rather than denying the conditional itself.

I now return to my main theme. Earlier I sketched a broad conception of perception on which it seemed obviously true that we do have introspective perception of a self and also obviously true that we have introspective perception of individual mental states and events.[27] This raised the question of what we must add to that conception, by way of narrowing it, to get the conception implicit in the thinking of those who have accepted, or at any rate taken seriously, the Humean denial that there is introspective perception of the self. I suggest that what must be added is something like the following: a mode of perception must be such that someone's perceiving something in that way can enter into the explanation of how it is that the person has knowledge of that thing, where part of the explanation is that perceiving the thing provides the person with identification information about it, which it does by producing in the person sense impressions of the thing. This seems to me a plausible way of narrowing the broad conception, and one that justifies the Humean denial without trivializing it.

---

27 The "broad conception" on which it seems "obviously true" that we have introspective awareness of the self and of individual mental states and events is not the same as the "broad perceptual model" I oppose in Essay 11. The difference is that the latter incorporates, while the former does not, the idea that the existence of the mental states and events to which we have introspective access is independent of their being known in this way, and even of there existing the mechanisms that make such knowledge possible.

Let me now return briefly to the view of David Armstrong, according to which what is "given" in introspection is "the occurrence of individual mental happenings" and according to which the mind or self is something postulated to "link together all the individual happenings of which introspection makes us aware," the postulation involving a theory that is embodied in ordinary language.[28] The most natural reading of Armstrong is one according to which we have introspective perception of individual mental happenings but not of a mind or self. This will not be defensible on the conception of perception just sketched, because on that conception we do not have introspective perception even of particular mental happenings (and I suggested earlier that if we reject the act-object conception, which a materialist like Armstrong seems to be committed to doing, then we cannot have introspective perception of mental particulars without having introspective perception of a self, or mental subject, on which they are "adjectival"). Is the view perhaps defensible on the broad conception of perception? I have said that on that conception it is obviously true that we do have introspective perception of the self; but that was on the assumption that in introspection we have "direct" knowledge of facts about ourselves, and Armstrong may be denying this assumption in claiming that the self (he says "mind") is something "postulated" in accordance with a theory. But it is hard to see why Armstrong should think that the notion of the mind is any more theoretical than notions of particular mental happenings like thoughts and pains (especially given his view that the latter have rather complex causal definitions).[29] And if he does think that first-person beliefs are the results of theory-mediated inferences from more primitive beliefs in which the notion of a self or mind does not figure, he owes us an account of how such beliefs might be formulated (obviously they cannot refer to pains, desires, and beliefs *qua* states, since the notion of a state is correlative with the notion of a subject of states) and of how the inference would go (in particular, of how "*I*" would make its appearance). In any case, such a view is thoroughly implausible on the naturalistic approach to epistemology of which Armstrong himself has been a champion. If we were wired by evolution (or, for that matter, by God) so that our being in various mental states directly produces in us beliefs about them, then the job

---

28 Armstrong 1968, p. 337.
29 Indeed, it is arguable that a satisfactory causal, or functional definition of particular mental states must invoke a relation of "copersonality" and so (implicitly) the notion of a self. See Shoemaker 1979 and 1984b.

was hopelessly botched unless the beliefs thus produced are beliefs to the effect that we ourselves are in those states – and only a philosophical picture (probably one involving the act-object conception) could make it plausible to suppose that they are anything else.

It seems to me, then, that whether we interpret "perceive" in the broad sense or in the narrow sense, the view that we have introspective perceptions of individual mental happenings but not of a self is indefensible. If we interpret it in the broad sense, we have introspective perception of both; if we interpret it in the narrow sense, we have introspective perception of neither. In the latter sense, indeed, introspective awareness does not involve perception of anything at all. And I think that this puts the Humean denial in an interesting new light. For it completely undermines the view, which motivates "bundle," "logical construction," and "no subject" theories of the self, that from an empiricist standpoint the status of the self (the subject of experience) is suspect compared with that of such things as sensations, feelings, images, and the like. What of the bearing of the Humean denial on Cartesian dualism? Although I think that there are lots of good reasons for rejecting Cartesian dualism, I do not think that the truth of the Humean denial is one of them. For I see no reason to think that the Cartesian dualist is committed to there being self-perception in the narrow, as opposed to the broad, sense. What does seem to be true, however, is the suggestion, implicit in the passages quoted earlier from Kant and Wittgenstein, that the Humean denial undercuts one argument in favor of Cartesian dualism, namely the argument from the fact that we do not in introspection perceive the self as having bodily properties; for the argument goes through only on the assumption that in introspection we do perceive the self in the narrow sense.

2

On knowing one's own mind

I

One of the views associated with Descartes is that it is of the essence of mind that each mind has a special, privileged access to its own contents. Recently, I think, this view has been very much out of favor. Those who have rejected it have not, in general, denied that there is something that might be called a "special access" to one's own mental states. Usually they have not denied that normally a person knows of his own beliefs, desires, sensations, thoughts, etc. in a way that is utterly different from that in which one person knows of such mental states in another person. And in the case of at least some mental phenomena, in particular sensations and occurrent thoughts, it would generally be allowed that a person's access to those phenomena in himself is both more comprehensive and less subject to error than his access to the same sorts of phenomena in other persons. What is denied, when this Cartesian doctrine is rejected, is, first, that the special access a person has to his own mental states is necessarily infallible or "incorrigible," or at least yields knowledge having a kind of certainty which empirical knowledge about other matters cannot attain, and second, that it is in any way constitutive or definitive of mental states, or of minds, or of the concepts of these, that these states intimate their existence to their possessors in a special and direct way.

In the present essay I shall assume, at least for the sake of discussion, that the first of these denials is correct – that it is logically possible for a person to be mistaken about his own mental states, of whatever kind, and that the certainty we can attain about our own mental states is not of a different order than that we can attain about other matters of fact. The anti-Cartesian view that concerns me here is the second denial – the denial that having a special access to its mental states, what I will sometimes call "self-acquaintance," is of the essence of mind, or that being accessible

[margin handwritten note: self-acquaintance is of the essence of mind]

I am grateful to Carl Ginet, Richard Moran, and Robert Stalnaker, and to members of my 1985 NEH Summer Seminar on "Self-Consciousness and Self-Reference," for helpful comments and criticisms.

in this special way is any way definitive of mental states. The anti-Cartesian sees self-acquaintance as analogous to sense-perception in one important respect; just as the existence of a tree or mountain is logically independent of its being perceived, and even of there being creatures who could perceive it, so, on the anti-Cartesian view, the existence of a belief or desire or sensation is logically independent of its being actually, or even potentially, the object of self-acquaintance. Typically the anti-Cartesian will see self-acquaintance as analogous to sense-perception in another respect as well. He will see it as involving a mechanism whereby, under certain circumstances, the existence of a certain states of affairs causes in a person a belief in the existence of that state of affairs, the cause and the effect being logically independent. And the important thing, for him, is that the existence of this belief-producing mechanism is something over and above the existence of the mental states about which it yields belief and knowledge, in the same sense in which the existence of our perceptual mechanisms is something over and above the external facts about which they yield belief and knowledge.

It is approximately true that it is only the mental states of a person that directly produce in that person beliefs in their occurrence. To be sure, excess acidity in my stomach may produce in me the belief that there is excess acidity in my stomach; but it is natural to suppose that here the belief production is mediated by the production of a sensation, something mental, and requires the background belief that sensations of that sort indicate excess acidity in the stomach.[1] Now it seems perfectly conceivable that there should be creatures, otherwise like ourselves, who have a "special access" to physical states of themselves which is not in this way mediated by sensations and background beliefs. We can imagine, for example, that the blood pressure of these creatures varies from one moment to the next, but that if you ask one of them what his blood pressure is he is always able (after some preliminary training) to answer correctly, and is unable to give any account of how he is able to do this, except by saying that once the question is put to him he "just knows" that his blood pressure is such and such. The anti-Cartesian, as I am conceiving him, sees no

---

1 Here I seem to overlook the knowledge one has of one's posture and the position of one's limbs. This is not inferential in the way knowledge of excess acidity in one's stomach is. But it also seems different from the knowledge one has of one's own mental states. It is usually classified as perceptual knowledge, and like other perceptual knowledge it is grounded on a perceptual experience – a state of being "appeared to" in a certain way – which is distinct from the state known about. As I emphasize in Essays 1 and 10, knowledge of one's own mental states is not so grounded.

important difference between the special access we in fact have to our own mental states and the access these creatures would have to their blood pressure, or which analogous creatures might have to their pulse rates, their body temperatures, their blood sugar levels, and so on. And it is on his view just a contingent fact that we have the one sort of access and not the other; logically speaking, it could just as well have been the other way around.

As is probably apparent by now, I have set up this anti-Cartesian position so as to oppose it. In opposing it I will be embracing a moderate Cartesianism – a version of the view that it is of the essence of mind that each mind has a special access to its own contents, or more soberly expressed, that each person has a special access to his own mental states. Embracing this Cartesian thesis does not, of course, commit me to holding the other thesis about the mental which is most commonly associated with Descartes, namely mind-body dualism. The Cartesianism I accept is perfectly compatible with materialism.

II

As a preliminary to arguing for the essentiality of this special access, i.e., of self-acquaintance, I want to say something about its utility – about the role it plays in our lives.

The self-knowledge I will focus on in the present essay is knowledge of our own beliefs, desires, and intentions. There are at least two areas in which this is important. One is in our dealings with other persons. When one is engaged in a cooperative endeavor with another, it is essential to the efficient pursuit of the shared goal that one be able to communicate to the other information about one's beliefs, desires, and intentions; and in order to communicate this information one must possess it. Often an action of one's own will contribute to the shared goal only if it is followed up by an appropriate action by the other – and for the other to know what action is appropriate it may be necessary for him to know with what intention one does what one does, what one expects its consequences to be, and what one intends to do next. When in such circumstances one conveys one's beliefs to another, this is not merely for the purpose of conveying what one takes to be information about the world, namely the contents of the beliefs; it is also for the purpose of giving him information about oneself which will assist him in predicting one's behavior and so in coordinating his own behavior with it, and also to enable him to correct those of one's beliefs he knows to be mistaken. To be sure, one needn't say "I believe that *P*" in order to convey to another that one believes that *P* – usually just saying "*P*" will serve as well. But if one doesn't believe that one believes that *P*, one cannot say either of these things with the intention of conveying to the other person that one believes this. And unless that second-order belief is true, one cannot succeed in fulfilling this intention. In the absence of self-knowledge, information about a person's mental states could not be conveyed to others as the result of speech acts aimed at facilitating cooperative endeavors by conveying such information. In such circumstances, cooperative endeavor would be considerably more difficult, to say the least. And here the utility of self-knowledge depends crucially on its being acquired by self-acquaintance; if I had to figure out from my behavior what my beliefs, goals, intentions, etc. are, then in most cases it would be more efficient for others to figure this out for themselves than to wait for me to figure it out and then tell them about it.

The other useful role of self-knowledge I am going to comment on is its role in deliberation, both about what to do and about what to believe. (It may seem tempting to view deliberation about what to do as a battle in which one's various desires are pitted against one another, the strongest prevailing and determining one's course of action.) Similarly, one might try to view deliberation about what to believe as a battle between contending beliefs or inclinations to believe.) If this were right, it would seem unnecessary that the deliberator should have knowledge of the contending beliefs and desires; he would merely be the subject of them, and the battleground on which the struggle between them takes place. But this model seems hopelessly unrealistic, in part because it leaves out entirely the role of the person as an *agent* in deliberation; it represents deliberation as something that happens in a person, rather than as an intentional activity on the part of the person. That this is wrong seems obvious; what is perhaps not quite so obvious is that the agency involved in deliberation essentially involves self-knowledge.

Deliberation is a self-critical enterprise. One's beliefs, desires, and intentions are up for review, and for this to occur one must not only have them but be aware of having them. Suppose that one's standing beliefs include the belief that *P* and the belief that if *P* then *Q*, and that one now comes up against evidence that *Q* is false. To see that there is a problem here that calls for resolution, it is not enough to be aware that the propositions "*P*," "If *P*, then *Q*," and "Not-*Q*" form an inconsistent triad; one must also be aware that these are all propositions one believes or is disposed to believe or has prima facie reason to believe. It is this aware-

28

ness, plus one's desire to avoid error, that motivates the various intentional activities involved in putting one's beliefs in rational order – the review of one's reasons for believing the various propositions, and perhaps the conducting of tests and the collection of new evidence. Someone who had no idea what he believed could not entertain the possibility that any specific one of his beliefs was wrong, and could not be led by doing so to initiate activities aimed at testing that possibility. If such a person's beliefs were inconsistent, and he were aware of the inconsistency between the propositions believed, he would have to think, incoherently, that the *facts* were inconsistent! As long as he remained ignorant of the fact that these propositions were believed by him, the objective of changing his beliefs so that they are no longer inconsistent would be one that he would have no way of forming or pursuing.

Similar remarks apply to deliberation about what to do. This often stems from competing desires. But the mere fact that certain of one's desires are in conflict will not by itself motivate activity directed at resolving the conflict. The activity I have in mind involves a critical assessment of one's desires, aimed either at deferring satisfaction of certain of them, or at denying satisfaction to some of them and if possible, extinguishing them. This obviously involves the operation of what Harry Frankfurt has called "second-order desires" – desires to the effect that certain first-order desires, and not others, be operative in the determination of one's behavior.[2] But to the extent that the influence of desires is rational, desires will influence behavior, including mental behavior, only in conjunction with appropriate beliefs; and where the operative desires are second-order desires, the beliefs would have to include beliefs about what one desires. Suppose that I have a desire for something the pursuit of which would conflict with other aims I have, or with fundamental values I have, and that as a result of deliberation I suppress the desire or at least deny it satisfaction. This can scarcely be a direct effect of the operation of my first-order desires together with relevant beliefs. It cannot be that the offending desire simply lost out in a tug of war between first-order desires. What we may suppose to have happened is that I noticed the conflict between this desire and others that I had, and that I then drew upon my knowledge of the world to calculate the consequences of pursuing these various competing goals (this would involve both calling up memories of relevant facts, and reasoning on the basis of what one takes to be the facts), and that I called to mind my more basic values, second-order de-

2 See Frankfurt 1971.

29

sires, and the like, and, viewing the results of my empirical reasoning in the light of these desires, "identified" (as Frankfurt would put it) with certain of my first-order desires and resolved to restrain or suppress others of them. Like any other rational activity, this activity must have been motivated by a set of desires and beliefs which "rationalized" it. The desires will have included a higher-order desire aimed at maximizing my utility or desire satisfaction in the long run, or something of the sort. The only sort of belief which could combine with this desire in such a way as to rationalize the activities involved in deliberation is a belief about one's system of desires, namely that it involves conflicts that are bound to give rise to imprudent action unless one engages in effective deliberation. And some of what goes on in the deliberative process requires for its explanation more specific beliefs about one's desires, namely beliefs to the effect that one has desires with such and such objects; only so could one be motivated to find out how the pursuit of certain objects would affect one's ability to pursue certain other objects.

III

Nothing I have said about the utility of self-knowledge and self-acquaintance entails the Cartesian thesis that it is of the essence of mental states, or of any central kind of mental states, that they be accessible to their possessor by self-acquaintance.) It seems offhand that it is open to the anti-Cartesian to hold that while the higher-order intentions involved in at least some communication are no doubt useful, and while they do require a capacity for self-acquaintance, they are not essential to mentality. Likewise, even if deliberation, as it exists is in us, requires self-acquaintance, it may be, for all I have argued so far, that one could have the benefits of deliberation without such self-acquaintance.

Now on one understanding of the claim that self-acquaintance is not essential to mentality I am prepared to concede it. I am prepared to ascribe beliefs, desires, and intentions to such lower animals as chimpanzees and dogs. And offhand it seems outrageous to ascribe to such creatures beliefs about their mental states. Such animals do not engage in the sorts of communicative and cooperative endeavors that would warrant such ascriptions. Nor is there any reason to think that they go in much for deliberation. This requires me to refine the Cartesian thesis I wish to defend.

What I wish to maintain is the impossibility of something I shall call "self-blindness." A self-blind creature would be one which has the conception of the various mental states, and can entertain the thought that it has this or that belief, desire, intention, etc., but which is unable to become aware of the truth of such a thought except in a third-person way. In other words, a self-blind creature could frame and understand ascriptions to itself of various mental states, but would be incapable of knowing by self-acquaintance whether such self-ascriptions were true. Only if self-blindness were a (conceptual possibility) would it be appropriate to think of the capacity for self-acquaintance as a quasi-perceptual capacity, which is something over and above the capacity to have and conceive of the mental states in question. And it is the appropriateness of so thinking of it that I am anxious to deny. Now, whatever else may be the case with dogs and chimpanzees, there is no reason to think that they are self-blind in this sense. If it is true that dogs lack knowledge of their beliefs, this is not because a dog can wonder whether it has a certain belief but has no way (except by observing its behavior) of establishing whether what it wonders is true!

To deny the possibility of self-blindness is to hold that it is implicit in the nature of certain mental states that any subject of such states that has the capacity to conceive of itself as having them will be aware of having them when it does, or at least will become aware of this under certain conditions (e.g., if it reflects on the matter). And this seems to me to qualify as a Cartesian thesis. In the remainder of this essay I shall be arguing in its support.

IV

Suppose a man confronts evidence which contradicts things he believes, and he makes suitable modifications in his beliefs – he modifies them in the way rationality dictates, or at any rate in one of the ways rationality allows, instead of sticking with an inconsistent or incoherent set of beliefs. Does this show self-knowledge? Specifically, does it show awareness that there was inconsistency in his beliefs and that modification was called for? I think it plainly does if the modification of belief is the effect of deliberation or reflection – we have already seen the central role self-knowledge plays here. But I wish to argue that even if no explicit rationalization or deliberation went on, such a readjustment of one's beliefs requires self-knowledge, or at least something very much like it. The man, or something in him, must be sensitive to the fact that there is the inconsistency, and must know what changes in his body of belief would remove it – and this requires knowledge (or something like it) of what beliefs he has.

31

Someone might object that self-knowledge is no more involved here than in any other case in which a man acts on his beliefs and desires. Suppose that my beliefs and desires call for (i.e., they "rationalize," to use Donald Davidson's term) a certain course of action, and I undertake that course of action, from those beliefs and desires. Does this show that I am aware that my beliefs and desires call for that course of action? It might be thought that the fact that I so act shows that I, or something in me, is sensitive to the fact that these beliefs and desires call for that course of action. But this is true only in the sense in which a bomb, in going off, shows that it, or something in it, is sensitive to the fact that the combustion in the fuse has reached the explosive. In the case of the bomb, the "sensitivity" is nothing over and above the various properties of the bomb having their natural effects. And in the case of the person acting on his beliefs and desires, the sensitivity is nothing over and above the particular beliefs and desires having their natural effects. Roughly speaking, it is the *existence* of the beliefs and desires, not *knowledge* of their existence, that gives rise to the behavior they rationalize. This needs to be qualified, since someone who was irrational could have had those beliefs and desires and not so acted. Perhaps, then, we should add the rationality to the causal factors. The fact that the person is rational might be compared to the fact that the powder in the bomb was dry. In order that the dryness of the powder should play its enabling role, it is not necessary that the bomb, or anything in it, should *know* that the combustion in the fuse has reached the powder. And no more is it necessary that I or something in me should *know* that my beliefs and desires are such and such in order for my rationality to play its enabling role. Indeed, you might say that for me to be rational just *is* for me to be such that my desires and beliefs tend to give rise to behavior they rationalize. Perhaps what is comparable in the bomb to the rationality of the person is its "explodability" – a property which is realized in, among other things, the dryness of its powder.

Applying this to the readjustment of my beliefs in the face of new evidence, someone might say that just as we need no self-awareness in order to explain my acting on my beliefs and desires, we need none in order to explain my modifying my beliefs and desires in the light of new experience. What produces the modifications is just the existence of the beliefs and desires and experiences, plus the fact that I am rational.

But the cases seem to me importantly different. I agree that we don't need any self-awareness in order to explain why beliefs and desires jointly produce effects which they rationalize – i.e., actions which it is rational for the subject of such a set of beliefs and desires to perform. Given that the agent is rational, the mere existence of such beliefs and desires is sufficient to explain their having the appropriate effects. But if the beliefs and desires are all first-order beliefs and desires, i.e., beliefs and desires that are not themselves *about* the agent's beliefs and desires, then one thing they do not rationalize is changes in themselves. For such changes to be rationalized, the beliefs and desires would have to include second-order beliefs and desires – desires to promote consistency and coherence in the system of beliefs and desires, and beliefs about what changes in the beliefs and desires would be needed in order to satisfy the second-order desires, which in turn would require beliefs about what the current beliefs and desires are.

In a rational being, there are two sorts of causal efficacy exerted by the first-order beliefs and desires. They jointly produce such effects as their contents make it rational for them to produce. And they jointly produce such effects as are needed in order to preserve or promote consistency and coherence in the belief-desire system. The latter may require the initiation of investigations aimed at discovering which of two inconsistent propositions is true, and of reasoning aimed at discovering which of two such propositions coheres best with certain other propositions, which are the contents of beliefs that are part of the system. Now it seems to me that the least we can say of this case is that it is *as if* the system contained a desire to be a rational and coherent belief-desire system, and beliefs (true beliefs) about what beliefs and desires it contains. If it is viewed as containing such second-order desires and beliefs, then the second sort of effect of beliefs and desires (the changes in the belief-desire system) can in a sense be assimilated to the first (the production of effects "rationalized" by the belief-desire system). The first-order desires and beliefs will be seen as producing knowledge of themselves, this knowledge of course consisting of true second-order beliefs. And this knowledge, given the rationality of the system and the desire to be rational (a second order desire), will produce the behavior (perhaps only "mental behavior," like reasoning) which it, together with the second-order desire, rationalizes, and which eventually results in changes in the system of beliefs and desires. But perhaps we needn't suppose that each belief or desire produces a separate state which is the knowledge or belief in its own existence. Perhaps instead it is the case that insofar as a person is rational, each belief and desire tends to double as knowledge or belief in its own existence. For perhaps in making its contribution to the preservation or restoration of consistency and coherence in the system, each desire and belief plays

[margin note: do 2nd order beliefs have to be conscious?]

[bottom handwritten note: At this juncture self-acquaint.33 becomes merely self-knowledge/-belief; whereas prior to this it seemed also to involve self-consciousness → or at least it was an open question whether it nec. involved self-consc. Apparently the self-acquaint. that Shoemaker argues is essential to mind need not be conscious.]

the causal role appropriate to a second-order belief to the effect that one has the first-order belief or desire in question. Either way, rationality would be seen as requiring self-knowledge.

I am tempted to say that if everything is as *if* a creature has knowledge of its beliefs and desires, then it *does* have knowledge of them. There is no phenomenology of self-knowledge of such states that is in danger of being ignored if we say this – there is nothing it is like to believe something, and there need not be anything it is like to know or believe that one believes something. What I am inclined to say is that second-order belief, and the knowledge it typically embodies, is supervenient on first order beliefs and desires – or rather, it is supervenient on these plus a certain degree of rationality, intelligence, and conceptual capacity. By this I mean that one has the former *in* having the latter – that having the former is nothing over and above having the latter.[3]

2nd order beliefs supervene on 1st order beliefs

If this is right, then of course the "self-blind man" is an impossibility. But I realize that some will be skeptical about what I have just been saying. Why couldn't there be a creature which is simply "hardwired" to make, in the light of new experience, the adjustments in its belief-desire system that are required to preserve rationality, without there being any second-order beliefs and desires that rationalize these adjustments? And why couldn't this show itself in the creature's behavior, in particular in its unwillingness to avow the relevant second-order beliefs and desires? To meet this challenge, I want to present an argument aimed more directly at showing the impossibility of self-blindness. I will call it the argument from Moore's paradox.

V

To say "It is raining, but I don't believe that it is raining" is not to assert an explicit contradiction, for both conjuncts may be true – it can be raining even though the speaker believes that it is not. But some sort of logical impropriety has been committed if this sentence is assertively uttered. This sort of impropriety – that manifested in utterances of the form "*P*, but I don't believe that *P*" – was first noticed by G. E. Moore, and has come to be discussed under the heading "Moore's paradox."[4]

Now there are, it seems offhand, conceivable circumstances in which

---

3 A very similar view is expressed in McGinn 1982, pp. 20–21.
4 Moore's paradox, and its bearing on the nature of self-knowledge, is the subject of Essay 4.

such an utterance might be expected from someone who was self-blind. Assuming that self-blindness is possible, it would not of course prevent its victim from having beliefs about his environment, such as that it is raining. And offhand it would seem that it should not prevent him from expressing such beliefs by making assertions. But since he would have plenty of information about his behavior, and can be presumed not to be cognitively or conceptually deficient in any way (his deficiency is supposed to be quasi-perceptual), it ought also to be possible for him to have, and give verbal expression to, behaviorally based beliefs about his own beliefs – first-person beliefs he acquires in a "third-person way." Now it seems possible that the total evidence available to a man at a given time should support the proposition that it is raining, while the total "third-person" evidence available to him should support the proposition that he does not believe that it is raining. This could happen even if the third-person evidence included the fact that he had just said "It is raining"; for the rest of the third-person evidence might support the proposition that in circumstances like these he is likely to lie! So if a self-blind man were in such circumstances, it seems that he might be led, on perfectly reasonable grounds, to assert the Moore-paradoxical sentence "It is raining, but I do not believe that it is raining."

Let us call our self-blind man George. As I have said, George's deficiency is supposed to be perceptual, or quasi-perceptual, rather than cognitive or conceptual. And this provides a reason for thinking that, contrary to what I just said, he would *not* make Moore-paradoxical utterances in such circumstances. Being as conceptually sophisticated as any of us, George ought to be as capable as anyone of recognizing the paradoxical character of Moore-paradoxical sentences. Unfortunately, there appears to be no generally agreed upon account of what exactly the logical impropriety involved in asserting such sentences is. But I suppose it would be generally agreed that the assertive utterance of such a sentence would be self-defeating. Since in asserting the first conjunct one would, if sincere, be expressing the belief which the second conjunct denies one has, one could not hope to get one's audience to accept both conjuncts on one's say so, and could have little hope of getting them to accept either. In any case, whatever the details of the right account, it ought to be possible to get George to recognize that the assertive utterance of Moore-paradoxical sentences involves some sort of logical impropriety, and defeats the normal purposes of assertion. Since we can assume him to be a rational man, we can assume that this recognition would lead him to avoid Moore-paradoxical utterances.

35

But let us suppose that it does so. What leads him to avoid such utterances is, presumably, his grasp of the nature of assertion and its relation to belief. But it would seem offhand that if George's conceptual grasp could have the effect of leading him to avoid Moore-paradoxical utterances, it should also have certain related effects. If asked "Do you believe that *P*?" he ought to answer "yes" just in case he would answer "yes" to the question "Is it true that *P*?" (and this should be so whether his intention is to tell the truth or to lie). Moreover, he will recognize that the meaning of "believe" makes it appropriate for the words "I believe" to function as a kind of assertion sign, but will be capable of appreciating the Gricean considerations that lead to its omission except when there are special reasons for including it (e.g., when the assertion is guarded or hesitant); so it is to be expected that he will preface his assertions with "I believe" in just the circumstances in which this is pragmatically appropriate. But now George is beginning to look just like a normal person. It would appear that there would be nothing in his behavior, verbal or otherwise, that would give away the fact that he lacks self-acquaintance. This seems to conflict with what I said earlier about the benefits of self-acquaintance; for on the supposition we are now making, those same benefits would be available to a self-blind man whose cognitive and conceptual resources were comparable with ours. And how can we be sure, if this is so, that self-blindness is not the normal condition of mankind? But rather than conclude that self-acquaintance provides no benefits that would not be available without it, and that it is questionable whether we have it, it seems better to take the considerations just mentioned as a reductio ad absurdum of the view that self-blindness is a possibility.

What I just said was all on the supposition that George's awareness of the logical impropriety of Moore-paradoxical utterances, and in general his grasp of the concepts involved, would lead him to avoid such utterances. And it may be objected that this is unwarranted. George's conceptual grasp does lead him to see the following as a sensible rule: "If you have the intentions (Gricean or whatever) that make appropriate an assertive utterance of a sentence '*P*,' don't conjoin this utterance with an assertive utterance of the sentence 'I don't believe that *P*.'" The trouble, it may be said, is that because of his self-blindness George is incapable of recognizing (except on third-person evidence) that the antecedent of this rule is true, and so is incapable of being guided by the rule in his linguistic activity.

But there is something peculiar about this view of the matter, if it is legitimate to suppose that George is capable of making assertive uses of language. If he has this capability he has to be capable of acting in accordance with, and in some sense following, rules of the form "If you have such and such intentions, utter '*P*' assertively," even though he would, if self-blind, be incapable of detecting (except on third-person evidence, which would usually be unavailable) whether the antecedents of such rules were true. Suppose, now, that we accept the general claim that if a creature is capable of following a rule of the form "If you are in circumstances *C*, do *X*," it is in some sense capable of recognizing that it is in circumstances *C*. It follows right away that a self-blind creature could not possess the assertive use of language.

Here a natural rejoinder is that this general claim about rule following is false. A well constructed Celsius thermometer "acts in accordance with" the rule "When your temperature is *X* degrees Celsius, register *X* degrees Celsius," but it does not literally recognize anything at all. Why shouldn't the following of linguistic rules sometimes be like this? Someone's being taught the assertive use of language is just a matter of certain causal connections being set up between person's mental states and certain behavior, namely the making of certain sorts of utterances. And it might be said that for a person to be such that certain mental states cause him to make certain utterances, so that he acts in accordance with rules of the form "When in mental state *M*, do *X*," it is not necessary that he be able to *establish* that he has those mental states – any more than a thermometer must be able to *establish* that it has a certain temperature in order for it to be such that its having that temperature causes it to register that temperature.

This rejoinder sounds prima facie plausible. But if it applies to rules of the form "If you have such and such intentions, utter '*P*' assertively," why shouldn't it apply to the only slightly more complicated rules which enjoin the avoidance of Moore-paradoxical utterances, require one to assent to "I believe that *P*" if one assents to "*P*," and so on? It is conceivable, I suppose, that a creature might be capable of being taught to act in accordance with rules of the first sort while being incapable of being taught to act in accordance with rules of the second sort. The additional complexity of the latter might be the straw that breaks the camel's back. But this additional complexity should not tax the abilities of our man George, whom we are supposing to have cognitive and conceptual capacities comparable to our own. It therefore seems to me that if despite his self-blindness George could acquire the assertive use of language, then in doing so he would also learn to use "believe" in such a way as to avoid pragmatic paradox, and what goes with this, to give appropriate answers to questions of the form "Do you believe that *P*?", to preface certain kinds of assertions with the words "I believe," and in general, to be indistinguishable from someone having the faculty of self-acquaintance. But the truth of this conditional seems to me a reductio ad absurdum of its antecedent. So the immediate conclusion of the argument from Moore's paradox is that for creatures having cognitive and conceptual capacities comparable with our own, the ability to acquire the assertive use of language excludes self-blindness – more specifically, this ability necessarily goes with a capacity for self-acquaintance with respect to beliefs.

Anyone persuaded of the view that self-blindness is possible will of course reply that the most this argument shows is not that there could not be a self-blind man but only that such a man could not have the assertive use of language – or, more guardedly, that he could use language assertively only in cases in which he had third-person knowledge (i.e., behaviorally grounded knowledge) of his own beliefs. This goes with the view that assertion is an expression of second-order beliefs (beliefs about one's beliefs) rather than first-order beliefs. This is, indeed, in line with one version of H.P. Grice's account of meaning – that according to which (leaving out some complications) meaning that *P* is doing something with the intention to bring about in one's audience the belief that one believes that *P*, through their recognition that one has this intention. Assuming that asserting involves meaning what one says, this account would suggest that sincerely asserting that *P* involves believing that one believes that *P* while insincerely asserting that *P* involves believing that one does not believe that *P*. And assuming that assertion must be sincere or insincere, this would imply that assertion involves a second-order belief as to whether one believes the thing asserted.

Now *in a way* this is what I hold myself. Since I think that anyone with the relevant conceptual and cognitive abilities will have the second-order beliefs if he has the corresponding first-order beliefs, I think that the person who makes sincere assertions expressive of his first-order beliefs will believe that he has those beliefs. But the opponent I have in mind thinks of assertion as directly the expression of second-order beliefs; and given that he thinks this, he thinks that there is a possibility which my argument cannot rule out without begging the question – namely that the self-blind man would not have the assertive use of language, except insofar as he gets second-order beliefs by third-person means, and that he would be distinguishable from normal persons by just that fact.

38

What I need to support my case is a reason for thinking that someone with first-order beliefs plus human conceptual capacity and normal rationality would thereby have the use of language, where this reason does not beg the question by assuming from the start that such a person would have to have second order beliefs as well. I will now try to present such a reason. As before, George will be a supposedly self-blind man who has human intelligence and conceptual capacity. My aim will be to reduce to absurdity the supposition that he is self-blind.

Given his intelligence and conceptual capacity, George should have no difficulty coming to understand language – i.e., learning rules that enable him to know what the truth conditions are for utterances of indicative sentences, what intentions, desires, feelings, etc. are expressed by utterances in the various moods, and what the standard effects of such utterances are. The question is whether he could employ this knowledge in the making of assertions. Well, it would seem that he could see that certain ends he has would be furthered by his saying certain things, and that this could motivate him to say those things, in just the way in which in other cases he is motivated to do what tends, according to his beliefs, to bring about the satisfaction of his ends. More specifically, he could know that the standard effect of hearing a sentence uttered in certain circumstances is to come to believe a certain proposition, and this could lead him in certain circumstances to utter a sentence with the object of making his audience believe the proposition expressed by it. (It may be objected that he can use language to further his aims only if he knows what his aims are. But if it is true in general that purposive action requires knowledge of what one's aims are, then I need argue no further, since this implies the impossibility of self-blindness. I have been assuming, however, that at least sometimes it is one's *having* an end, not one's knowing that one has it, that combines with one's beliefs to produce action, and that this can be true when the action is one of uttering a sentence assertively.)

Earlier I mentioned a version of Grice's theory of meaning according to which the intended effect, when one means that P by uttering something, is that one's audience believe that one believes that P. But in Grice's first formulation of the theory the intended effect was said to be that the audience believe that P.[5] Obviously both sorts of intentions are possible. If someone intends by doing something to bring it about that

5 For Grice's earlier formulation, see Grice 1957. For his later formulation, see Grice 1969.

his audience believes that it is raining, and intends that this effect come about through his audience's coming to believe that he has this intention, let us say that he has a Grice-1 intention. If the intention is that the audience should believe, through recognizing the intention, that the speaker believes that it is raining, let us say that the speaker has a Grice-2 intention. I do not wish to deny that our intentions in speaking are often Grice-2 intentions. But what I have argued is that given a general ability to engage in practical reasoning, Grice-1 intentions are enough to account for a good deal of what looks like assertion. If the self-blind man is a possibility at all, he will be capable of such intentions, and will have (or appear to have) an assertive use of language.

Does it follow that George would be indistinguishable from a normal person — and thus that we get a reductio ad absurdum of the supposition that he is self-blind? Well, not immediately. For what about cases in which there would be a point in his speaking with Grice-2 intentions (if only he had them), but no point in his speaking with Grice-1 intentions? Consider, for example, a case in which he knows that his hearer already believes that P (so there would be no point in his saying "P" with the object of getting his hearer to believe this), but in which there would be a point in his conveying to his hearer that he believes that P — perhaps he knows that his hearer is looking for a fellow P-believer with whom to start a partnership, so that it would be to his advantage that his hearer believe that he is a P-believer if, but only if, he actually is one. It might seem that this is the case that would provide a behavioral difference between George and the normal man. The normal man, who has self-acquaintance, would straightforwardly express his belief (either by saying "I believe that P" or by saying "P"), while George, being self-blind, would just stand there — knowing that the other already believes that P, he has no motive to assert P in order to get him to believe this, and not knowing his own belief he lacks a motive for trying to get his hearer to believe that he believes that P.

But it seems to me that George would have a motive for saying "P," or "I believe that P," in this case. He could reason as follows. "P is true. [This expresses his belief, but it of course doesn't say that he has it.] It is therefore to anyone's advantage, by and large, to act on the assumption that P is true, for, ceteris paribus, one is most likely to achieve one's ends if one acts on assumptions that are true. Since this applies to anyone, it applies to me — ceteris paribus it is to my advantage to act on this assumption. But that means acting as if I believed that it is true. In this instance so acting would mean saying 'I believe that P,' or just 'P.' And

40

plainly this would have good consequences for me. For it would lead this man to choose me as his partner, and given that what this man believes is true, a team consisting of him and someone else who will likewise act on the assumption that P is likely to be successful (since they will be acting on the assumption of a truth)."[6] Having given himself a good reason for saying "P" or "I believe that P," he then says one of these. It seems to me that he would always have such an argument available to him, in any case in which it would be rational for a self-aware believer to avow his belief. So again it looks as if he would speak, as well as act, just as a rational self-aware man would. And this calls into question the supposition that he lacks something the self-aware man has.

I should mention in passing that one thing this reasoning assumes is that having concluded that it is to his advantage to act on the assumption that P is true, George has reason to think that he will so act. Only so does he have reason to think that if he teams up with the other, the two together will act as if P were true. But if he can't do this, i.e., if his beliefs about what is the case and how he ought to behave in the future (given what he takes to be the case) give him no indication of how he will in fact behave in the future, then it seems to me that we don't have the rational sort of creature we are supposed to have. We don't have the sort of creature who can plan, or who can undertake projects that take time to execute − i.e., ones such that the initial stages make sense only on the supposition that they will be followed up in certain ways. Perhaps what we have uncovered here is a connection between knowledge of one's own mental states and intentional knowledge of one's own future behavior − knowledge that one will do something because one has excellent reasons for doing it and for that reason intends to do it. What I am inclined to think is that one cannot have the latter without the former, and

---

6 Our (putatively) self-blind man would of course have to contend with the point that acting as if one believed a true proposition may not conduce to the attainment of one's goals if at the same time one is acting on other beliefs that are false. But here he is no worse off than someone who is not self-blind. Many philosophers (e.g., Davidson) have offered more or less a priori arguments in favor of the presumption that beliefs are generally true; and our man is as entitled as anyone to avail himself of such arguments. And even if this presumption cannot be supported on a priori grounds, there would seem to be good empirical evidence in its favor, which likewise would be available to our man, even if (ex hypothesi) he doesn't know what in particular his own beliefs are. And of course the argument I imagine him giving about P is one he can give about any proposition which in fact he believes—so if someone points out that acting on P will advance his aims only if Q is true and he acts on it, then if in fact he believes that P, he will be able, arguing as above, to give himself a reason for acting as if he believes that both P and Q are true.

that the capacity to have the latter is indispensable for any creature to which anything like human rationality can be ascribed.

One might think that George's self-blindness could show itself in his response to a request like "Tell me some things you believe." But there is no reason why this should leave him speechless. He could be sure of making an appropriate and correct response to this request by treating it as equivalent to the request "Tell me some things that are true." Interestingly enough, *trying* to satisfy the latter request, whether successful or not, guarantees *successfully* satisfying the earlier one. And there is no reason why George should not realize this.

VI

Before going on to consider how the argument from Moore's paradox applies to states other than belief, I want to consider a pair of objections to the argument as stated so far. One of these will require me to qualify the conclusion I have drawn from it.

I began by saying that is seems offhand that there are conceivable circumstances in which the total evidence available to a man supports the proposition that it is raining while the total third-person evidence supports the proposition that he does not believe that it is raining, and that if the man were self-blind he might well come up, in such circumstances, with the Moore-paradoxical utterance "It is raining but I don't believe that it is raining." I then went on to argue that it follows from the stipulation that the self-blind man is not in any way conceptually deficient that he would avoid such utterances, would assent to "I believe that it is raining" just in case he would assent to "It is raining," and in general would use "believe" in first-person utterances in pragmatically appropriate ways. And I wrote as if this showed that even in the sort of case envisioned, his behavior would be indistinguishable from that of a normal person. The first objection is that it does not show this. As before, let George be the putatively self-blind man. If George is self-blind, then in the envisaged circumstance he is going to be very puzzled. He knows that Moore-paradoxical utterances are to be avoided. Yet it will seem to him that such an utterance is warranted by the evidence. His grasp of the concepts of belief, assertion, etc. may prevent him from making such an utterance. But it doesn't appear that there is anything that would prevent him from giving expression to his puzzlement. And now there will be something – namely his expression of puzzlement – that distinguishes him from the normal person. This may seem to ruin my attempt to re-duce to absurdity the supposition that he is self-blind.[7]

The answer to this is that the case envisioned is not really conceivable. There is a contradiction involved in the idea that the total evidence available to someone might unambiguously support the proposition that it is raining and that the total third-person evidence might unambiguously support the proposition that the person does not believe that it is raining. For the total third-person evidence concerning what someone believes about the weather should include what evidence he has about the weather – and if it includes the fact that his total evidence concerning the weather points unambiguously toward the conclusion that it is raining, then it cannot point unambiguously toward the conclusion that he doesn't believe that it is raining. So the situation I said seems "off-hand" to be conceivable is not really conceivable. Since the objection now under consideration depends on the conceivability of that situation, and none of my own claims depend on it, the objection would seem to be answered.

But a related objection is not so easily answered. Consider George's knowledge of his *past* beliefs. To a large extent it can be just like the knowledge a normal person has of his past beliefs. Often one knows of one's past beliefs on the basis of "third-person evidence." One remembers what one did and said, and draws conclusions from that about what one believed. Or one knows things about what evidence was then available to one (perhaps because it was the evidence available to everyone), and concludes from that that one must have believed that such and such. Such ways of knowing about past beliefs will be available to George. But there is an additional way normal people can know about past beliefs. Sometimes a belief does not manifest itself in any behavior, verbal or otherwise. And in some such cases information about what evidence was available concerning a certain matter may be insufficient to indicate what the person believed about it. This might be because the belief was due to wishful thinking, or it might be because it arose from complex inferences which the person's behavior gave no indication that he was performing or capable of performing. Now in some such cases a normal person will nevertheless know later on what he believed – he will have known this by "self-acquaintance" at the time, and will have retained this

---

7 This objection was raised by a member of the audience when I read an earlier version of this essay at Berkeley. At the time I had no answer to it.

43

knowledge in memory. This is the sort of memory one expresses by saying "I remember thinking at that time that . . . ," or "I remember that despite the evidence to the contrary, I was convinced that . . . ." But if George is self-blind, and lacks the faculty of self-acquaintance, then he won't have this sort of knowledge of his past beliefs. And this is a difference between him and other people that should be detectable; if a person never has beliefs about his past beliefs that are not grounded on third-person evidence, this fact should reveal itself. Of course, George might make himself indistinguishable from other people by *pretending* to have such beliefs. But the claim that he might be indistinguishable from normal people for *this* reason can hardly be used as part of a reductio ad absurdum argument against the supposition that he is self-blind.

I think that this objection does require me to quality my claims. If someone's access to his own past beliefs is completely a third-person access, let us say that he suffers from DAPB (for direct access to past beliefs) deficiency. It does seem that self-blindness would bring DAPB deficiency with it, and that DAPB deficiency would be detectable. It doesn't follow, however, that there is self-blindness wherever there is DAPB deficiency. For why couldn't there be someone whose faculty of self-acquaintance is unimpaired, but who has a memory impairment that results in DAPB deficiency but does not interfere with the memory of facts known otherwise than on the basis of self-acquaintance? If there could be, then I can modify my claim as follows: while the self-blind man would not be indistinguishable from a normal person, he would be indistinguishable from someone who has self-acquaintance but suffers from DAPB deficiency.

Let's come at this from another direction. Our earlier discussion suggests that when George has the belief that *P*, his behavior will be that of someone who believes that he believes that *P*. This implies that George has a state that plays at least a good part of the causal role of the second-order belief expressed by "I believe that *P*." That is, he has a state that combines with his desires and other beliefs to produce the sorts of behavior that that second-order belief, together with those other beliefs and desires, would rationalize. All of this he would have simply in virtue of being rational, having normal conceptual capacities, and having the relevant first-order beliefs. Let's call this a "quasi" second-order belief, where this leaves it open whether it is a genuine second-order belief or an "ersatz" one. The supposition that George is self-blind is the supposition that it is ersatz. What the objection just raised comes to is that on this supposition this quasi second-order belief would lack one part of the

But one may generate a memory of past belief by having gone through the inferential steps to get to the conclusion that one holds the belief — going through those steps only "in one's head," so to speak

causal role of the genuine second-order belief that one believes that *P*. Part of the causal role of such a second-order belief is to have, to borrow a term of David Kaplan's, a certain sort of "cognitive dynamics" – such a state produces, or turns into, a past tense second-order belief to the effect that one did at the time in question have the first-order belief in question. And this state will be causally independent of the corresponding past tense first-order belief. For example, if at *t* I believe that it is raining, and believe that I believe this, then the latter belief will turn into a belief that I believed at *t* that it was raining, and this is a belief I may continue to have even if I cease to believe that it was raining at *t*. But now let us imagine someone, call him George★, who is just like George except that when he believes that *P*, his quasi-belief that he believes that *P* not only plays the causal role that George's plays but also has the cognitive dynamics of a genuine second order belief – it produces, or turns into, a state that plays the causal role of a past tense belief on his part that he previously believed such and such. Anyone who thinks George★'s present tense quasi second-order beliefs are ersatz will probably think that his past tense ones are ersatz too. And anyone who thinks that George's present tense quasi second-order beliefs are ersatz will probably think that George★'s are ersatz too. For it hardly seems plausible that adding this additional bit to the causal role of a state turns it from an ersatz belief to a real one, and bestows on its possessor a faculty of self-acquaintance – especially if, as I suggested earlier, someone possessing such a faculty could suffer from DAPB deficiency. But George★ will not be distinguishable from a normal person even in the way George was. It does not seem to me at all plausible to deny that George★ has a faculty of self-acquaintance. And I think that if we allow that he has one, we should allow that George has one as well, and that self-blindness with respect to belief is an impossibility.

VII

At best, the argument I have given so far shows that George, the putatively self-blind man, would give every indication of having knowledge of him own *beliefs* – it says nothing about his situation *vis à vis* his other propositional attitudes, such as desire, hope, intention, etc. Now there are counterparts to Moore's paradox in the case of these other propositional attitudes. In the case of desire, the Moore-paradoxical utterances would be ones like "Please close the window, but I don't want you to" and "How old are you? – but I don't want you to tell me." In the case of hope there is "Would that he would come, but I hope that he doesn't." For the case of intention there is "I'll be there, but I intend not to be." Will my argument from Moore's paradox, and the related points I have made, show that George will give indications of having knowledge of his own desires, hopes and intentions?

Up to a point it will. Given his intellectual abilities, George will see the advisability of avoiding the Moore-paradoxical utterances relating to desire, etc., just as he saw the advisability of avoiding those relating to belief. So, for example, even when the behavioral evidence indicates that he doesn't want something, and he does in fact want it and so is disposed to ask for it, he will not come up with the likes of "Please close the window, but I don't want you to." But as in the case of belief, if he is capable of avoiding Moore-paradoxical utterances, he should in other ways be capable of using the verbs of propositional attitude in pragmatically appropriate ways. He should answer affirmatively to "Do you want X" if he answers affirmatively to "Shall I give you X?" If he is capable of using language at all, he should be capable of giving linguistic expression to his desires, e.g., by making requests and other speech acts aimed at the attainment of things he wants. And if he is capable of doing this, he should be capable of learning to do it by saying things of the form "I want X" or "I would like X." Similar considerations suggest that words like "hope" and "intend" will turn up in his first-person utterances, used in pragmatically appropriate ways.

But there are two parts of my argument about belief for which there are no counterpart arguments about desire and other propositional attitudes (from now on, I will talk only about desire). I could claim without begging any questions that simply in having the belief that P, George has a premise, namely P, from which he can reason that it is to his advantage to act in ways expressive of belief that P, including saying that he believes it. But belief is unique among propositional attitudes in being such that having the attitude entails having available as a premise the proposition that is the "object" of the attitude. Obviously this is not true of desire. Also, and what goes with this, there seems to be no formula for satisfying the request "Tell me some of your desires" that is comparable with the one I suggested for satisfying the request "Tell me some of your beliefs," namely treating this as equivalent to "Tell me some things that are true."

Perhaps, however, these differences between belief and desire are made up for by another one. As practical reasoning is usually represented, in the basic case statements about the agent's beliefs will not figure among the premises — the premises will of course be expressions of the agent's beliefs, but what they will be about is the nature of the world and the agent's situation in it. With desire, however, it seems different; it is natural to include among the premises statements about the agent's desires or goals. So, in a simple case, the premises might be "I want X" and "The most efficient way of getting X is to do A," and the conclusion "I should do A." Earlier I said that it seems that it is the *having* of beliefs and desires, not believing that one has them, that leads to action. But when the action is the result of practical reasoning, this seems at best half true – the premises need not express a belief about the agent's beliefs, but they must, it may seem, express a belief about his desires. If we further claim that rationality plus human conceptual and intellectual capacity requires engaging, on appropriate occasions, in practical reasoning which results in actions rationalized by the agent's desires, we get the conclusion that it requires self-knowledge with respect to desire, and hence that self-blindness is impossible. This is of course a much quicker argument than the one I gave about belief, and bypasses the argument from Moore's paradox.

It can be objected, however, that the premises in practical reasoning need not be explicitly about the agent's desires. The work done by premises about the agent's desires or goals can be done instead by premises about what is good or desirable. Instead of "I want X" we might have "It is desirable that I should have X." This brings us to a tangled issue: the connection between regarding something as desirable and actually desiring it. If the former entailed the latter, we could have our man George reasoning as follows: "X is desirable. Therefore [by my earlier argument] I should act as if I believed that X is desirable, and so, among other things, should include the claim that I believe this among the premises I employ in my reasoning. From this premise it follows that I desire X. So if I am asked what I desire I should say that I desire X, in the absence of reasons for doing otherwise." In that case George's behavior would presumably be that of a normal person. And assuming that regarding something as desirable and desiring it generally go together, it would seem that such reasoning would for the most part lead to George's acting as if he has self-acquaintance with respect to his desires. Indeed, if we could suppose that George is a perfectly rational being, we would have no problem – for (in a perfectly rational being, presumably, desiring and regarding as desirable would always go together.) But all I have been supposing is that George is rational to the extent that normal human beings are – it is on that degree of rationality, plus first-order beliefs and desires and normal human intelligence, that I want to claim that self-acquain-

47

tance supervenes. And in normal human beings desiring and regarding-as-desirable do sometimes come apart. So I need an argument to show that in the exceptional cases in which this happens, George will still behave as if he had knowledge of his desires – or as much such knowledge as the rest of us do.

I have no argument for this that satisfies me. Still, the claim seems to me plausible. We have already seen that George can be expected to say things of the form "I want X" as the expression of his desires, and it is to be expected that he will sometimes say this even when he would admit that the thing wanted is not objectively desirable. Similarly, it is to be expected that he will sometimes say "I don't want X" as the expression of a desire not to have something, say a painful medical treatment, even when he would admit that the thing is objectively desirable. The difficulty of producing a decisive argument here is due in part to the fact that, issues about self-knowledge aside, it is difficult to know what to say about cases in which there seems to be a discrepancy between what a person wants and what he thinks is objectively desirable, valuable, or worthwhile. It is natural to say that if the person really does regard something as objectively desirable then in some sense he wants the thing, although in another sense he doesn't. Given what I have said about George, it does not appear to me that the conflicting indications about what he wants, and about what he thinks about what he wants, would be different from what we find in normal people.

Although I do not claim to have a decisive argument, I think that my consideration of Moore's paradox gives support to the claim that normal human rationality and intelligence plus first-order beliefs and desires gives you everything, in the way of explanation of behavior, that second-order beliefs can give you – from which we should conclude either that second-order beliefs are superfluous or, what I think is the correct conclusion, that second-order beliefs, and the self-knowledge they constitute, are supervenient on first-order beliefs and desires plus human rationality and intelligence. To accept the latter conclusion is to reject the possibility of self-blindness, and with it the perceptual model of self-awareness.

VIII

Let me end by trying to forestall one possible objection to what I have been saying. It may be thought that in denying the possibility of the self-blind man I am denying the possibility of unconscious beliefs, desires,

and intentions. And it may be objected that we know, from the work of
Freud and others, that any such denial has to be wrong. Fortunately, the
question of whether self-blindness is a possibility is not the same as that
of whether there can be unconscious beliefs, desires, etc. Clearly, a man
with the unconscious belief that he is a failure is not someone who is
prepared to assert "I am a failure" but not "I believe that I am a failure."
Presumably he will be no more disposed to assert the first than the second, and in fact can be expected to deny both. Nor, presumably, will he
be someone whose nonverbal behavior is always, or normally, what
rationality would dictate for someone having the beliefs and desires he
has, including the belief that he is a failure. That belief may manifest itself
in his behavior in devious ways, but it is not to be expected that he will
act on it, in the sense of performing actions which it, in conjunction
with his other beliefs and desires, "rationalizes." Here, admittedly, things
begin to get messy, for it is arguable that there is a *kind* of rationality, al-
beit very limited rationality, involved in self-deception about such matters – in failing to face up to what deep down he knows, the man is pro-
tecting himself against situations that would be very painful. Still, I take it
that overall such a man's actions, in relation to his beliefs, values, etc., exhibit a failure of rationality. What I have asserted, in denying the possibility of self-blindness, is a connection between self-knowledge and rationality; that given certain conceptual capacities, rationality necessarily
goes with self-knowledge. It is entirely compatible with this that there
are failures of rationality that manifest themselves in failures of self-
knowledge. And such I assume we have in cases of unconscious belief. All
of this, I realize, puts a rather heavy burden on the concept of rationality.
Fortunately, that is a matter for another essay, which I haven't the slightest idea of how to write.

[margin handwritten note:] But even here, a zombie might say, "I believe I am a failure."

3

First-person access

I

A distinctive feature of recent philosophy of mind has been the repudiation of "Cartesianism." With one part of this repudiation, namely the rejection of mind-body dualism, I am in complete agreement. But my concern in the present essay is with a different part of it, namely the rejection of the Cartesian conception of the mind's epistemic access to itself – as a first approximation, the view that each of us has a logically "privileged access" to his or her own mental states, and that it is of the essence of mind that his should be so.

Like the repudiation of Cartesian dualism, the repudiation of the Cartesian privileged access thesis is nothing new, and stems at least as much from scientific as from philosophical considerations. An extreme version of the privileged access thesis is the "transparency thesis" – the view, apparently held by Descartes, that nothing can occur in a mind of which that mind is not conscious. It is not easy to see, now, how this ever could have been plausible. In any case, it is widely seen as having been refuted by Freud, as well as by recent psychological research of a distinctly non-Freudian character which seems to show both that a vast amount of what goes on in a person's mind is completely inaccessible to that person's introspective consciousness, and, what is equally shocking to Cartesian preconceptions, that when people do report on their own mental operations, these reports are often wrong.[1] There are, however, weaker forms of the privileged access thesis that do not seem to be undermined, at least directly, either by acceptance of the Freudian unconscious, or by acceptance of the existence of unconscious mental processing *a la* modern cognitive psychology, or by the psychological evidence of the fallibility of people's "introspective" judgments about their own mental processes. These concern the nature of "first-person access" to two sorts of mental states: sensory states, including both sensation (e.g., pain) and

My thanks to Carl Ginet, Richard Moran, and David Velleman for helpful comments.
1 See Nisbett and Wilson 1977.

perceptual states (e.g., seeming to see red), and intentional states, such as beliefs, desires, and intentions. One claim is that such states are necessarily "self-intimating": that it belongs to their very nature that having them leads to the belief, and knowledge, that one has them, or at any rate that it normally does so under certain circumstances. Another claim is that a person has "special authority" about what such states he or she has. Sometimes this is taken to mean that a person's self-ascriptions of such states are infallible or incorrigible – that it is impossible in principle that they should be mistaken. But weaker forms of the claim are possible; at a minimum it is the claim that it is in some sense necessary that our beliefs about our own mental states of these kinds be for the most part correct, and that a person's belief that she has such a state creates a presumption that she has it, in a sense in which it is not true that someone's having a belief that some *other* person has such a state creates a presumption that that other person does indeed have the state.

The self-intimation claim and the special authority claim are closely related. If the presence of a certain mental state intimates itself to its possessor, let us say that it is *weakly* self-intimating. If both the presence of the mental state and the lack of it intimate themselves, let us say that it is *strongly* self-intimating. If a state is strongly self-intimating, then assuming the impossibility of blatantly contradictory beliefs (e.g., someone believing both that he is in pain and that he is not) self-ascriptions of that mental state will be generally correct, and so also will be claims to the effect that one lacks that mental state. Likewise, if both claims to the effect that that one has a certain mental state and claims to the effect that one lacks that state are infallible, or even for the most part true, then, assuming the impossibility of what I shall call first-person agnosticism concerning that mental state, both the presence of that mental state in a person and its absence will normally be intimated to that person. Concerning some sorts of mental states, first-person agnosticism is clearly a possibility; someone may just have no opinion, even when he reflects on the matter, about whether he has an oedipus complex, or whether a certain sort of information-processing is going on in him. But offhand it seems as little possible that someone should have this sort of agnosticism regarding sensations and ordinary beliefs and desires, the states about which self-intimation and infallibility claims are made, as it is that someone should have blatantly contradictory beliefs about his mental states of these sorts. We might sum up the situation as follows. If it is necessarily the case that if one addresses the question of whether one has mental state M one has an opinion about whether one does (call this the ban on first-person agnosticism), and if in addition it is impossible for someone to believe both that he has M and that he doesn't (call this the ban on blatant self-contradiction), then the strong self-intimation claim about M is true just in case the infallibility claim is true about first-person M judgments. If the strong self-intimation claim is weakened slightly, so as to say that it is of the essence of M that its presence or absence normally intimates itself to the person, then what it is equivalent to, assuming the ban on blatant self-contradiction and first-person agnosticism, is a special authority thesis slightly weaker than infallibilism, namely that it is necessarily the case that self-ascriptions of M and non-M are normally correct.

I think that the current anti-Cartesian consensus is such that most philosophers of mind, or at any rate a substantial number of them, reject all self-intimation, infallibility, and special authority theses, along with the stronger "transparency thesis" that is nowadays rejected by everyone. It would not be denied by most of these philosophers that *in fact* we are normally right in our self-ascriptions of sensory and intentional states, and are seldom in a state of ignorance or first-person agnosticism about them. It *would* be denied that it is in any way conceptually necessary that this be so. And it would be denied that there is any sort of special certainty that attaches to first-person mental state ascriptions and sets them apart from other beliefs about the world – a kind of certainty that gives them a unique foundational role *vis à vis* the rest of our knowledge and beliefs.

You have probably surmised by now that I have not taken the trouble to lay out this consensus position only to say that I agree with it. I do agree with part of it. In particular, I agree with the denial that first-person mental state ascriptions have a kind of supercertainty that bestows on them a special and unique foundational role. But I think that there are defensible versions of the self-intimation and special authority claims. So to a limited extent the essay will be a defense of Cartesianism.

II

The version of the special authority thesis I endorse is not the infallibility claim. But the infallibility claim does have a good deal of intuitive plausibility, and it is useful to consider why this is. The very vehemence with which some recent philosophers attack it testifies to the initial pull it has on us.

To some extent, I think, the attractiveness of the infallibility claim is the product of the compelling force of Descartes' "Cogito argument." An interesting slide occurs in the Second Meditation. Early on Descartes asserts the indubitability of "I think," along with "I exist." A few pages later he asserts, in effect, the indubitability of a wide range of first-person mental state ascriptions, including such judgments as that it seems to one that one sees light, that one hears noise and that one feels heat, this on the grounds that what these ascribe "is simply thinking."[2] Recent philosophers who have reflected on why "I think" is immune even to the radical doubt of the First Meditation, based on the idea that one may be deceived by an all powerful demon, have generally seen that "It seems to me that I feel heat" cannot be immune to doubt for the same reason. "I think" is indubitable for a logical reason; it is a logically necessary condition of my being deceived about anything that I think, since being deceived is a matter of having false beliefs, which in turn is a special case of thinking – in the sense of "think" in question. "I think," like "I exist," is necessarily self-verifying, in the sense that it is a necessary condition of its being asserted, or even entertained in thought, that it be true. But it is obvious that attributions to oneself of particular thoughts, such as "I think that I am breathing," and also attributions to oneself of perceptual states, such as "It seems to me that I feel heat," do not have this status. The truth of these is not a necessary condition of their being asserted or entertained. Nevertheless, the slide from claiming the indubitability of "I think" to claiming the indubitability of propositions ascribing particular thoughts and conscious states is a very natural one. It is natural to suppose that one's belief in the truth of what is expressed by "I think" and one's other beliefs about one's current mental states are all products of some common mental faculty of self-knowledge – e.g., are all deliverance of "inner sense." If one sees *that* "I think" is indubitable, without seeing clearly *why* it is, it is very natural to suppose that its indubitability must reflect the infallibility of that faculty. And then it is natural to suppose that other deliverances of that faculty share the same indubitability. I hope it will be agreed that insofar as the infallibility thesis has this source, it is grounded on confusion.

But the thesis has another source of plausibility. We are accustomed to using imaginability as a test of possibility. And often the task of imagining so and so is equated with the task of imagining something that would *show* so and so to be the case. Suppose, then, that we are asked to consider whether it is possible for someone to believe that he is in pain when he is not. There are two ways in which one might try to imagine this –

2 Cottington et al. 1984, Vol. II, P. 18.

from the first-person perspective, and from the third-person perspective. Let's begin with the former.

The demand here cannot be that one imagine believing that one is in pain while having decisive evidence that one is not; arguably there is no proposition whatever that one can imagine believing while having what one regards as decisive evidence that it is false, and it does not follow from this that there is no proposition whatever that one can imagine falsely believing. What I can do with the proposition that the sun is shining is imagine believing it and at the same time imagine that there is decisive evidence, though not evidence available at the time to me, that it is false. (So it is only the having of the belief, not its falsity, that is imagined from the first-person perspective.) So let us see if I can imagine falsely believing that I am in pain in this way. Now if one is asked to imagine believing something, one is bound to imagine having *evidence* of the thing in question, or at least being in circumstances that entitle one to believe it. For example, if asked to try to imagine believing that the sun is shining, I will imagine having certain visual experiences, certain feelings, and so on. But what am I to do when asked to try to imagine believing that I am in pain? It is natural to say that insofar as anything is my evidence that I am in pain, it is the pain itself. And indeed, the instructions "Imagine *believing* that you are in pain without imagining that you *are* in pain" seem impossible to follow. But of course, it is impossible to imagine being in pain while imagining there being, at the same time, decisive evidence that one is not in pain — at any rate, this is impossible if imaginability is taken to imply possibility. Our question concerns the possibility of someone's believing that he is in pain when he is not; and the attempt to imagine this from the first-person point of view seems necessarily to fail.

So let us see if we can imagine this situation from the third-person perspective. We are to imagine there being evidence that decisively shows that someone believes that he is in pain, together with there being evidence that decisively shows that that person is not in pain. Again the difficulty is obvious. The most decisive third-person evidence that the person believes that he is in pain would include his saying, with every indication of sincerity, that he is in pain. But that is precisely what we would ordinarily take as decisive evidence that the person *is* in pain; so how can we imagine a case in which there is this evidence *together with* evidence that decisively shows that the person is *not* in pain? To be sure, we can suppose that while the person says "I am in pain," all of the facts about his nonverbal behavior and circumstances point to the conclusion that he

54

is not in pain. But it is precisely in such circumstances that we would be led to question either the person's sincerity in saying "I am in pain" or his understanding of the meaning of those words; and evidence that would lead us to question either of these would undercut the putative evidence that he believed that he was in pain. It should be added that an important part of our nonverbal evidence that someone is in pain is so through being evidence that he believes that he is in pain; this is true of such things as taking aspirin, going to the doctor, etc. This compounds the difficulty of imagining there being decisive evidence that someone believes he is in pain together with there being decisive evidence that he is in fact not in pain. So our attempt to imagine there being the belief without the pain seems no more successful when conducted from the third-person perspective than when conducted from the first-person perspective. Insofar as imaginability can be taken as a test of possibility, this seems to support the claim that such a case is not a possibility.

This argument from imaginability for the infallibility thesis would take a somewhat different form if we took some state other than pain as our example – e.g., an intentional state such as believing that it is sunny outdoors. But I think the argument has equal force when applied to a number of different states. Since I do not endorse the infallibility thesis, I do not of course claim that the argument is decisive. The connection between imaginability and possibility will not bear that much weight. Moreover, I will concede later on that we may after all be able to imagine cases in which someone is mistaken about his own sensory or intentional states. But at the very least the argument is of diagnostic interest; I think that the difficulty of imagining cases of mistaken self-ascription of sensory or intentional states (especially, I think, the difficulty of imagining such cases from the first-person perspective) is a major source of the plausibility of the infallibility thesis. Moreover, the argument brings out some points of importance. The first-person version reminds us that first-person ascriptions of such mental states are typically not grounded on evidence of any sort, unless we count a pain or belief as evidence of itself. The third-person version reminds us of the close connections, sometimes amounting to identity, between the behavioral manifestations of mental states and the behavioral manifestations of first-person belief in such states. Finally, while the conclusion of this argument is one I reject, similar arguments provide part of the case for a conclusion I accept. If it is difficult to imagine counterexamples to the infallibility thesis, it is even more difficult, I think impossible, to imagine counterexamples to the special authority thesis which asserts the for-the-most-part-truth of first-person mental state ascriptions – and in my view this is because the latter is indeed necessarily true.

It will be complained, with some justice, that in discussing the possible evidence about a person's mental states and his beliefs about his mental states I did not consider facts about the person's inner physiology. It is sometimes suggested that we could discover that someone was mistaken in thinking he was in pain by finding that although he asserts with every indication of sincerity that he is in pain, he is not in some physiological state (C-fiber firing, say) that we have found to be correlated with pain – or, alternatively, that he is in a physiological state we have found to be correlated with belief that one is in pain while not in any physiological state we have found to be correlated with pain. I shall return to this later on, and will argue that while there could (perhaps) be physiological evidence that a first-person ascription of pain was mistaken, this does not jeopardize the special authority thesis I shall defend, or the imaginability argument for it.

III

One way of putting the imaginability argument for the special authority thesis is to say that on any imaginable basis for assigning to people beliefs concerning their own mental states, those beliefs would have to be for the most part true. This should be reminiscent of a more general claim that has had some prominence in recent philosophy. Donald Davidson has argued in a number of places that, to put it crudely, it is a necessary constraint on the "interpretation" of the utterances and attitudes of others that we regard their beliefs as by and large true, and has used this as a sort of transcendental argument to show that most beliefs must be true.[3] A natural thought, for anyone who finds Davidson's claim plausible, is that the special authority thesis is true just as a special case of the Davidsonian claim. This of course would cast the special authority claim in a rather non-Cartesian light; it would obliterate the sharp distinction Descartes saw between the epistemological status of beliefs about one's own mental states and beliefs about other matters, and it would make inappropriate the application of the word "special" to the authority one has about one's own mental states. I hasten to add that this is not how Davidson himself views first-person authority about mental states; he

3 See Davidson 1974, Davidson 1977, and especially Davidson 1986.

thinks that there is something special to the first-person case, and that it is rooted in a difference between a speaker's knowledge of the meanings of his own utterances and the knowledge an "interpreter" has of this.[4] Nevertheless, the relation between the special authority thesis and the more general Davidsonian claim is worth investigating.

I think that the strongest considerations in favor of the Davidsonian claim are the considerations that have been taken to support causal theories of reference and causal theories of mental representation. Hilary Putnam has argued that the skeptical hypothesis that we are brains in vats is incoherent, and presumably he would also regard as incoherent, on the same grounds, the skeptical hypothesis that we are all victims of systematic deception by a Cartesian evil demon.[5] The basic idea behind his argument is that the reference of our terms, and the representational content of our mental states, is determined in part by what sorts of things we stand in certain causal relations to, these being the sorts of causal relations that are involved in perceptual and other sorts of epistemic access. To put the point in terms of Putnam's well known "Twin Earth" example, what makes it the case that my term "water" refers to H_2O, rather than to the phenomenally identical substance XYZ which my doppleganger on Twin Earth uses "water" to refer to, is that my perceptual and other causal interactions have been with H_2O rather than with XYZ.[6] Applying this to the case of the brain in the vat, if there were brains in vats, receiving their sensory inputs from computers, their words could not have the same referents as ours have and their mental states could not have the same contents ours have. Even if a brain in a vat were just like me "inside the head," i.e., its neurophysiological states were just like mine, its beliefs could not be about trees and tables and vats − at best they would be about states of the computer that play the same role in producing its beliefs as trees, tables, and vats play in producing mine.[7] It follows from such an account that our beliefs could not be systematically false, since it is a necessary condition of their having the contents they do that we stand in certain sorts of causal relations to the things or states of affairs

4 See Davidson 1984.
5 See Putnam 1981, Chapter 1.
6 See Putnam 1975.
7 This will be true if the brain has always been in the vat, i.e., has never been embodied, and so related to the world in the normal way. If until recently a brain has been normally embodied, it could be argued that its states have contents bestowed on them by its recent connections with the world, and are about trees and the like.

they are about, these relations being apt for producing in us true beliefs about those things or states of affairs. As Davidson has put it, "we can't in general first identify beliefs and meanings and then ask what caused them. The causality plays an indispensable role in determining the content of what we say and believe."[8] Much the same sort of conclusion follows from the account of mental representation advanced by Dennis Stampe and Robert Stalnaker.[9]

These views have it in common that their account of what makes it the case that mental states have the representational content they do, namely certain causal or counterfactual relation between states of mind and states of the world, guarantee that what our beliefs are about is something we have epistemic access to, and rule out that our beliefs about the world should be systematically false. If we are guided in interpreting people's attitudes by what such accounts say we should be guided by, we will attribute a large measure of truth to their beliefs. But this supports only a qualified form of the Davidsonian thesis that beliefs must be by and large true. Surely there could be people who devote most of their time spouting false sentences which they "hold true." Where it seems most plausible that beliefs must be by and large true in order to have the contents they do is where their connections with the world are most direct – i.e., this is most plausible where we can suppose the beliefs to be generated, for the most part, by the states of affairs that make them true, and in a way that involves minimal dependence on reasoning and background theory. I shall sometimes refer to these as "foundational beliefs" (not meaning thereby to endorse a foundationalist account of knowledge). Perceptual beliefs about the environment constitute one category of beliefs of this kind – and it seems plausible that the determination of the content of these plays a central role in the determination of the contents of representational states generally.[10] But first-person ascriptions of sensory and intentional states would seem to be another such category. Like perceptual beliefs they are (mostly) uninferred, and are taken to be the products of the very states of affairs they report. The suggestion to be considered is that the basis of the special authority thesis about first-person mental state ascriptions lies in the same sorts of considerations that support the quasi-Davidsonian claim that perceptual beliefs must be gen-

8 Davidson 1986, p. 317.
9 See Stampe 1977 and Stalnaker 1984.
10 In Shoemaker 1963 I maintained that it is a necessary truth that sincere memory and perceptual claims are generally true; but I can no longer endorse the arguments I gave there.

erally true – roughly that it lies in the truth of a causal theory of refer-ence and mental representation.[11]

It would be compatible with this suggestion that as a matter of contin-gent fact, first-person mental state ascriptions are less subject to error than perceptual judgments about the environment, perhaps because the causal connections between beliefs and the states of affairs they are about are more direct in the former case than in the latter. But the claim would be that insofar as it is conceptually necessary that the "for the most part true" claim holds for the former, it does so for reasons that apply to the latter as well.

I have, of course, done no more than hint at the considerations that support a causal theory of content, and at those that support the infer-ence from such a theory to the conclusion that beliefs, or some subcate-gory of beliefs, must be generally true. While I am sympathetic to such claims, I shall not attempt to establish them here. What I want to consid-er is whether, supposing that some view along these lines is right, the first-person authority claim can be regarded as a special case of it.

That it is not *just* a special case of it is suggested by the following consideration about the thought experiments Putnam uses to support his claims about the content of mental states. What happens in these, e.g., the Twin Earth case and the Brain-in-the-vat case, is that what is "inside the head" is held fixed through a number of situations while the environment is varied; our intuitions about the different situations are then held to show that the content of mental states is not determined solely by what is inside the head, as it is on "individualistic" accounts of mental content, and that instead it is determined in part by causal and epistemic relations to things in the environment. As we vary the nature of the environment, we must change our content assignments in such a way as to preserve, at least, the general truth of perceptual beliefs formed in normal circumstances, and of other beliefs closely related to them. Thus it is that my thoughts are about H_2O and the thoughts of my doppleganger on Twin Earth are about XYZ, even though we are alike "inside the head." But of course, when the contents of someone's thoughts are about that very same person's mental states, we cannot hold fixed what is "inside the head" while varying the part of reality the

11 I suggested this view in my comments on Frederick Kaufman's paper "Self-ascription of Sensations and Causal Theories of Mind," delivered at the meetings of the Eastern Division of the American Philosophical Association in 1986, and came to doubt it as the result of questions raised by Stephen Schwartz on that occasion.

thoughts are supposed to be about, since that part of reality is, precisely, what is inside the head.[12]

It may seem that this is easily gotten around. We might redescribe what happens in the Putnam examples as follows: we hold fixed the intrinsic, nonrelational features of beliefs "about the environment" while varying the environment, and we see as we do this that the content of the beliefs changes in such a way as to preserve the general truth of the beliefs. To make the same point about first-person mental state ascriptions, we will hold fixed the intrinsic, nonrelational features of beliefs "about one's own mental states," thereby holding fixed *part* of what is "inside the head," while varying other parts of what is inside the head, and we will claim that as we do this the content of the first-person beliefs changes in such a way as to preserve the truth of the beliefs. As we might put it, following a number of recent theorists, in both cases we hold fixed the "narrow content" of certain beliefs, and alter their "wide content" by altering their causal relations to other parts of the world.[13]

The distinction between narrow and wide content, which is problematic enough as applied to beliefs about the environment, is especially problematic as applied to beliefs about one's own mental states. But let us suppose for the moment that the distinction can be drawn. Even so, if we try to construct examples involving first-person mental state ascriptions that parallel Putnam's examples, we will find that the parallel breaks down at a crucial point.

If we could have here a parallel to Putnam's Twin Earth example, or his brain in a vat example, it would have to go something like this. In the actual situation "believe" in one's first-person utterances refers to *belief*, and the propositions expressed by those utterances, and so the first-person beliefs expressed by them, are by and large true. In an alternative situation (on Twin Earth, or in another possible world) in which the intrinsic, nonrelational features (the "narrow contents") of one's first-person psychological beliefs are the same, the beliefs would be false if assigned their actual world (wide) content – e.g., when one says or thinks "I believe that the sun is shining," one doesn't (usually) believe that the sun is shining. However, in the alternative situation "believe" means something

---

12 Here I am indebted to Stephen Schwartz.
13 Roughly, narrow content is supposed to be what is shared by mental states when the states are individuated by their intrinsic, nonrelational features, while wide content is what is ascribed in ordinary "folk psychological" content ascriptions, and is determined by causal, etc., relations to what the states are about. See Putnam 1975, p. 220, and Fodor 1987, *passim*.

different, and what is *there* meant by these first-person utterances are generally things that are true, and hence the beliefs *there* expressed by them are generally true.[14] This parallels the fact that the assertions of my doppleganger on Twin Earth would be false if "water" in them had the meaning it has in my assertions, but are true given the meaning they have in his.

That the parallel breaks down is shown by the fact that one thing I will certainly believe in any situation in which my narrow first-person beliefs are the same as my actual ones is that the attitude I have toward "The sun is shining" is the *same* as that I have toward "I believe that the sun is shining" – that I believe the one in the same sense in which I believe the other. But in the envisaged alternative situation, supposing it to be a possibility, this will not be true. By hypothesis, it is *belief* I have toward whatever content is there expressed by "I believe that the sun is shining" – it is precisely in order to preserve the general truth of my *beliefs* about my own states that we are supposed to assign that sentence a different content in the alternative situation than in the actual one. But since, in that situation, the "believe" in the sentence doesn't refer to *belief*, I will be wrong in thinking that my attitude toward whatever is there expressed by "The sun is shining" is the same as my attitude toward whatever is there expressed by "I believe that the sun is shining." And to be wrong about that is to be wrong about something rather fundamental.[15]

This shows that *if* the meaning and reference of "believe" could

14 To a large extent, of course, what determines the (wide) content of first-person mental state ascriptions is the same as what determines the content of beliefs about the environment. If my relations to my environment bestow a certain content on the thought I express by "The sun is shining," they thereby determine a large part of the content of the thought I express by "I believe that the sun is shining." So the content of the second (and of the thoughts expressed by it), being in part determined by my causal and epistemic relations to my environment, cannot be determined entirely by my causal and epistemic relations to my own internal states. What can be determined in this way is, at best, what state or relation the word "believe" refers to in that sentence. More generally, it is the reference of the distinctively mental terms – "belief," "fear," "pain," etc. – that we might try to suppose is determined by causal and epistemic relations to mental states in a way parallel to that in which the reference of terms like "tree" and "water" is determined by causal and epistemic relations to items in the environment.

15 David Velleman has suggested to me that the strategy of reinterpreting beliefs so as to make them true might be reapplied to circumvent this difficulty. Perhaps someone could come up with a reinterpretation of "same" (or "same attitude") which makes true (in the envisaged situation) the belief I express by saying "The attitude I have toward 'The sun is shining' is the same as that I have toward 'I believe that the sun is shining,'" and claim that the envisaged shift in the reference of "believe" is accompanied by a shift to this sense of "same." I have my doubts as to whether a satisfactory such reinterpretation could be worked out, but have no proof that it could not be.

change in such a way as to leave unchanged the narrow content of first-person mental state ascriptions, this would preserve the truth of one set of first-person beliefs (those expressed by sentences like "I believe that the sun is shining") only at the cost of falsifying others (those expressed by sentences like "I believe that I believe that the sun is shining in the same sense in which I believe that the sun is shining"). This is enough to show that the strategy of preserving the general truth of beliefs by reinterpreting contents so as to make beliefs come out true does not work in the case of first-person belief ascriptions. But in addition, there are reasons for doubting that such a change is possible. As "Moore's paradox" brings out, sentences like "The sun is shining but I don't believe that the sun is shining" have a distinctive sort of logical oddity. Such sentences can be true, but they are not rationally assertible. Let us call such sentences "Moore-paradoxical." Now suppose that the meaning and reference of "believe" changes, so that it refers to some other relation belief*, and that otherwise the "wide" content of mental states remains the same. Will sentences of the form "*P* but I don't believe [i.e., believe*] that *P*" be Moore-paradoxical? If not, there should be circumstances in which such sentences are rationally assertible. But on any plausible account of narrow content, if what someone means by "believe" is such that he is disposed to assert such sentences in some circumstances, the narrow contents of the states he uses "believe" to express cannot be the same as those of someone who uses "believe" to refer to belief. On the other hand, if such sentences are Moore-paradoxical, that seems a strong reason for saying that belief* is, or at any rate includes, *belief*, contrary to our supposition – for how can such a sentence be Moore-paradoxical except through there being an incompatibility between what its second conjunct asserts and what the speaker in some sense implies in asserting the first conjunct, namely that he *believes* the proposition in question? So in either case, we do not have a change in the meaning and reference of "believe" accompanied by no change in narrow content.

This does not mean that first-person belief ascriptions do not share with perceptual beliefs about the world the property of being such that the way their content is determined makes it impossible that they should be generally false. It only means that the basis of this property cannot be the same in both cases. Of course, first-person *belief* ascriptions are only one kind among many of first-person mental state ascriptions; so it may be, for all I have shown, that for some or all of the other kinds the basis of this property (the property of being for the most part true because of the way their content is determined) is the same as it is in the case of percep-

tual beliefs about the world. And, indeed, I do not deny that this may be
so in some cases. But it cannot be so in all.

IV

Here is a sketch of an alternative explanation. Consider again the case in
which we hold fixed across some range of different situations someone's
beliefs "about his own mental states" (where these beliefs are individuated "narrowly") while varying their causal relations to other internal
states. The strategy we have rejected says that insofar as we can do this,
the beliefs have different contents in the different situations, and are for-
the-most-part-true in each. The alternative account says that insofar as
we can do this, the different internal states a given first-person belief is
caused by, in the different situations, are merely different "realizations" of
the *same* mental state, and the first-person belief retains the same content, and remains for-the-most-part-true, across all of the different situations.

What this requires is a version of the functionalist or causal account of
mind that incorporates into the functional definitions of certain sorts of
mental states connections between being in a certain state and believing
that one is in that state. Functionalist accounts define mental states in
terms of their causal relations to inputs (sensory stimuli and the like),
outputs (behavior), and other mental states. The claim would have to be
that in the case of the mental states about which the special authority
claim is made, i.e., sensory and intentional states, the nature of these
defining causal relations is such as to guarantee the truth of the infallibility thesis that self-ascriptions of these states must always be true, or at
least of the special authority thesis that weakens "always" to "for the most
part."

David Lewis has shown how one can, given certain suppositions, make
one's functional definition of a mental state such that the infallibility thesis is true of it. On his approach, what I call the "Ramsey-Lewis technique," mental states are defined in terms of the Ramsey sentence of a
common sense psychological theory made up of a number of "platitudes" about the relations of mental states to one another and to inputs
and outputs. He asks us to suppose that among the platitudes "are some
to the effect that introspection is reliable: 'belief that one is in pain never
occurs unless pain occurs' or the like,"[16] and that these platitudes play a

16 Lewis 1972, p. 214 in Block.

certain role in the "term-introducing postulate" for our common sense theory. Given these suppositions,

> ... the necessary infallibility of introspection is assured. Two states cannot be pain and belief that one is in pain, respectively (in the case of a given individual or species) if the second *ever* occurs without the first. The state that *usually* occupies the role of belief that one is in pain may, of course, occur without the state that *usually* occupies the role of pain; but in that case (under the suppositions above) the former is no longer the state of belief that one is in pain, and the latter no longer is pain. Indeed, the victim no longer is in any mental state whatever, since his states no longer realize (or nearly realize) common-sense psychology. Therefore it is impossible to believe that one is in pain and not be in pain.

Lewis does not himself endorse the infallibility thesis or the suppositions here used to generate it.[17] Nor do I. Later I shall argue that an approach somewhat along the lines he suggests gives us a defensible version of the special authority thesis. But first let me indicate why I do not accept the version presented here.

First of all, while it is a virtue of the Ramsey-Lewis technique that it acknowledges, and invokes, the "holism of the mental," this particular version seems to exaggerate it. It is true, and one of the insights behind functionalism, that a creature will be capable of having a certain mental state only if it is capable of having countless others, and that mental states are partly defined and individuated by their relations to other mental states. But this surely ought not to be taken to imply that, for example, a creature that did not have pain in its repertoire of mental states could not have mental states of any sort. So failure to have states that play the causal role of pain, where that role is taken to guarantee first-person infallibility about these states, should not be taken to disqualify a creature from having any mental states whatever.

But this renders it unclear how the "platitude" that belief that one is in pain never occurs in the absence of pain is to play a role in defining mental states or the terms that designate them. If "believes that he is in pain" were not semantically complex, we could think of it and "pain" as designating two states that are definable in terms of each other in somewhat the way "positive charge" and "negative charge" are definable in terms of each other, and in that case this platitude could play a central role in the definition. But of course it is not like this. It is not an orthographic accident that "believes" occurs both in "believes that he is in

---

17 He says that he neither endorses nor repudiates the supposition (p. 215), and begins his discussion by saying "I do not know whether introspection is (in some or all cases) infallible . . ." (pp. 214–215).

pain" and predicates like "believes that it is sunny outdoors," or, for that matter, that "pain" occurs both in "is in pain" and "believes that he is in pain."[18] In general, the meaning of expressions of the form "believes that P" should be a function of the meaning of "believes" and the meaning of P – so the meaning of "believes that he is in pain" should be a function of the meanings of "believes" and "is in pain." If, as seems plausible, "believes" is applicable to creatures that don't have pain in their repertoire of states at all, it is hard to see how the above "platitude" can enter into the determination of *its* meaning. And in any case, it would seem that it ought to be possible to define the concept of belief without mentioning particular contents; obviously it would be impossible to mention in the definition all of the contents that can be believed, and it is hard to see why our definition should have to mention some and not others.

What these considerations suggest is that if Lewis's "platitude" belongs to common-sense psychological theory, its status must be, as it were, that of a theorem rather than that of an axiom or postulate – it must be a consequence of more fundamental principles. But I think that my earlier remarks about the connection between infallibility and self-intimation suggest what these more fundamental principles might be. We can take as one of the constitutive principles of the common-sense psychological theory that, for the class of mental states in question, and for creatures having the conceptual resources for entertaining first-person thoughts about these states, the normal "default" condition *vis à vis* any state in that class is believing or being disposed to believe that one does *not* have it – other things being equal, this is the belief one will have if one considers whether one has the state. We can then take the theory to say that this default condition is overridden when and only when the subject comes to have the state in question – coming to have it replaces the belief (or disposition to believe) that one does not have it with the belief (or disposition to believe) that one has it. This would guarantee, of course, that there would be no blatant contradiction with respect to the possession of states of the sort in question. And it would guarantee that beliefs that one is in that state are always correct: it would imply the infallibility thesis with respect to them.

But now imagine a creature having a set of physical states that by and large conform to the principles of common sense psychology as here envisaged, and fall short of perfect conformity only in the following respect: it very occasionally happens that the state that (by and large) plays

18 For discussion of the view that this is just an orthographic accident, see Field 1978.

the functional role of belief that one is in pain occurs without being caused by the state (suppose there is only one) that plays (by and large) the causal role of pain – perhaps it occurs as a spontaneous, uncaused event, or perhaps it is produced by some chance confluence of antecedent conditions. We can suppose that our account differs from Lewis's in not implying that this creature lacks mental states altogether; but like Lewis's it would imply that the creature never has pain, and never has the belief that it is in pain. And this is a highly implausible consequence. For one thing, it is not credible that our own justified confidence that we ourselves sometimes have pain, and that we sometimes believe that we do, justifies us in believing that we are not creatures of that sort.

But suppose that we weaken slightly the provision in our functional account that gives us strong self-intimation about a certain mental state. As before the account will say that the normal, default condition is believing (or being disposed to believe) that one lacks the state. But instead of saying that this will be overridden when and only when the subject comes to be in the state, it says that the system in which the states are realized is so constituted as to make it highly unlikely that this default condition should be overridden except through the subject's coming to be in the state. Suppose that for a given creature C-fiber firing is a candidate for being the realization of pain and Z-fiber firing is a candidate for being the realization of belief that one is in pain; on our modified account, the fact that Z-fiber firing occasionally occurs without C-fiber firing will not disqualify these as realizations of those states. Nevertheless, while the modified account does not imply the infallibility thesis, it does imply the special authority thesis. It will be not only true but necessarily true that self-ascriptions of the states in question are normally true, and that someone's ascribing such a state to himself creates a strong presumption that he has it.

Let us return to the "imaginability" argument discussed earlier, and to the rebuttal of it which claims that special access theses can be undermined by imaginable discoveries about the physiological bases of mental states. Obviously the possibility of discovering about someone who claims to be in pain that he lacks some physiological state that we had found in the past to be correlated with pain would not do much to refute the infallibility thesis; it might more plausibly be said to show that the correlation between pain and that physiological state is not invariable. It is different, however, if what we imagine discovering is that someone is in a physiological state that "realizes," i.e., plays the defining causal role of, belief that one is in pain while lacking any state that plays the causal role of pain. I have just conceded that this seems imaginable, and that this refutes the infallibility thesis, or at least undermines the imaginability argument in its support. But it might seem that if this is imaginable, it is also imaginable that we should discover creatures who *regularly* are in a state that realizes the defining causal role of belief that one is in pain without being in any state that plays the causal role of pain. If we can imagine a case in which there is Z-fiber firing without C-fiber firing, surely we can imagine a run of such cases. This might seem to refute not only the incorrigibility thesis but the special authority thesis. Similar imaginings might seem to refute any version of the self-intimation thesis; it is as easy to imagine a run of cases in which there is C-fiber firing without Z-fiber firing as it is to imagine the reverse. This might be reinforced by the "distinct existences argument," that has been advanced by David Armstrong and others.[19] If, as seems plausible, awarenesses of mental states are caused by the mental states of which they are awarenesses, these must be distinct existences in the sense in which Hume held that causes and effects are distinct existences, and this means that it can only be contingent that these are "constantly conjoined" to any degree.

One thing wrong with this whole line of thought is that it ignores a distinction between different senses in which a physical state can be a "realization" of a mental one. In one sense a certain pattern of C-fiber firing could be a realization of pain. Given a certain overall organization of the brain and nervous system, such a pattern of firing of C-fibers is, we can suppose, what is produced by the standard causes of pain (cuts, burns, etc.), and is what produces its standard effects. Where this is so, let us say that C-fiber firing is a "core realization" of pain. But there is plainly a sense in which what realizes pain (in such a case) is not C-fiber firing by itself but C-fiber firing *plus* a certain overall organization of the brain and nervous system, one that guarantees that C-fiber firing will "play the causal role" of pain, i.e., will be produced by its standard causes and will produce its standard effects. This more encompassing state, call it "C-fiber firing plus," could be called a "total realization" of pain.[20] If any token of a physical

19 See Armstrong 1968, pp. 106–107.
20 See Shoemaker 1981, especially pp. 264–267, where the core realization/total realization distinction is introduced. To guard against misunderstanding, I should point out that I am not committed to the claim that there will always be some physiologically salient part of the total realization of a mental state that is the core realization – nor, indeed, am I committed to the claim that total realizations will be physiologically salient. It may be that, as John Haugeland has said, "decisions are not distinguishable (even in

state is a total realization of a given mental state, every token of it will be a total realization of that state. But this is not true of core realizations; in a brain "wired" differently from ours C-fiber firing might not play the causal role of pain, and would not be a core realization of pain.

Once this distinction is seen, it is clear that it is perfectly consistent to hold (1) that in us C-fiber firing and Z-fiber firing are realizations of, respectively, pain and belief that one is in pain, and (2) that there could be creatures in which one of these regularly occurs without the other, and in which the second regularly occurs without any realization of pain occurring, while maintaining (3) that pain is necessarily self-intimating and that self-ascriptions of pain are, as a matter of conceptual necessity, normally, or even always, true. For one could maintain that (1) is true if "realization" means "core realization," but not if it means "total realization."

I have in fact conceded that there could be creatures in which occasionally a total realization of belief that one is in pain occurs without being caused, or accompanied, by a total realization of pain – as it might be, Z-fiber-firing-plus without C-fiber-firing-plus or any other total realization. But it by no means follows from the possibility of this that there could be creatures in which the normal state of affairs is that total realizations of belief that one is in pain are unaccompanied by pain. For what the "plus" in "Z-fiber firing plus" might ensure is, precisely, that the overall physical makeup of the creature is such that normally Z-fiber firing will not occur unless it is caused to occur by some realization of pain.[21]

As for the "distinct existences" argument, it is perhaps sufficient to say that while core realizations may be distinct existences in the Humean

principle) as separate individuals *at the level of microphysics* (Haugeland 1983, p. 8), and that what Haugeland says about the level of microphysics also applies to the neurophysiological level. My point is only that *if* some physiologically salient sort of state is found to be associated with a given sort of mental state, and *if* this has a claim to be a realization (rather than a mere correlate) of the mental state, we must carefully distinguish the claim that this is a core realization of the mental state from the claim that it is a total realization of it.

21 This needn't mean that it can never happen that there is a run of cases in which a total realization of belief that one is in pain occurs unaccompanied by any realization of pain. What is required by the special authority thesis, as applied to pain, is that every total realization of belief that one is in pain involve the creature's being so constituted that it is highly unlikely that the creature be in that state without instantiating a realization of pain. That something is highly unlikely does not mean that there cannot be a run of cases of its occurrence. It is possible, though fantastically unlikely, for a "fair" die to turn up six a thousand times in a row, and in that sense, perhaps, it may be possible for someone to be regularly wrong in his self-ascriptions of pain. So even the imaginability of a run of cases in which there are total realizations of belief that one is in pain without realizations of pain does not undermine the special authority thesis.

sense, total realizations are not. Total realizations are individuated by their causal roles in a way that constrains the relations between different ones of them. To use a loose analogy, while loans and repayments are distinct events, they are not distinct existences in the Humean sense – there is no possible world in which a repayment is not always preceded by a loan.

V

I think that it is in fact true that for a large number of mental states, we cannot imagine discovering counterexamples to the special authority claim, even though we can (with some difficulty) imagine discovering counterexamples to the infallibility thesis. This is explicable on the supposition that the mental concepts involved are defined, more or less on the lines suggested by Lewis, in such a way as to make the truth of the special authority thesis constitutive of the mental states in question. But can we give any reasons, other than the imaginability argument for thinking that these concepts are so defined? I think that we can, although here I can give no more than a brief sketch of these reasons.

Several recent writers, including Donald Davidson, Daniel Dennett, and Robert Stalnaker, have laid stress on the point that the attribution of mental states, in particular intentional ones, is possible only on the assumption that the creature to which they are applied is to a certain degree rational.[22] This is a constitutive claim as well as an epistemological one. It is a necessary condition of a creature's having beliefs at all that it exhibit some sensitivity to evidence, i.e., that what beliefs it has is influenced by its sensory input and its other beliefs in at least minimally rational ways. It is also a necessary condition of a creature's having beliefs and desires that there be at least a tendency for its beliefs and desires to lead jointly to the kinds of behavior they jointly make rational, i.e., behavior which, given the truth of the beliefs, should tend to promote the satisfaction of the desires. These patterns of sensitivity to evidence, and tendencies to influence behavior, are arguably part of what determines the identity of states as beliefs and desires, and part of what determines their content. Thus the defining "functional roles" of mental states intimately involve the requirement that the subject of the states be minimally rational – call this the "rationality constraint."

We have seen that the special authority thesis follows from the strong self-intimation thesis and the ban on blatant self-contradiction. It is obvi-

22 See Davidson 1970, Dennett 1971, and Stalnaker 1984, especially p. 15ff.

ous enough that the ban on blatant self-contradiction can be seen as a special case of the rationality constraint. I want to suggest that the strong self-intimation thesis can also be seen as a special case of it.

An essential part of rationality, for creatures with the conceptual capacities of human beings, is the appropriate adjustment of beliefs and desires in the light of new information about the world, and, as a necessary means to such adjustment, the conducting of appropriate tests and reasoning. For someone to know what sorts of tests and reasoning are called for it is essential that he know what his current beliefs are − only so can he know which of them are called into question by new information, and so what questions about the world his tests and reasoning should be focused on. Similar points apply to desires; one cannot rationally revise one's desire system in the light of experience without having knowledge of what desires one currently has. This seems to require that beliefs and desires be self-intimating.[23] To show that this self-intimation has to be *strong* self-intimation, so that the lack of a belief or desire yields belief that one lacks it, would require more space than I have here. One point is that this (in conjunction with the ban on blatant contradiction) would ensure that one's true beliefs about one's beliefs and desires are not swamped by false ones in a way that disqualifies them from being knowledge. One might wonder why there couldn't be a person whose beliefs and desires were weakly self-intimating, so that if she has a belief or desire she believes that she has it, who seldom or never believes falsely that she has a certain belief or desire, but who is frequently in a state of "first-person agnosticism" about whether she has a certain belief or desire (virtually always, as it happens, in cases in which she doesn't have the belief or desire in question). But it is worth asking what such a person would do if asked "Is it true that *P*?" in cases in which she doesn't believe that *P* and doesn't believe anything incompatible with *P*. She won't, if sincere, answer either "yes" or "no." And her answering "I don't know," or "I have no opinion," would seem incompatible with her first-person agnosticism. This suggests that this case involves an incoherence, or at any rate a violation of the rationality constraint; but I shall not attempt to establish this here.[24]

---

23 See Essay 2. See also McGinn 1982, pp. 20–21.

24 In Essays 2 and 11, I attempt to demonstrate the incoherence of the supposition that someone might be "self-blind," in the sense that while otherwise possessed of normal human conceptual and cognitive capacities, including normal rationality, he lacks the normal first-person access to his own intentional states. I think there is a similar incoherence in the supposition that any appreciable degree of first-person agnosticism might occur in an otherwise normal human being.

If our special access to our mental states is tied to rationality in the way indicated, we have an explanation of how it can be the case both that the access must be appreciable and that it is less than perfect. It must be appreciable because an appreciable degree of rationality, and the first-person access that comes with it, is required for the very existence of mental states of the sort we have. It is less than perfect because our rationality is less than perfect. Failures of rationality, such as those involved in self-deception, can bring with them failures in access. But if we try to suppose such failure the rule rather than the exception, we overstep the bounds of intelligibility.

In talking about the connection between special access to mental states and rationality, I have focused on our access to intentional states like belief and desire. It is less obvious how there can be such a connection in the case of our access to sensory states and, especially, to sensations such as pain. I shall limit myself to just one brief remark about this.

There could be a state to which there is no special first-person access and which performs some of the functions of pain. We can suppose that this state is caused by situations that are actually or potentially damaging to the subject's body, and that its effect is to produce involuntary movements that tend to remove the subject from the dangerous situation. So, for example, when produced by proximity to a hot stove, the state causes muscular contractions which send the person's body reeling to the opposite side of the room. If this were all there were to the causal role of this state, no one would be inclined to think that it was a kind of pain, or, indeed, that it was any sort of *mental* state at all. It is also obvious that this state would be considerably less efficient than pain in performing the function it shares with pain, namely that of getting people out of dangerous situations. While the role of pain in producing reflex actions, like withdrawing one's hand from something hot or sharp, approximates to the role of my imagined state, this is the limiting case. Normally the behavioral effects of pain are partly a function of the subject's beliefs and desires. In leaping from the frying pan one tries to avoid leaping into the fire. The bodily protection system of which pain is a part exploits the rationality of the creature. Pain does not simply cause bodily movements apt to be advantageous to the creature; it gives the creature a *reason* for acting in certain ways – and like any other reason, this has the effects it does in combination with the creature's beliefs and desires. It is, I suggest, the fact that the explanatory role of pain is of this sort, i.e., that it is a reason giving role, that qualifies pain as a mental state. And I suggest that its playing this role requires that we have a special first-person access to it.

71

Let me return to the comparison made earlier of the special authority thesis and the Davidson-Putnam thesis that perceptual beliefs, and beliefs closely related to them, must be generally true. I gave a reason earlier for rejecting the view that the truth of the former is *just* a special case of the truth of the latter. And in the course of my discussion a further difference has emerged between these two kinds of "authority." If I am right, special authority about one's mental states can be seen as a consequence of strong self-intimation and the ban on blatant self-contradiction, and as crucially involving the fact that, as I put it, the "default" condition with respect to mental states (of the kinds in question) is being disposed to believe that one does not have them – this is the state one is in (normally) unless one has them. Nothing like this is true of beliefs about the environment. The default condition *vis à vis* environmental states of affairs is not disbelief but "agnosticism" – neither believing that the state of affairs obtains nor believing that it doesn't. Of course, it is now true of me that in the absence of strong evidence that there is a hippopotamus in the house I will believe that there isn't, rather than merely suspending judgment. But this is because of contingent background beliefs I have about the distribution of hippopotami in this part of the world. It is not because of such background beliefs that I believe now that I do not have a headache, or that I believe that I have no opinion as to whether the next president of United States will be a Democrat or a Republican.

Another difference is that in the case of mental states there is a much tighter connection between the obtaining of a state of affairs and the overriding of the default condition with respect to belief in it. If I come to be in pain, the default condition will be overridden automatically, and I will come to believe that I am in pain. But it is not automatic that if there comes to be a hippopotamus in the house, the default condition will be overridden and I will come to believe that there is. To get that belief I will have to get myself in right situation and do the right things.

But despite these differences, I think there is something right about the suggestion that first-person authority and Davidson-Putnam authority about the environment are special cases of something more general. Beliefs about our own mental states and beliefs about the environment are *beliefs* in the very same sense, and there ought to be a general account of belief that applies to both. A satisfactory account of belief should include an account of how the contents of beliefs are determined. Considerations of the sort Putnam and Davidson have emphasized make it plausible that the contents of uninferred "foundational" beliefs are determined in part by their causal relations to the things and states of affairs they are "about." This should apply to first-person "introspective" beliefs as well as to perceptual beliefs about the environment. On a broad construal of "functional," all of this would be part of a functional account of belief. What accounts for what is distinctive about first-person authority stems from the functional nature of the contents believed, i.e., the mental states ascribed, rather than the functional nature of belief *per se*.[25] It is this that makes certain mental states strongly self-intimating. It is, of course, a consequence of a state's being strongly self-intimating (together with the ban on blatant contradiction) that self-ascriptions of it are generally true. But this is just the particular way in which those self-ascriptions, those first-person beliefs, satisfy the general requirement on foundational uninferred beliefs that they be causally related to the states of affairs they are about in such a way as to constitute, normally, knowledge of them. So first-person authority is a special case of the more general phenomenon, but not *just* a special case of it.

25 This relates to a difference between first-person access and sense perception, which seems to me to provide one reason for not construing the former on the model of the latter. From an evolutionary standpoint it seems plausible to say that our repertoire of mental states and our faculty of knowing them "introspectively" were "made for each other." With minor exceptions, this could not be said of environmental states of affairs and our faculty of knowing them perceptually; the latter was "made for" the former, but not conversely – we evolved so as to be capable of having perceptual knowledge of the world, but the world did not evolve so as to be knowable by us. I am suggesting that there is a conceptual difference that, as it were, corresponds to this: whereas in both cases the identity of the beliefs (introspective in the one case, perceptual in the other) is determined in part by their causal and counterfactual relations to the states of affairs known about, the converse relation holds only in the introspective case and not in the perceptual one; it is true of introspectively knowable mental states, but not of perceptually knowable environmental states, that their identity is determined in part by their causal and counterfactual relations to a faculty of knowing them. (But on some theories of secondary qualities, environmental states of affairs involving the instantiation of such qualities constitute an exception to this.)

4

Moore's paradox and self-knowledge

I

Moore's paradox is usually presented by pointing to the puzzling character of certain sentences, or of imagined utterances or assertions involving these sentences. Conjunctive sentences such as Max Black's "Oysters are edible, but I don't believe that they are,"[1] or the more usual "It is raining but I don't believe that it is raining," I will call "Moore-paradoxical sentences." These are seen as having a logically anomalous character because their assertive utterance would involve some kind of logical impropriety, despite the fact that both of their conjuncts could be true. And I think it is widely assumed that both the paradox and its resolution have to do with the linguistic expression of belief.

A natural first move to make in explaining it is to say that while what someone actually *says* in uttering a Moore-paradoxical sentence is not self-contradictory, since both conjuncts could be true, there is nevertheless a contradiction between what the speaker in some way *implies* in asserting the first conjunct, namely that she believes the thing asserted, and what she explicitly *says* in asserting the second, namely that she does not believe that thing. This is also put by saying that there is a contradiction between something *expressed* by the first conjunct and what is *asserted* by the second.

If "expressing" a belief requires actually having it, then saying "It is raining" does not always express the belief that it is raining – not all assertion is sincere. And in any case, what contradicts the second conjunct, namely "I don't believe that it is raining," is not the belief the first conjunct expresses (beliefs *qua* mental states do not contradict anything), and not the proposition that is the content of that belief, but the proposition that the speaker has that belief. So it needs to be explained in what sense

I have had helpful comments and criticisms from Rogers Albritton, Kent Bach, Mark Crimmins, Jennifer Dworkin, Carl Ginet, Richard Moran, Richard Miller, David Rosenthal, and Allen Wood.
1 See Black 1954, p. 56.

assertive utterances, whether sincere or not, express beliefs, and in what sense someone who expresses a belief is committed to, and can be said to imply, the truth of the proposition that she has the belief expressed.

One explanation would be along Gricean lines. If linguistic meaning is a matter of having higher-order intentions to influence the beliefs and behavior of an audience through their recognition of these intentions, then meaningful assertion must be a matter of intending either to make one's audience believe the thing asserted or to make them believe that one believes it, through their recognizing that one has this intention, and in either case it must involve intending to make them believe that one believes it. That gives us an explanation of the sense in which someone who asserts something, sincerely or not, expresses belief in the thing asserted. The assertion is an action done with the intention of (perhaps among other things) producing the belief that one has that belief. And if one does something that others will recognize, and that one knows others will recognize, as aimed at making one's audience believe that one believes that *P*, it seems fair to say that one thereby commits oneself to having that belief and implies that one has it.

The intention that really does the work here is the intention to make one's audience believe that one believes something. Grice saw this intention as embedded in a more complex intention; but one could agree that assertion involves having intentions of this sort without accepting the rest of Grice's account. And one could see this intention as the byproduct of the intention to make one's audience believe the thing asserted – in our example, believe that it is raining – without following Grice in thinking of that intention as necessarily embedded in the higher order intention that this belief should come about through the recognition of the intention. Anyone capable of instrumental reasoning and aware of the rudiments of folk psychology should be able to appreciate that, except in very peculiar circumstances, others will be unlikely to accept something as true because one says it if they don't believe that one believes what one is saying.

I think that there is a good deal of truth in accounts along these lines, and I do not intend to quibble with their specific claims. However, I do want to question the claim that Moore's paradox has to do solely or primarily with the linguistic expression of beliefs, and that its resolution lies in speech act theory – in considerations about the nature of assertion, the nature of linguistic intentions, and the like. What seems to me too little noticed is that there is something paradoxical or logically peculiar about idea of someone's *believing* the propositional content of a Moore-paradoxical sentence, whether or not the person gives linguistic expression to this belief. What really needs to be explained is why someone cannot coherently *believe* that it is raining and that she doesn't believe that it is, despite the fact that the conjuncts of this belief can both be true. If we can show that such beliefs are impossible, or at least logically defective, and if we can come up with an explanation of this, then an explanation of why one cannot (coherently) *assert* a Moore-paradoxical sentence will come along for free, via the principle that what can be (coherently) believed constrains what one can be (coherently) asserted.

II

Consider the Moore-paradoxical sentence "It is raining, but I don't believe that it is raining." If this could be asserted it would be the (ostensible) expression of a conjunctive belief, namely that it is raining and that the speaker, identified in a first-person way, does not believe that it is raining. The content of that belief is not a self-contradiction, as we have seen – both conjuncts could be true. But, consider the proposition that is the conjunction of this proposition and the proposition that the speaker believes this proposition, i.e., that expressed by the sentence "It is raining and I don't believe that it is raining, and that this is so (viz, that it is raining and I don't believe that it is) is something I believe." That *is* self-contradictory.[2] So it is a feature of the contents of Moore-paradoxical sentences that if they can be believed at all, the subject of such a belief could not, logically, believe that she had it.[3]

Given that this is so, there would seem to be two possible explanations of why Moore-paradoxical sentences are paradoxical, i.e., why there is an absurdity involved in any putative attempt to assert them. One explanation would crucially involve the idea of consciousness. Assertion, on this view, requires that the speaker be conscious of the belief being expressed by the assertion – or, to allow for insincere assertion, that the speaker present herself as conscious of that belief. Let's assume with D.H. Mellor and David Rosenthal that a belief's being conscious consists in the sub-

---

2 On the assumption, which seems reasonable, that the proposition that one believes a conjunction entails that one believes each of the conjuncts.

3 In the previously published version of this essay (Shoemaker 1995) I wrote here "could not believe that she had it without believing a contradiction." But that was too weak; it mistook the self-contradictoriness of saying that the content is truly believed for the self-contradictoriness of what is believed.

ject's having a higher order belief, or higher order thought, to the effect that she has it.[4] The content expressed by a Moore-paradoxical sentence could not be the content of a conscious belief – or, at any rate, it could not be the subject of a conscious belief that is not logically incoherent.[5] This view does not deny that the content of a Moore paradoxical sentence can be believed, only that it can be *consciously* believed.

The other view, as you might expect, says that the content of such a sentence cannot be believed at all – or, on a slightly milder version of the view, that such a content cannot be believed without the subject believing a self-contradiction. The reason for this is that believing something commits one to believing that one believes it, in the sense that in some kind of circumstances, yet to be specified, if one believes something, and considers whether one does, one must, on pain of irrationality, believe that one believes it. Whereas on the first view the explanation of Moore's paradox lies in a constitutive connection between assertion and conscious belief, on the second view it lies in a constitutive connection between believing and believing that one believes.

One advantage of the second of these views over the first is that it gives a better explanation of something that the logical oddity of Moore-paradoxical sentences brings out. David Rosenthal has said that while "It is raining" and "I believe that it is raining" have different *truth* conditions, they have the same *performance* conditions.[6] This points to something important, but I would put it somewhat differently. Certainly the conditions under which one can appropriately *say* "It is raining" are not identical with those in which one can appropriately *say* "I believe that it is raining." The conditions of pragmatic appropriateness are different; utterances of these sentences often have different "implicatures." And of course it would not do to say that the sentences are asserted on the basis of the same evidence, since (so I would claim) "I believe that it is raining," understood as a belief report, is not said on the basis of evidence at all, and evidence concerning the weather can in any case be only partial and indirect evidence concerning anyone's state of mind. I would prefer to talk of "assent conditions" rather than "performance conditions," and

---

4 See Mellor 1978 and Rosenthal 1986.
5 As observed above, it is self-contradictory to suppose that the content of a Moore-paradoxical sentence could be *truly* believed. But could it be *falsely* believed? Well, since it is demonstrably true that it could not be truly believed, anyone who believed it would be in a position to see that his belief had to be false. Such a belief would be, to say the least, logically incoherent.
6 See Rosenthal 1993.

say that the propositional contents expressed by "It is raining" and "I believe that it is raining" have the same assent conditions. But for reasons that will appear later, I think it is better to say that the assent conditions for the former entail those for the latter, without committing oneself to the converse.[7]

One thing that can be meant by assent is a kind of linguistic performance. One assents to a propositional content in this sense if one asserts it or answers affirmatively to the question whether it is true. And it seems clear that for any propositional content P, anyone who has the concept of belief must be disposed to assent to the content that she believes that P if she is disposed to assent to the content P. If someone answers "yes" to the question "Is it raining?", but in the same circumstances answers "No" or "I don't know" to the question "Do you believe that it is raining?", then either she is joking or she has, at best, a very imperfect grasp of the concept of belief. This is of course true independently of what the person's beliefs actually are. Assent, in this sense, can be either sincere or insincere; but whether one is telling the truth or lying, one had better assent to "I believe that P" if one assents to "P."

But one can think of this kind of assent, call it linguistic assent, as the ostensible expression of something, call it mental assent, that can occur without there being any linguistic performance at all. A thought occurs to me, and I either assent to its content or not. Mental assent is an episodic instantiation of belief, and cannot be insincere, just as beliefs cannot be insincere. And here too the assent conditions for "P" entail those for "I believe that P" – if both the contents *It is raining* and *I believe that it is raining* present themselves as candidates for assent, I cannot assent to the first without assenting to the second. Arguably, it is *because* the mental assent conditions of these contents are related as they are that their linguistic assent conditions are related as they are. When linguistic assent is sincere, it involves mental assent. And all linguistic assent offers itself *as* sincere, whether it is or not. So, taking "assent" to mean "mental assent," we need to ask why it is that the assent conditions for P entail those for *I believe that P*.

---

7 In the earlier published version of this essay (Shoemaker 1995) I did commit myself to the converse. But as I pointed out in the "note added in proof," nothing in the main argument of the essay explained the holding of the converse, and the only thing I say that suggests an explanation is a claim at the end of the essay that I put forward only tentatively. I discuss my current reservations about the converse, and about that claim, in Section V.

It might be thought that the answer to this lies in the fact, or what for now I will suppose to be a fact, that assent, unlike belief generally, is necessarily conscious. Supposing, again, that a first-order belief's being conscious consists in the subject's having a higher-order belief, or higher-order thought, to the effect that she has that first-order belief, assenting to P involves having the higher-order belief that one believes that P. So, if one assents to P, thereby manifesting a conscious belief that P, one must believe that one believes that P. But of course, to say that one has this second-order belief, the belief that one believes that P, isn't yet to say that one *assents* to its content. For all that has been shown so far, this might be a belief that is not conscious and so is not manifesting itself in assent. Now it might seem that this is easily gotten around. What is to be explained is why, given that both P and *I believe that P* are given as candidates for assent, I must assent to the second if I assent to the first. Let's equate a content's being given as a candidate for assent with one's having a thought with that content. If one assumes that such a thought must be conscious, and assumes that if one has a conscious thought with the content P at a time at which one believes that P, one must assent to P, then the explanation will be complete. If both P and *I believe that P* are given to me as candidates for assent, and I assent to P, then I must believe that I believe it, and since the content of that belief, that I believe that P, is the content of a current conscious thought of mine, I must assent to it as well.

But besides assuming that assent is conscious and that thoughts are conscious (at any rate, that thoughts whose contents are candidates for assent are conscious), this line of thought assumes that if one believes that P, and has the thought that P – i.e., has the content P presented as a candidate for assent – one will assent to P, and so (on the assumption that assent is conscious) will have the higher-order belief that one believes that P. It is important to see that this is a strong self-intimation claim, asserting a constitutive relation between believing and believing that one believes. And without something like this, the explanation does not go through. I think that if one focuses only on the constitutive relation between conscious belief and assertion, and does not recognize a constitutive relation between belief and believing that one believes (or, if you like, between belief and conscious belief), one will be without a satisfactory explanation of why the assent conditions for "P" entail those for "I believe that P."

But in fact the self-intimation claim invoked in the explanation just given is too strong. There would seem to be cases of self-deception in which someone believes that P and yet, when the content P is presented as a candidate for assent, sincerely denies that she believes it. Presumably this happens in cases of repressed belief. And I think that there are more ordinary cases, not involving even garden variety self-deception, in which this can happen. For lots of the beliefs that one can be said to have at a time are not available to one at that time. To borrow an example from Mark Crimmins, before doing the dishes or washing the dog I put my wrist watch in my pocket.[8] Later on I start looking all over for it. Then it comes to me that of course I put it in my pocket. The information that it was in my pocket was in my memory the whole time, and in some sense I believed it. But during the first part of my search it was not available. Now it seems likely that if at any point during my search I had considered the possibility that the watch was in my pocket, this would have immediately made the belief available and elicited assent to the proposition that it was there. But it does not seem to me inevitable that this be so. I might initially think "I wouldn't have done that," only to realize a minute later that that is what I did do. Again, if I have stored in my memory a belief in some proposition about physics, or about medieval history, it does not seem inevitable that on now being confronted with that proposition I will immediately assent to it. It might take some time, and some thought, for me to realize that I do believe it; and it might even be that my initial, prereflective, response to it is to dissent from it. Yet in a good sense I do believe it.

But the central, paradigmatic, case of believing is that in which the belief is available in a way it is not in these cases – in which it is apt to serve as a guide to action, and, what goes with this, in which its content is apt to be among the premises of the subject's reasoning, including practical reasoning. Other cases of believing count as cases of believing because of their relation to these cases, e.g., because they are disposed to turn into cases of this sort as the result of mental activities – those that go on when one searches or prods one's memory – that are within the repertoire of normal human beings.

This suggests an amendment of the self-intimation thesis that was found wanting. The self-intimation thesis we need to complete our explanation has two parts to it. First, if a belief is available, then its subject has the belief that she has that belief, and that second-order belief is

8 See Crimmins 1992b.

available as well.[9] Second, if a belief is available, then if its content is presented as a candidate for assent, the subject will assent to it. Given this, we can be assured that if I assent to P, I will assent to the proposition that I believe that P. If I assent to P, it goes without question that the belief that P was available. But then the belief that I believe that P must also be available. And then I must assent to it if it is presented as a candidate for assent. Notice that we can now retire the assumption that assent is always conscious; this assumption is true, I think, but it is no longer being appealed to in the explanation.

The second part of this thesis, that if a belief is available then its content will be assented to if presented as a candidate for assent, seems to me to need no argument; it partly defines what is meant by availability. My next job is to argue for the first part of the thesis, that if a belief is available then the subject will have the belief that she has it, and this belief will also be available.

III

My argument for this is one that I have used elsewhere.[10] I will first formulate it in a way that does not involve the notion of availability of be-

---

9 In commenting on the earlier version of this essay (Shoemaker 1995) presented at a symposium at the Pacific Division of the APA in 1994, Rogers Albritton pointed out that this seems to generate an infinite regress—in believing something one believes that one believes it, believes that one so believes, and so on ad infinitum. The regress is avoided if the claim is modified to read: if one believes that P, *and considers whether one does*, one will believe that one believes that P. This threatens no regress, because there is no threat of an infinity of considerings. But I do not think such a modification is necessary or appropriate for the case that primarily concerns me, namely where the belief that P is a first-order belief, and where (as I maintain in Section III) the belief that one believes that P can be only tacit. I can avoid the regress by restricting the claim to such cases, and to cases, if there are such, in which explanatory work can be done by attributing to a subject the belief that she has some higher-order belief – roughly, these will be the cases to which the argument of Section III applies.

Albritton will have none of this, and seems skeptical even of the view that someone who candidly *says* that she believes that it is raining must have the higher-order belief that she believes that it is raining: "Where is it written that it takes *two* beliefs, or even one with two contents, to confess that one believes it's raining? Why can't I just bare my soul, in the matter?" But it is surely clear that in confessing that one has that belief, one manifests a propositional attitude toward the content *I believe it is raining*, in addition to the propositional attitude one has toward the content *It is raining*. And this attitude looks an *awful* lot like belief. Like belief, it disposes one to use that content as a premise in one's reasonings, where it is relevant. For example, in counting the people in the room who believe that it is raining, one includes oneself in the total.

10 See Essays 2 and 11.

lief, as a general argument for a constitutive relation between believing and believing that one believes, and will then argue that it supports the self-intimation thesis just formulated.

A rational agent who believes that P will be disposed to use the proposition that P as a premise in her reasonings. Moreover, she will know that for any proposition whatever, if that proposition is true then, other things being equal, it is in anyone's interest to act on the assumption that it is true – for one is most likely to achieve one's aims if one acts on assumptions that are true. She will also know that to act on the assumption that something is true is to act as if one believes the thing; and she will know that if it is in one's interest to act in this way it will normally be in one's interest to make manifest to others that one is so acting – this will increase the likelihood that other believers in the truth of the proposition will cooperate with her in endeavors whose success depends on the truth of the proposition, and it will tend to promote belief in that proposition within her community and so to promote the success of endeavors whose success depends both on the proposition being true and on its being believed to be true by participants in the endeavors. Knowing that it is in anyone's interest to act in these ways if a proposition is true, she will know that it is in her own interest to so act. So she can reason as follows: "P is true. So it is in my interest to act as if I believed that P and, in normal circumstances, to act in ways that would make others believe that I believe that P. Since the circumstances are normal, I should so act." Assuming that she is rational enough to act in conformity with the conclusions of her own practical reasoning, and to know what will make others believe that she believes something, this should lead her to behave in the ways characteristic of someone trying to manifest to others that she believes that P, including saying "I believe that P."

The reason for pointing out that such reasoning is available is not to suggest that it regularly goes on in us – obviously it doesn't – but rather to point out that in order to explain the behavior we take as showing that people have certain higher-order beliefs, beliefs about their first-order beliefs, we do not need to attribute to them anything beyond what is needed in order to give them first-order beliefs plus normal intelligence, rationality, and conceptual capacity. What the availability of the reasoning shows is that the first-order states rationalize the behavior. And in supposing that a creature is rational, what one is supposing is that it is such that its being in certain intentional states tends to result in effects, behavior or other internal states, that are rationalized by those states. Sometimes this requires actually going through a process of reasoning in which one gets from one proposition to another by a series of steps, and where special reasoning skills are involved. But usually it does not.

I should add that if we distinguish between "explicit" beliefs and "tacit" beliefs, all that I mean to commit myself to by this argument is the view that a rational person who believes that P at least tacitly believes that she believes that P. The best account of tacit belief I know of is that of Mark Crimmins.[11] He suggests that "A at-least-tacitly believes P just in case it is as if A has an explicit belief in P," where the right hand side of this can be paraphrased "A's cognitive dispositions are relevantly as if A has an explicit belief in P." My claim is that to the extent that a subject is rational, and in possession of the relevant concepts (most importantly, the concept of belief), believing that P brings with it the cognitive dispositions that an explicit belief that one has that belief would bring, and so brings with it the at least tacit belief that one has it. And it does so in virtue of what it is to believe and to be rational.

Elsewhere I have used this argument as part of an attack on the perceptual model of introspective self-knowledge.[12] Were such a model appropriate, then just as one could lack a perceptual capacity, such as vision, without being in any way cognitively impaired, it ought to be possible for someone to lack the quasi-perceptual capacity for knowing one's own beliefs without being in any way cognitively impaired. But if I am right, such "self-blindness" is not a possibility.

But now let me show how this argument supports the self-intimation thesis formulated earlier. I argued that a rational person who believes that P will be disposed to behave in ways that indicate possession of the second order belief that she believes that P. But this is true because a rational person will be disposed to have her beliefs available when their contents are relevant to the situation in which she finds herself. The reasoning I said is available to the rational believer of P is of course reasoning that would occur only if the belief that P were available to the believer. So what in the first instance is shown by the argument is that if the belief that P is available to a subject, the subject will be disposed to behave in ways that indicate that the belief that she believes that P is available, and in ways that manifest assent both to the proposition P and to the proposition that she believes that P. And that, I submit, is strong support for the self-intimation claim formulated earlier.

---

11 See Crimmins 1992a.   12 See Essays 2 and 11.

IV

We saw earlier that the self-intimation claim just argued for can be used to vindicate the claim that where *P* and *I believe that P* are offered as candidates for assent, the subject who assents to the first must assent to the second. And that claim, if supplemented with the premise that for any possible belief it is possible for that belief to become available, can be used to show that belief in the conjunctive proposition "*P* and I don't believe that *P*" is impossible. Suppose that belief in "It is raining and I don't believe that it is raining" is available. Then, by the self-intimation claim, the subject will be disposed to assent to it, and presumably this requires that she will be disposed to assent to both conjuncts. But assent to the first conjunct, "It is raining," commits her to assenting to "I believe that it is raining," and that contradicts what she assents to in assenting to the second conjunct.

But I want to present another argument to show that belief in such a proposition is impossible. This argument will not involve the notion of mental assent, and will not depend on the assumption that assent is necessarily conscious.

Let us approach the question of whether someone could believe that it is raining and that she doesn't believe that it is by considering a slightly different question, namely whether one could believe the conjunctive proposition that it is raining and that one believes that it isn't raining. This is not of course the same as having two separate beliefs, one that is raining and one that one believes that it is not raining. The latter I will allow to be possible. Perhaps it could be a case of self-deception. Someone's desire that the picnic will succeed generates the belief that it is not raining, and with it the belief that she believes this, but does not manage to eradicate the belief that it is raining. She has incompatible beliefs, one that it is raining and one that it is not raining, but that doesn't mean that she believes the conjunction of these – perhaps these incompatible beliefs are in different "compartments" of her mind. And no more does having the belief that it is raining and the belief that she believes that it is not raining mean that she believes the conjunction of their contents – perhaps these beliefs are in different compartments of her mind.

Our question now is whether one could believe such a conjunction as that expressed by "It is raining and I believe that it is not raining." Here is an argument, which I do not fully endorse, that one could not. We can begin with the following pair of claims: first, if someone believes a proposition, she will be disposed to use that proposition as a premise in her reasonings, and second, if someone believes that she believes a proposition, she will be disposed to use that proposition as a premise in her reasonings. Now as we have already observed, it is possible to believe something in such a way that it is not, at a given time, available to one for use as a premise or as a guide to action; the putative information in its content may be stored in one's memory, but not in a way that makes it currently accessible. But part of what it is to believe the conjunction of two propositions is for one's beliefs in the conjuncts to be so linked that neither can be available without the other being available. So if one believes the conjunction of "It is raining" and "I believe that it is not raining," then in any case in which the belief in either conjunct is available, one should be prepared to use both "It is raining" and "It is not raining" as premises in one's reasonings. I take it that this is not possible. I also take it that if one has a belief, then there must be some possible circumstances in which the thing one believes, or the thing one believes one believes, is available to one as a premise in one's reasonings. It follows that there cannot be a belief in the proposition "It is raining and I believe that it is not raining."

The reason I do not fully endorse the argument just given[13] is that I have reservations about the claim that if one believes that one believes a proposition, one will be disposed to use that proposition as a premise in one's reasonings. I will discuss these in Section V. I think that the claim is true if amended to read "If one believes that one believes a proposition, one will be disposed to use that proposition as a premise in one's reasonings *if there is no inconsistency in one's belief system*." But then the argument will yield only the weaker conclusion that if one's beliefs are consistent, one cannot have a belief in the proposition "It is raining but I believe that it is not raining."

But now consider a claim related to this one, namely that if one believes that one does *not* believe a proposition, this will dispose one to *refrain* from using that proposition as a premise in one's reasonings. That, I think, is defensible as it stands. And this provides a basis for the claim that there cannot be a belief in the proposition "It is raining, but I don't believe that it is raining." If one believes the first conjunct, one will be disposed to use the proposition *it is raining* as a premise in one's reasonings. If one believes the second conjunct, one will be disposed *not* to use that same proposition as a premise in one's reasonings. And if one believes the conjunction, neither of these beliefs can be available without the other

13 I did endorse it in the previously published version of this essay.

85

being available. Now it is of course possible to have dispositions to do incompatible things as long as the activation conditions for these dispositions are different. But the activation conditions for dispositions associated with beliefs and beliefs about beliefs are, first, these beliefs being available (whatever that comes to), and, second, one's being presented with a problem, practical or theoretical, to which the relevant content propositions appear relevant. So if one believes the conjunction *It is raining and I do not believe that it is raining*, the activation conditions for the dispositions associated with beliefs in the two conjuncts will be the same. This means that if the beliefs can ever be available and relevant to problems facing one, there will be circumstances in which one both uses and does not use the proposition *It is raining* as a premise in one's reasonings. And surely that is not possible.

The following objection may be raised to my claim that when one has a conjunctive belief, one's beliefs in the conjuncts are linked in the way I have described. Surely one could repress a conjunctive belief without repressing both conjuncts. Or, more generally, surely a conjunctive belief could become relatively inaccessible, tucked away in the recesses of one's memory and recoverable only with difficulty, without both conjuncts becoming thus inaccessible. Someone might have the available belief that his wife is vacationing in the Bahamas, and the available belief that his wife's former lover is vacationing in the Bahamas, without having the available belief that his wife and his wife's former lover are both vacationing in the Bahamas – that conjunctive belief might have been repressed. I agree, but I do not think that this conflicts with my claim. Suppose that I believe that *P*, believe that *Q*, and believe the conjunction of *P* and *Q*, and that I could repress the latter belief without repressing either of the former. In such a case both *P* and *Q* are, as we might say,, believed by me twice. They are believed separately, and they are believed together. The belief that *P* that is a component of the conjunctive belief is linked with the belief that *Q* that is a component of the conjunctive belief; these beliefs are so related that neither could become available without the other becoming available.

But I needn't put the matter in a way that requires me to speak of having the same belief twice. Instead of saying that having a conjunctive belief involves having beliefs in the conjuncts that are linked in a certain way, I can say that it involves having a single belief that combines the dispositions that the beliefs in the conjuncts have individually. Such a single belief is impossible when the dispositions are those of the belief that *P* and those of the belief that one does not believe that *P*.

V

In a previous version of this essay[14] I offered the arguments given up to this point as an explanation of the fact, or what I took to be a fact, that the assent conditions for P and those for *I believe that P* are always and necessarily the same. In fact they explain only half of this, namely that the assent conditions for P entail those *I believe that P*. I did tentatively maintain in that version that belief that one believes that P entails belief that P. And that, if true, would explain the other half of what I took as my *explicandum*, namely that the assent conditions for *I believe that P* entail those for P – although I did not offer it as an explanation of that. But I am now doubtful both about this claim about assent conditions and the claim that would explain it.

In thinking that assent to "I believe that P" entails assent to P, I was tacitly assuming that "I believe that P, but not-P" is paradoxical in the same way as "P but I don't believe that P." But there is an important logical difference between them. As I indicated earlier, the conjunction of "P but I don't believe that P" with the proposition that the subject, identified in a first person way, believes that proposition is self-contradictory. But no contradiction follows if we conjoin "I believe that P, but not-P" with the proposition that the subject (identified in a first-person way) believes this. It does follow that the subject has inconsistent beliefs – that she both believes that P and believes that not-P. But it is not self-contradictory to say that someone has contradictory beliefs, and it is not obviously self-contradictory to say this of oneself, even if one spells out what the beliefs are. So while it is logically impossible for someone to truly believe the content *P and I do not believe that P*, there is not the same case for its being logically impossible for someone to truly believe the content *I believe that P, but not P*.

My case for the claim that believing that one believes that P entails believing that P rested on the claim, already mentioned in section IV, that if one believes that one believes that P one will be disposed, insofar as one is rational, to use the proposition that P as a premise in one's reasonings. After all, it seem a general truth that someone who believes a proposition should be prepared to use that proposition as a premise in her reasonings; so the rational person who believes that she believes that P will be in a position to give herself an argument having that general truth as one premise and the proposition that she believes that P as an-

14 Shoemaker 1995.

87

other, and having as its conclusion that she should be prepared to use the proposition that P as a premise in her reasonings. And if she is rational, she will be disposed to conform to that conclusion – i.e., to use P as a premise in her reasonings. And these will include her practical reasonings – her reasonings about what to do. If she uses P as a premise in her practical reasonings, she will act on the assumption that P. And that, of course, is what a believer in P will do. So a rational person who believes that she believes that P will behave in just the ways that would be taken to indicate that she believes that P. This suggests that such a person would believe that P.[15]

This may seem to clash with the obvious fact that people engage in self-deception, and among other things deceive themselves about their own beliefs. If people can be mistaken about their beliefs, how can it be that someone who believes that she believes that P necessarily believes that P? But the argument does not claim that if one believes that one does *not* believe that P, then one does not believe that P. And it is possible to maintain that *positive* second-order beliefs, to the effect that one has certain first-order beliefs, are always true, while denying that *negative* second-order beliefs, to the effect that one lacks certain first-order beliefs, are always true. If one believes that one does not believe that P, it does follow, I think, that one does not have an *available* belief that P, but it does not follow that one does not have a belief that P at all. So it could be maintained (and I did maintain in the earlier version of this essay) that clear cases of self-deception about one's beliefs are cases in which one sincerely denies having a belief one has, not cases in which one sincerely claims to have a belief that one does not have. It may be true in some cases of self-deception that the subject sincerely claims to believe that P and in fact has a belief that not-P. But in such a case (the claim would be) the subject will also believe that she does not have a belief that not-P. What may well be true in such a case is that the subject has inconsistent beliefs – with one part of her mind she believes that P, and with another part she believes that not-P. And the self-deception consists in her having the mistaken negative belief that she does not have the belief that not-P.

But there are apparent counterexamples to the claim that belief that one believes that P entails belief that P, and some of these also seem to be counterexamples to the claim that the assent conditions for *I believe that P* entail those for P, and to the claim that someone who believes that she believes a proposition is thereby disposed to use that proposition as a

15 I first presented this argument in Shoemaker 1991.

premise in her reasonings. These seem to fall into two sorts. In one sort of case, a person spontaneously avows that she believes that P, and also avows P, but given what we know about the case we find it natural to say that she doesn't really believe that P. In the other sort of case, a person comes to believe on the authority of someone else (say a psychiatrist), or on the basis of behavioral evidence available to anyone, that she has a certain belief, where this is a belief whose content she declines to avow.

As an example of the first sort of case, imagine someone who is fond of saying that she believes that everyone is inherently good. Here we can suppose that she is also prepared to assent, verbally, to the content proposition "Everyone is inherently good." But we might doubt that she really believes it. One wouldn't guess that she did from the way she talks about other people in concrete situations. And she makes no attempt to reconcile her claim with the condemnations of other people we often hear from her. We might suspect that she says this because it sounds to her like something she ought to believe, or because she likes the idea of being someone who believes (or is viewed by others as believing) the thing in question.

I am not persuaded by this sort of case. To begin with, if we say here "She doesn't really believe that," this may be akin to saying "He doesn't really want that," where what is meant is that the person's desire won't survive his being enlightened in certain ways e.g., about the consequences of the thing wanted. That is, we are saying that the person's belief would not survive certain kinds of reflection and certain kinds of confrontation with the facts. In such a case, not "really" believing something is compatible with believing it, although in such a way that the belief would not hold up to close examination. Second, someone who says "She doesn't really believe that" may be voicing the suspicion that if we pressed the person as to what she means by "Everyone is inherently good," we would find that she does not mean anything at all determinate – which is why she sees no clash between saying this and saying what she does about other people when in her less irenic moods. And if that suspicion is right, then the person's mistaken belief is not what it superficially seems to be. It is not the belief that she believes a certain proposition, that expressed by "Everyone is inherently good," but rather the belief that there is a determinate proposition expressed by that sentence, and one that she believes.

As an example of the second sort of case, suppose that a psychiatrist tells me that I have the repressed belief that I was adopted as an infant. In fact, the psychiatrist has confused me with another patient (he has been reading the wrong case history), and has no good grounds for this belief attribution. But I accept it on his authority. It seems compatible with this that when I consider the proposition I am supposed to believe, that I was adopted, I find no evidence in its support, and am disposed to deny it. Here, it seems, I might be in a position to assert "I believe that I was adopted, but that's not true."

This is a puzzling case. For one thing, if I am prepared to say "That is not true," then it seems that I must also be prepared to say "I believe that it is not true that I was adopted." And then I will be attributing to myself inconsistent beliefs. There is of course no difficulty in supposing that I believe (truly or falsely) that *in the past* I believed that P while now affirming, and expressing belief in, the falsity of P. And there is perhaps no difficulty in supposing that I believe that I am *disposed* to believe that P – that it is a belief I am prone to fall into – while at the same time believing (and believing that I believe) that P is false.[16] But while having inconsistent beliefs is clearly possible, and believing that one has inconsistent beliefs (i.e., believing that among one's beliefs there are some that contradict others) is also clearly possible, there is something problematic, to say the least, about believing concerning a certain proposition both that one believes it and that one believes its negation.

There is a slight variation on this example on which it does not involve ascribing to oneself inconsistent beliefs. As before, I accept the psychiatrist's attribution to me of the belief that I was adopted. But instead of being disposed to deny the proposition that I was adopted, I might, when I consider the evidence for and against it, be unwilling either to affirm it or to deny it. This too would seem to be a counterexample to the claim that if one believes that one believes that P, one believes that P – and to the claim that if one assents to *I believe that P*, one must assent to P. But it too seems problematic. Suppose that I accept a conditional to the effect that if one was adopted, one should take a certain course of action. Do I take that course of action, or not? If I do, doesn't that amount to assenting to the antecedent of that conditional – despite my unwillingness to give verbal assent to it? And if I don't, doesn't that call into question whether I really believe the proposition that I say (on the authority of the psychiatrist) that I believe?

One way of trying to make sense of these cases is to invoke the idea that there can be a failure of unity of consciousness, or (better) unity of

16 In an earlier discussion of such examples I suggested that all my acceptance of what the psychiatrist tells me could amount to in this case is the belief that I am disposed to believe that I am adopted – that this is a belief I am prone to have on certain occasions. See Shoemaker 1991, p. 149, note 12. This no longer satisfies me.

mind. If my mind can house, perhaps only temporarily, two or more different subjects of mental states, there will be no problem (no *logical* or *conceptual* problem, that is) about one of these believing things another of them does not believe. On this conception, when I speak it will be, in the first instance, one of these "primary" subjects (as I will call them) that is speaking, but the "I" in my utterances may refer either to the person (the mind as a whole) or to the primary subject that is doing the speaking. The claim that believing that one believes that P entails believing that P can now be reformulated as the claim that if a primary subject believes that it, that primary subject, believes that P, then it, that primary subject, does believe that P. It would be compatible with this that a primary subject can believe that the person believes something which it, that primary subject, does not believe – it would believe that the person believes that thing in virtue of a primary subject other than itself believing it. That is what we would have in my example. When I say "I believe that I believe that I was adopted," the first "*I*" would refer both to the speaking primary subject and to the person, but the second would refer only to the person. And if I add "But I doubt whether that is true," the "*I*" refers to the speaking primary subject. Such a bifurcation of the mind would take some of the sting out of the attribution to oneself of inconsistent beliefs; for what such an attribution would come down to is the attribution of the inconsistent beliefs to different primary sub-subjects of oneself. Such a bifurcation of the mind would also explain why I do not take a certain course of action despite believing that I am adopted and believing that if I was adopted I should take that course of action. For the beliefs that rationalize that course of action would belong to different primary sub-subjects of my mind, and (so one might hold) only beliefs that belong to the same primary sub-subject of one's mind can be expected to lead to the behavior they jointly rationalize.

Allowing such a division of the mind would allow for the sensible utterance of the form "I believe that P, but not P." But it might seem that it would also allow for the sensible utterance of a paradigm Moore-paradoxical sentence of the form "P, but I do not believe that P." Can't this be believed in virtue of one's speaking primary subject believing P and believing that another primary subject does not believe that P? But it would seem that the possible referents for "I" on this view, while they include both the speaking primary subject and the person, do not include primary subjects other than the speaking subject. On this conception, the person has whatever beliefs and other attitudes the primary subjects have; it has them in virtue of the primary subjects having them. But it

91

doesn't lack whatever attitudes any of its primary subjects lack – otherwise it could both have and lack the same attitude. So while one of the primary subjects (other than the speaking one) lacks the belief that P, the person does not lack it, since the speaking subject has it. Thus, whether "I" refers to the speaking primary subject or to the person, the case in which the speaking primary subject believes that P while believing that another primary subject does not believe it does not give us a case in which the speaking subject can sensibly say "P but I don't believe it."

I have no idea whether an account involving this sort of division of the mind could be empirically adequate. Doubtless it could be so only if it were much more complex than what I have sketched here. But the very fact that the envisaged phenomena make it tempting to entertain something along these lines shows the kind of strain they put on our ordinary conception of persons as subjects of beliefs and other attitudes. While I am no longer willing to make the unqualified claim that believing that one believes that P entails believing that P, I am inclined to claim that this holds in conceptually central cases, those in which the concept of belief applies unproblematically.

VI

Let me conclude by saying what all this tells us about the nature of self-knowledge – specifically, knowledge of one's own beliefs.

I have spoken of beliefs as self-intimating. And we can think of this self-intimation as having two stages. The first stage is the transition from the mere possession of a belief to its being available. This has little if anything to do with Moore's Paradox, and I have had little to say about it. I have suggested, however, that it is of the essence of belief that someone who has a belief with a certain content thereby has a disposition that would manifest itself under certain conditions in her having an available belief with that content, i.e., in her believing it in such a way that it would serve, as need arises (or is perceived to arise), as a guide to action and a premise in her reasoning. The second stage is the transition from a belief's being available to the subject's having the available second-order belief that she has it. Here the word "transition" may be misleading, for I think that in some cases it may be wrong to think of the second-order belief as a distinct state that is caused by the available first-order belief. What my argument suggests, rather, is that where the subject has the concept of belief, and of herself, the first-order belief's being available *constitutes* her having the at least tacit belief that she has that first-order belief. But I think it is also true that where a belief that P is available, the subject will be disposed under certain conditions to form the explicit second-order belief that she believes that P. At any rate, the self-intimation of belief consists in there being these two constitutive links, one between believing a content and having an available belief in that content, and the other between having an available belief and having the (available) belief that one does. It is this that constitutes our distinctive first-person access to our beliefs. The higher-order beliefs from which this issues count as knowledge for a familiar reason; they are reliably produced, and we are entitled to regard them as reliably produced.

In Section V, I discussed the more problematical claim that positive second-order beliefs, beliefs ascribing beliefs to oneself, are infallible – or, as it might also be put, are self-verifying. Combined with the claim that beliefs are self-intimating, this would give us a very strong version of the view that we have a privileged access to our own beliefs. I think this is tantalizingly close to being true. But I think the most we can claim is that it is true in some conceptually central class of cases, ones blessed with more rationality than is usual in human affairs.

I have leaned in this discussion on a notion of "availability" of beliefs that needs more elucidation than I have given it. A fully satisfactory account of beliefs would have to say more fully than I have done just what it is for a belief to be available and how it is that beliefs become available.

PART II

Qualia

5

Qualities and qualia: What's in the mind?

Since the 17th century, a central issue in metaphysics and epistemology has concerned the status of what, following John Locke, have come to be called "secondary qualities": colors, odors, tastes, sounds, warmth and coldness, etc. The problem is posed by the fact that while these qualities are experienced as belonging to objects in our external environment – the apple is experienced as red, the rose as fragrant, the lemon as sour, etc. – the scientific world-view, as developed in the 17th century and subsequently, seems to allow no place for them among the objective properties of material bodies. A common solution has been to deny, in one way or another, that these qualities do objectively inhere in external things in the way we experience them as doing. Galileo seems to have held that colors, etc., are properties of our sensations rather than of external things. Locke sometimes wrote as if that were his view as well, although his official view, as I read him, was that colors and the like are "powers" in objects to produce certain sorts of "ideas" in us.

On a natural understanding of it, the difference between Locke's view and Galileo's is semantical rather than metaphysical. Both hold that our sensations or ideas have what for the moment I will call subjective properties, which are immediately accessible to our consciousness and have no resemblance to any properties inhering in external objects, and both would allow, no doubt, that in virtue of the properties that do inhere in external objects, what Locke called their "primary qualities," such objects have powers to produce in us sensations or ideas having certain of these subjective properties. But while the one view says that colors and the like are themselves these subjective properties, the other says that they are

My thanks to Paul Boghossian, Dan Dennett, Gil Harman, Chris Hill, Bill Taschek, David Velleman, and Steve Yablo for helpful comments and discussion.

powers to produce sensations or ideas having them. This appears to be a disagreement not about what sorts of things or properties there are in the world (including our minds) but about which of these are the referents of words like "color," "red," "taste," "sweet," etc. If we view the matter in this way, then in one way Locke's view seems clearly preferable to Galileo's, at least in the case of color; since in fact we apply color predicates to physical objects and never to sensations, ideas, experiences, etc., the account of their semantics recommended by the Principle of Charity is one that makes them truly applicable to tomatoes and lemons rather than to sense experiences thereof. But given the world picture both views share, there is a way in which Galileo's expression of it is more satisfying. It is natural to say that on both views colors, tastes, etc., *as we experience them*, exist only in the mind, and it is natural to say that on both views our sense experience misrepresents reality by projecting onto external objects, or somehow leading us to project onto them, qualities that in fact belong to items in our mind that are produced by them.

It is, at any rate, one of the cliches of the history of philosophy that the problem about secondary qualities first faced in the 17th century was solved, or swept under the rug, by relegating them to the "dustbin of the mind." It is also a cliche of recent discussion of these issues that this solution becomes problematic if one abandons the dualistic view of mind taken for granted by the 17th century writers in favor of a materialist or physicalist view. A dualist can hold that there is no place for redness-as-experienced in material bodies, and nevertheless allow for its existence, by locating it in the nonmaterial realm he takes the mind to be. A materialist obviously cannot do this, since according to him there is no nonmaterial realm. A materialist who does not deny that there is such a thing as redness-as-experienced must allow that there is, after all, a place for this property in the material world. And if he nevertheless agrees with the 17th century writers in holding that such properties are instantiated only in the mind, i.e., as properties of sense-experiences or the like, he must explain how they can be instantiated in one part of the material world, namely the neural substrate of our perceptual experience, if they cannot be instantiated in the parts of the material world in which we seem to experience them as being instantiated, namely the surfaces of objects like ripe tomatoes. In recent philosophy the term "qualia" is sometimes used for what I provisionally called "subjective properties" earlier – properties of sense-experiences that somehow correspond to secondary qualities, either by being identical with them (as on Galileo's view) or by being the properties whose instantiation is the mental effect of the activation of external powers that are identical with them (as on Locke's view). Or rather, it is used to cover these together with certain properties of such sensations as pains and itches, those the having of which by a sensation constitutes its phenomenal or qualitative character, or "what it is like" to have it. If one allows that there really are such properties – that they are not, like phlogiston, mere figments of mistaken theory – then the prima facie counterintuitiveness of the view that secondary qualities are just identical to primary qualities of external objects (e.g., that redness is just a microstructural property of physical surfaces, or that being sweet is just a matter of having a certain molecular structure) is matched by the prima facie counterintuitiveness of the view that qualia are just identical to certain neurophysiological properties. And of course the displacement maneuver by which the 17th century writers handled secondary qualities, namely the maneuver of relegating them to the mind, cannot be applied to qualia; they are already in the mind if anywhere, and there is no place else to relegate them. This point has been much emphasized by Thomas Nagel, who has been the most prominent exponent in recent years of the view that qualia, the subjective, phenomenal aspects of sensations that determine "what it is like" to have them, cannot be accommodated by physicalist accounts of mind.[1]

What options does a materialist have? One is to say that the 17th century writers got the whole discussion off on the wrong foot, and that there is no cogent objection to a straightforward identification of the secondary qualities with "primary" ones, i.e., with properties that have a place in the scientific world picture. One could, of course, combine this with a similar identification of qualia with neurophysiological properties; if the counterintuitiveness of the former reduction can be overcome, so, one might hold, can the counterintuitiveness of the latter. But there is another way of playing this view out, which is favored by some of its recent proponents. It may seem that if we allow that secondary qualities are out in the world where we experience them as being, and if we hold that their status there is not that of being mere powers to produce experiences in us, then there is no need for us to encumber our ontology with "qualia" at all. We must allow, of course, that there is a difference, accessible to introspection, between an experience "as of red" and an experience "as of green." But this difference, it may be held, is purely a difference in the intentional, i.e., representational, properties of the experiences. While qualia are held to play a role in determining the intentional

1 See Nagel 1974.

content of experiences, they are not thought of as being themselves intentional properties. This comes out in the idea that "spectrum inversion" is a possibility. If you and I are spectrum inverted relative to each other, so that your experiences of red things are like my experiences of green things, and vice versa, and likewise for other pairs of colors, then the visual experience I have when I look at a ripe tomato will have the same intentional (representational) content as the visual experience you have in the same circumstances when you look at a ripe tomato – both will be experiences "of," i.e., will represent, something as red. So the difference between them will be a difference in their qualitative character, i.e., in what qualia they have, that does not yield a difference in their intentional properties. A consequence of the rejection of qualia is the rejection of the possibility of spectrum inversion, and other sorts of "qualia inversion." And to many this will seem a benefit; not only do we get rid of some troublesome entities, but we avoid the epistemological problems that beset anyone who allows that spectrum inversion is a possibility. Among recent philosophers who hold that we can and should deny the existence of qualia, if these are regarded as introspectably accessible but nonintentional features of mental states, are Daniel Dennett and Gilbert Harman.[2] Although their arguments are different, both clearly think that an acceptable materialist and functionalist account of the mental must, in Dennett's words, "quine qualia." Here I am primarily concerned with Harman's version of this view.

Confronted with this position, the friend of qualia may at first be tempted to dismiss it by an appeal to introspection. Don't we find qualia staring us in the face, as it were, when we attend introspectively to our experiences? Well, not in a way that provides a quick knockdown refutation of the qualia quiners. Indeed, introspection can seem to provide confirmation rather than refutation of their view. The only thing that seems to answer to the description "attending introspectively to one's visual experience" is attending to how things appear to one visually; and offhand this seems to tell one what the representational content of one's experience is without telling one anything about what the nonintentional features of one's experience are that encode this content. One may be inclined to say that one is revelling in the qualitative or phenomenal character of one's experience when one "drinks in" the blue of a summer sky or the red of a ripe tomato. But neither the blue nor the red is an object of *introspective* awareness; these are experienced, perceptually

2 See Dennett 1988, and Harman 1990.

100

rather than introspectively, as located outside one, in the sky or in the tomato, not as features of one's experience.[3] G. E. Moore once complained that the sensation of blue is "as if it were diaphanous"; if one tries to introspect it one sees right through it, and sees only the blue.[4] In a similar vein one might say that qualia, if there are such, are diaphanous; if one tries to attend to them, all one finds is the representative content of the experience. Yet qualia were supposed to be features of experience that are immediately accessible to consciousness.

One might suppose that however it may be with visual experience, it is at least clear that one is attending to qualia when one attends to sensations of taste, or to bodily sensations such as pains, itches, and tingles. Yet the qualities one attends to when one savors the wine or the sauce are ones that one experiences as located in one's mouth; and if they are where they are experienced as being, they cannot be features of sensations, *qua* mental states. So perhaps the only objects of awareness here are, first, the objects of a certain sort of perceptual awareness, e.g., the tartness of the wine in one's mouth (which in turn might be identified with some chemical property), and, second, the intentional features of one's experiences, i.e., the fact that they have objects of the first sort as their intentional objects.

It is also true in the case of bodily sensations, such as pains, that when one attends to their qualitative character, or what one supposes is that, one seems to be attending to something having bodily location – something in one's foot, or back, or tooth. And sensations, *qua* mental states, cannot literally be in one's foot, back, or tooth. Insofar as my awareness of the location is awareness of the sensation, it seems to be awareness of an intentional property – the "pain in one's foot" is in some sense "of" one's foot. This fits with the view, which has been proposed by David Armstrong and George Pitcher, that pains should be thought of as somatic sense impressions of bodily conditions.[5] And on such a view there may seem to be no room for awareness of qualia, over and above the perceptual awareness of bodily conditions one has in having pain, and the awareness of the intentional features (the representative content) of these somatic sense experiences.

A possible view about all of these cases is the "projectivist" view that in our perceptual experience we in some sense project what are in fact

3 This is correctly emphasized by Harman in Harman 1990.
4 Moore 1922, p. 25. See also Wittgenstein 1953, para. 275.
5 See Armstrong 1968, and Pitcher 1970.

nonintentional features of our experiences, i.e., qualia, onto the states of affairs these represent. So when I revel in the blue of the sky, the quality to which I am responding aesthetically is really a feature of my experience, which I mistakenly take to be instantiated in front of me. When I taste the wine I project the qualia of my experience onto my tongue and palate. And when I feel pain I project the qualia of my sensation into my back or foot or tooth. This view reconciles the phenomenology of these cases – the fact that the nonintentional properties we are aware of in them are experienced as spatially located – with the claim that sensory experience involves qualia and awareness of qualia. But it does so at a cost; there is something profoundly unattractive about the view that there is something like a category mistake, the attribution to things of features they *could* not have, involved in the content of every sense experience.

It is not easy to reconcile the phenomenology of these cases with the existence of qualia without saying things that sound like the projectivist view. Nevertheless, I believe that we need an account of these matters that accepts the existence of qualia and shows how commitment to their existence is compatible with materialism and functionalism. Elsewhere I have tried to show how acceptance of qualia can be reconciled with functionalism and physicalism – here I am mainly concerned to argue that we should take qualia seriously enough to feel the need of such a reconciliation.[6]

II

My main argument will be that we need qualia to make sense of secondary qualities. But before I get to that, let me present a preliminary argument that forces a clarification of the view I am opposing, the "intentionalist view" (as I shall call it) which says that experiences have no introspectable properties other than intentional ones.

I like cabernet sauvignon. More specifically, I like the taste of this wine. But what I like is not the mere existence of cabernet sauvignon or its taste; what I like is *experiencing* its taste. But is even this a satisfactory characterization of what I like? Let's suppose for a moment that the taste of wine is some chemical property of it; that what one is detecting when one experiences that distinctive cabernet sauvignon taste is some complex combination of esters, acids, oils, etc., although of course one

6 See Shoemaker 1975a and 1982.

does not experience it *as* having such a chemical composition. I suppose that I might learn to detect this same property visually, with the aid of the apparatus in a chemistry laboratory, and so have an experience whose intentional content is the chemical property that is in fact the taste of cabernet sauvignon. But when I say that I like that taste of cabernet sauvignon, or like experiencing this taste, I don't mean that I would like having such a visual experience. So the object of my liking is not: the having of an experience that is "of" a certain property. Is it perhaps: the having of an experience of this property *in a certain sense modality*, i.e., having a gustatory experience of it? Well, given the way I in fact am, I do like having such experiences of that property. But what I like about them is not that they have a certain intentional content, not that they are produced by certain sense organs (and are in that sense gustatory), and not a combination of these. What I like about them is what it is like to have them – and it is just saying the same thing in an-other way to say that what I like about them is their qualitative or phe-nomenal character, which must be distinguished from their intentional content.

This argument seems to me decisive on one natural understanding of what intentional properties are, namely one on which such properties are individuated referentially. So, for example, the property of being "as of red" will be, on this conception, the property an experience has if it rep-resents something as having the property of being red. If the property of being red is in fact identical to physical property *P*, then this will also be the property something has if it represents something as having *P*. But it will be replied that if we can think of experiences and properties of ex-periences as having representational content, we can apply the sense-ref-erence distinction to them, and that representational properties are more appropriately individuated by their senses rather than by their referents. So, in the example just given, the property of being as-of-red and the property of being as-of-*P* will be different, even if redness and property *P* are in fact one and the same. Applying this to the cabernet sauvignon example, it will be conceded that what I like in liking the taste of caber-net sauvignon is not the having of an experience that has a certain refer-ence-individuated intentional property; but the intentionalist will point out that it does not follow that what I like is not the property of having a certain sense-individuated intentional property.[7] To claim that the latter

7 Here I am indebted to comments Gilbert Harman made on an earlier version of this es-say.

is what I like does not imply that, ceteris paribus, I would like any experience that represented that same property as being instantiated.

This reply is fair enough. But it raises the question of what sort of "sense" an experience (or a property of an experience) can have, if sense-individuated intentional properties are to be the objects of those of our likes and dislikes that are directed at our experiences. The view has to be that what we like is not (just) having an experience that represents some situation in the world, but having an experience that represents that situation *in a certain way*. If this view is to suit the needs of the qualia quiners, representing something "in a certain way" had better not mean representing it by having a certain qualitative character. And if the "sense-individuated intentional properties" of an experience are not themselves to be qualia under another name, they had better determine reference by themselves, and not merely in combination with other things, such as causal relations to things in the environment.

III

Now let's return to secondary qualities. One view about these seems clearly ruled out. Colors, for example, cannot be properties of objects over and above the microstructural properties of them that account for the ways they influence the physical features of the light that impacts on our visual systems, and tastes, or flavors, cannot be properties of substances over and above the chemical properties of them that account for the chemical and physiological changes they induce in our tastebuds. To suppose that the secondary properties of things are in this way over and above their physical properties is either to embrace a view about the causation of our perceptual experiences which is known to be false, namely the view that they are caused by something other than the microstructural physical properties of objects, or to embrace the view that secondary qualities are epiphenomenal and play no role in the production of our perceptual experiences, a view that seems to have the absurd consequence that our experience of the world would be as it is even if no secondary qualities were ever instantiated in it.

Given that this view is ruled out, why are we resistant to a straightforward identification of colors and other secondary qualities with physical properties of external objects? No doubt there are many reasons for this, and I shall not attempt to discuss all of them here. I want to focus on a consideration, or set of considerations, that *seems* (but I think only seems) to militate against such an identification, and which in my view *does* militate against the version of the anti-qualia view that has been advocated most explicitly by Harman, namely the intentionalist view that the only introspectable properties of sense experiences are intentional ones.

The scientific evidence seems to indicate that the microstructural properties associated with particular colors are a highly diverse lot.[8] If we are to identify redness, or some determinate shade of it, with a physical property, that property will have to be a highly disjunctive one. And what gives unity to the disjuncts will not be anything about their intrinsic physical nature that makes them a "natural kind," but rather their relation to creatures with perceptual systems like ours. What links all of these various microstructural properties together, as "realizations" of a single shade of color, is the fact that they are alike in their effects (that is, the effects of their instantiation in appropriate circumstances) on creatures having perceptual apparatus like ours.

If, begging the question here at issue, one puts this point in terms of qualia, it is natural to jump immediately to one or the other of two views, the view that colors just are qualia (and so exist only in our minds), and the view that colors are "powers" of objects to produce in us experiences having certain qualia, where this is interpreted as excluding their being identical with microstructural physical properties of objects, or even with disjunctions of such microstructural properties. The first of these views offends against my Moorean sensibilities; but since in any case it is not available to the qualia quiners, I shall not bother to argue against it here. The second view is also not available to the quiners of qualia, since it characterizes the powers as powers to produce qualia instantiations. But those who claim that colors are "powers" of objects sometimes have in mind a view that makes colors more "objective" than this view does, indeed that allows them to be microstructural properties of objects (or disjunctions thereof), and it would seem to be this view, if any, that would suit the needs of the qualia quiners.

We can distinguish two versions of the view that colors are powers of objects; let us call them the view that colors are "extrinsic powers" and the view that colors are "intrinsic powers."[9] On the first, the redness of a tomato is a power of it in the sense in which, in Robert Boyle's famous example, the power of a key to open my door is an extrinsic power. The key could be deprived of the latter power while remaining intrinsically

---

8 For a good summary of the scientific evidence, see Hardin 1988.
9 I think that this distinction is essentially the same as E.M. Curley's distinction between "individual powers" and "sortal powers" – see Curley 1972.

unchanged, namely if the lock is changed. And if redness is an extrinsic power, the tomato could be deprived of its redness while remaining intrinsically unchanged, namely if the sensory organs of human observers (and other color perceivers) are changed in such a way that ripe tomatoes no longer produce in them the sorts of sense experiences they do now – e.g., if they are changed so as to produce the sorts of sense experiences now produced by unripe tomatoes. On the view that colors are intrinsic powers, on the other hand, a red object cannot cease to be red without undergoing a change in its intrinsic properties. Redness, on this view, is the power of producing (under appropriate conditions) a certain sort of visual experience in creatures having sensory apparatus of the sort we in fact have. If we are replaced by, or turned into, creatures whose sensory apparatus is such that the presence of a ripe tomato causes in them the sort of visual experience which as things are is produced in us by the presence of an unripe tomato, then ripe tomatoes will continue to be red as long as they continue to be such that if they *were* presented to creatures of the sort we are now they *would* produce experiences of the sort they now produce in us.

The view that colors are extrinsic powers is incompatible with the view that they are identical with disjunctions of microstructural physical properties of objects, but the view that they are intrinsic powers is not. Indeed, given certain plausible assumptions it implies that they are. So let us assume that colors are disjunctions of microstructural properties – and let's not worry right now about how this applies to rainbows, sunsets, and the sky on a clear day. This allows colors to be "objective," in some good sense of that word.[10] Even so, it remains true that there is something subjective about colors.

10 David Lewis has pointed out to me that there are ways of being an objectivist about colors while holding that they are "extrinsic," although not in the way envisaged above. First, if the laws of nature could be different, then in some other possible world things intrinsically, just like red things in this world, might standardly present a very different appearance to observers just like the standard observers in this world. An objectivist about colors who allows this possibility could plausibly maintain that the colors of things depend on their intrinsic properties *plus* the laws of nature, rather than on their intrinsic properties alone. I am inclined to reject this possibility, on the grounds that properties should be individuated in terms of their causal features in such a way as to be internally related to the laws of nature (see Shoemaker 1980). Second, it might be that the character of the light reflected by objects under various conditions is affected not only by the intrinsic natures of the objects but also by what sort of "field" they are situated in; as a result, objects having a certain intrinsic nature standardly present one sort of visual appearance to observes like us in the actual world, whose spacetime is pervaded by the X-field, and standardly present a different sort of appearance to intrin-

I have already remarked that what unites the different disjuncts in these disjunctions, so as to make it appropriate for us to have a single word that applies just in case one or another of these disjuncts is instantiated, is their relation to our perceptual experience. This could be put by saying that the relation "is a token of the same shade of color as," holding between tokens of microstructural properties, is observer relative – or, more accurately, relative to a particular sort of perceptual apparatus. There could be creatures with perceptual systems more finely tuned than ours who see several shades of color where we see only one. Frank Jackson's Fred, who can easily discriminate red things the rest of us find indistinguishable, would be such a creature.[11]

A further point is that the similarity and difference relationships between different shades of colors are observer relative, or perceptual system relative. It seems clearly possible that there should be creatures who can make as many color discriminations as we can, indeed can make the same ones, but who see different similarity relations between the shades than we do; some shades we find easy to discriminate (e.g., a shade of red and one of green) they find difficult to discriminate, while some shades we find difficult to discriminate (e.g., an orangish yellow and a yellowish orange) they find it easy to discriminate, even under poor lighting conditions. One can even tell a story in which having this different "quality space" is advantageous to them, given their nutritional needs and given the way the colors are distributed among the foodstuffs in their environment. Given that colors as we see them do not seem to correspond to natural kinds, it is not plausible, I think, to maintain that possessors of alternative quality spaces would simply be misperceiving the "objective" similarity and difference relations between colors; it seems much better to allow that color similarity and color difference are observer relative, or perceptual-system relative.

What does it mean to say that certain colors are similar relative to observers of sort A and different relative to observers of sort B? A natural answer is that these colors produce phenomenally similar visual experi-

sically similar observers in another possible world, where the Y-field pervades spacetime. This possibility I think I must allow. Here an objectivist about color should probably identify colors not with intrinsic properties of objects (or disjunctions thereof) but with a certain sort of extrinsic property; so, e.g., where Ps and Qs are kinds of intrinsic properties, being red might be a matter of having one of $P1 \ldots Pn$ and being in an X-field, or having one of $Q1 \ldots Qn$ and being in a Y-field. For my purposes here, this sort of objectivist view does not differ from the one discussed in the text.

11 See Jackson 1982.

ences in observers of sort A and phenomenally different visual experiences in observers of sort B. This assumes that there are relations of phenomenal similarity and difference that hold between visual experiences. And this is turn suggests that visual experiences have features in virtue of which these similarity relations hold.

Could these features be merely intentional features of the experiences? It would seem not. For suppose that an observer of sort A and one of sort B both have experiences that are "of" a homogeneous expanse of red, occupying the entire visual field, and then, after an interval, both have experiences that are "of" a homogeneous expanse of green. If we describe their visual experience in intentional terms, i.e., in terms of what they are experiences *of*, it would seem that we can give the same description of both, namely the one I just gave. And if the intentional properties of the experience determine the phenomenal similarity relations between them, then the similarity relations should be the same for the two observers; for it is true of each that her first experience is of a homogeneous expanse of red, and her second experience is of a homogeneous expanse of green. But the similarity relations need not be the same; the A type observer might be one of us, and the B type observer might be one of the creatures imagined earlier, who has a visual quality space in which certain shades of red and certain shades of green are very similar.

It may be replied that we can get around this by invoking the distinction made earlier between reference-individuated and sense-individuated intentional properties. In the example just given the reference-individuated intentional properties will be the same in the experiences of the A type observer and those of the B type observer. But, it may be claimed, the sense-individuated intentional properties may be different. The idea is that senses are individuated by functional roles, and that if creatures differ in quality spaces in the way imagined then the senses of their color experiences will differ, even when they are experiences of what in fact are the same colors. So, it may be held, we can say that experiences are the same just in case they share the same sense-individuated intentional properties, that they are similar (or different) to a degree or an extent just in case they have sense-individuated intentional properties whose senses are similar (different) to that degree or extent, and that there is no need to invoke some set of properties over and above these – qualia or "phenomenal" properties – in virtue of which experiences are similar or different.

But I think that it can be shown that this will not do. Let Jack and Jill be, respectively, our *A* type and *B* type observers. Their quality spaces are alike with the following exception. Jill sees a certain shade of green, call it *G*, as standing in the similarity relations to other shades that Jack sees a certain shade of red, call it *R*, as standing in, and sees *R* as standing in the similarity relations that Jack sees *G* as standing in. Suppose now that Jack and Jill are both staring at something of a certain shade of *blue*. My question is: could it be the case that their experiences are exactly alike in their introspectable character – or, at any rate, that there is some good sense in which they are "phenomenally" exactly alike? I think that the intentionalist must answer "no." For suppose that these as-of-blue experiences are phenomenally exactly alike, and suppose that it is also true that if they were looking at something of any other shade of color, other than *R* or *G*, their experiences would be phenomenally exactly alike. Clearly, the phenomenal character of their experiences of blue and other colors, together with the similarity relations between their experiences of these colors and their experiences of *R* and *G*, will fix the phenomenal character of their experiences of *R* and *G*. So given our supposition, and given what we are supposing about these similarity relations, we know that Jill's experience of *R* is exactly like Jack's experience of *G*, and that her experience of *G* is exactly like Jack's experience of *R*. If this sameness is a matter of having the same sense-individuated intentional properties, then Jill's *G*-produced experiences have the same sense as Jack's *R*-produced experiences, and her *R*-produced experiences have the same sense as Jack's *G*-produced experiences. But if sense determines reference, then one or the other is misperceiving *R* and *G* things – either Jack is perceiving *R* things as *G* and vice versa, or Jill is perceiving *R* things as *G* and vice versa. And that seems wrong. We can suppose (although this is not essential) that both quality spaces differ from our own – that in some respects Jack's color similarity judgments are more like ours than Jill's are, while in other respects Jill's are more like ours than Jack's are. And we can suppose that each has a quality space that is well adapted to the environment in which his or her ancestors evolved, in the sense that given the way colors are distributed among things in that environment, it facilitates distinguishing edible from inedible substances, and the like. Given this, it would be implausible to maintain that one or the other must always and systematically misperceive these particular shades. Nor is it open to the intentionalist to hold that it is possible for Jack's *R*-produced experiences to have the same sense-individuated intentional properties as Jill's *G*-produced experiences without these experiences representing the same properties as being instantiated in objects, and so without one or the other of them misperceiving these shades. To hold that would be to hold that the so-called sense-individuated intentional properties do not determine reference; and to hold this, as I observed earlier, is just to make them qualia under another, and very misleading, name.

So, returning to our example, it seems that the intentionalist must say that it cannot be the case that Jack and Jill experience blue, and other colors besides R and G, in the same way – that they have experiences of them that are phenomenally exactly similar. This seems to me implausible even if we restrict our attention to cases, like this one, in which the difference in quality space is intersubjective. And it seems even more implausible if we consider a case in which the difference in quality space is intrasubjective – i.e., a case in which someone changes from being a type A observer to being a type B observer.

Suppose this happens to Emily. First let me say what is the case with Emily's experience of *blue*, and her experience of most other shades, during the series of changes I describe. At t_1, before undergoing an operation in which her perceptual mechanisms are rewired, Emily calls blue things "blue," and says that they look blue. At t_2, after the operation, she calls blue things "blue," says that they look blue, and says that they look just as they did before the operation. At t_3, some months later, she calls blue things "blue," says that they look blue, and says that their appearance is unchanged from what it was at t_1 and t_2. Throughout her ability to identify blue things by color is unimpaired. The same is true, mutatis mutandi, of her experience of other shades of color – with the exception of the shades of red and green we are calling, respectively, R and G. Which brings us to the effects of the operation.

We will suppose that Emily is conscious during the operation, and is staring at a blue wall throughout. There is a prearranged signal she is to give if there is any change in how the wall appears to her. The signal is never given. After the operation Emily confirms that there was no change in the appearance of the wall, and initially doubts whether her color experience has been affected at all. But when we show her R and G things, she reports that the R things look the way G things used to look, and the G things look the way R things used to look. Moreover discrimination tests reveal that she has changed from being an A type observer to being a B type observer; and from this and the fact that the appearance of blue things (and things of most other shades) has remained unchanged, we can deduce that the appearance of R and G things has been reversed.

So far this does not directly challenge the view of the intentionalist. He can allow that at this point Emily's R-produced experiences exactly resemble her G-produced experiences before the operation, and likewise that her G-produced experiences exactly resemble her R-produced experiences before the operation. For he can hold that at this point her R-produced experiences have exactly the same sense-individuated intentional properties as her G-produced experiences had in the past, and that her G-produced experiences have exactly the same sense-individuated intentional properties as her R-produced experiences had in the past. Her R-produced experiences are "as of" G things, for they lead her to say that the R things she sees are, or at least look, G, and her G-produced experiences are "as of" R things, for they lead her to say that the G things she sees are, or at least look, R. The intentionalist can also say, of course, that Emily's blue-produced experiences after the operation have the same sense-individuated intentional properties as her blue-produced experiences before the operation. So at this point he can apparently hold onto his view that the only introspectively accessible properties we need to ascribe to experiences in order to account for the similarity and difference relationships between them are sense-individuated intentional properties.

But now consider the situation as it is a few months later. Emily has become accustomed to being a B-type observer. She has become just like Jill. No longer is she inclined to say that R things look G, or vice versa. We can suppose that she now says of R things that they look, as well as are, R. The intentionalist will say, and we can agree, that now her R-produced and G-produced experiences have different sense-individuated intentional properties than they did right after the operation. This being so, he cannot allow (consistently with his intentionalism) that there is any good sense in which her current R-produced experiences are phenomenally just like her R-produced experiences right after the operation. But what about her current *blue* produced experiences? Can the intentionalist allow that *these* might be phenomenally just like her blue-produced experiences right after the operation? Suppose he does. Then he will have to allow the same thing about her yellow-produced experiences, her orange-produced experiences, and so on. But this, together with the current structure of Emily's quality space, and the fact that her quality space has the same structure as it did right after the operation, will imply that her current R-produced experiences might be phenomenally just like her R-produced experiences right after the operation, and likewise that her current G-produced experiences might be phenomenally just

111

like her G-produced experiences right after the operation. And this the intentionalist cannot allow, given his claim that the intentional content of these experiences has changed.

Yet as I described the case, throughout it, from before the operation till after the accommodation to it, Emily claims that the appearance of blue things (also yellow things, orange things, etc.) has remained unchanged, and manifests recognitional capacities that are in line with these claims. Surely we would have every reason to accept these claims at face value. But if we accept them, we must also accept her claim, if she makes it, that R things now look to her the way G things looked to her before the operation, and vice versa; or, in other words, that her current as-of-R experiences are phenomenally just like her as-of-G experiences before the operation, and vice versa. But that, given the rest of the story, is just what one would expect her to claim. And if that claim is true, the intentionalist view is false. In the terminology I have used elsewhere, an adequate description of the case must invoke a relation of qualitative, or phenomenal, similarity that is distinct from (even if normally coextensive with) the relation of "intentional similarity"; and with this it must invoke qualia in addition to intentional properties of experiences.[12]

What we have in this case might be called a partial spectrum inversion. If what I have said about this case is right, we get the result that if a creature has a quality space that is symmetrical in certain ways, then a series of changes of the sort I have imagined would add up to a total spectrum inversion.[13] Each change involves a change in the structure of the quality space in which two shades "change places," each coming to appear the way the other did previously, the appearance of all of the other shades remaining unchanged, this being followed by an "accommodation" in which the intentional content of the experiences adjusts to the change. Two different shades are involved in each change. After the final change, all shades have changed their appearance, the original structure of the quality space has been restored, and for every shade S the S-produced experiences have (in normal circumstances) the intentional content of being as-of-S.

The possibility of total spectrum inversion, if indeed it is possible, dramatizes the need to distinguish qualia, or phenomenal properties of experiences, from sense-individuated intentional properties of them. But it is not necessary to insist on this possibility in order to demonstrate this

12 See Shoemaker 1982.
13 I present an example of such total intrasubjective spectrum inversion "by stages" in Shoemaker 1982. See also Essay 7.

need. All that is needed to show it is the possibility of the partial inversion Emily was described as undergoing. The claim from which this follows is a simple one: it is that it is possible for there to be a change in the structure of someone's color quality space (like that from being an *A* type observer to being a *B* type observer), and that it is possible for this to happen in such a way that there are some colors whose appearance to the person remains unchanged through both the change in the structure of the quality space and the subject's accommodation to that change.

IV

The argument of the last section rested in part on a thought experiment involving partial spectrum inversion. Such thought experiments raise obvious questions. From the fact that we can imagine Emily undergoing, and accommodating to, a partial spectrum inversion it certainly does not *follow* that it is in any sense possible that any of *us* should undergo such a series of changes. At most it follows that there could be creatures, similar to us on the folk psychological level, who are capable of undergoing such changes. For certain philosophical purposes I think that the latter conclusion is all that we need to establish. It, or a natural extension of it, is all we need to establish in order to refute those who claim that the idea of spectrum inversion is incoherent, or that the notion of a quale is one of which we can make no clear sense. But it isn't obvious how a conclusion about what sorts of creatures there could be tells us anything about *us*. Finding that there could be creatures whose experiences have qualia as well as intentional properties doesn't tell us that our experiences do, for it doesn't tell us that we are such creatures.

But I think that my thought experiment does support, even if it does not entail, a conclusion stronger than that there could be creatures capable of undergoing the changes Emily was described as going through. I think we can say, first of all, that *for all we know* we are such creatures. Moreover, it is worth noting that such changes needn't be the result of rewiring inside the head. It seems clearly possible that our visual perception of the world should be by means of a miniaturized TV camera plus receiver attached to the head – such devices might be used to protect the eyes from dangerous sorts of radiation in the environment. And then the rewiring could be inside the camera or receiver, not inside the head, and would not be constrained by immutable aspects of our biological nature. This suggests that the experience change that is possible for Emily is also a possibility for us.

But instead of pursuing this line of thought I want to raise a consideration that does not depend on thought experiments at all. Let me return to the issue of the connection between the similarity and difference relations between sense-experiences, on the one hand, and their intentional properties, on the other. It is true that simultaneous experiences belonging to a single person are similar to the extent that their sense-individuated intentional properties are the same or similar in intentional content, and different to the extent that these properties are different in their intentional content. But quite apart from the arguments given earlier, it seems to get things exactly backwards to say that it is in virtue of the intentional properties they have that the experiences are similar or different to the extent that they are. On the contrary, it is in virtue of, among other things, the similarity relations between experiences that they have the "senses," and representational content, that they do. Consider, for example, my experiences of two red surfaces which Frank Jackson's Fred can discriminate visually but I cannot. My experiences are exactly alike, and represent these surfaces as being exactly alike in color; and it is because they are exactly alike that they have the same representational content, rather than vice versa. Similarly, in a case in which someone can barely, but only barely, distinguish otherwise similar things of two different colors, it is the phenomenal similarity of the experiences that underlies their similarity of intentional content, rather than vice versa.

I have made free use in this essay of Quine's notion of a "quality space." The structure of a quality space is in part a matter of our having or lacking the ability to discriminate among different sensory stimuli, and of the ease or difficulty with which we make such discriminations. It is of course an empirical question to what extent this is innate, and to what extent it is modifiable by experience. But it seems beyond question that it is to some extent innate, and that it is only to a limited extent that it is modifiable and "cognitively permeable." We can become sensitive to differences in taste or color to which we were initially insensitive, but there will always remain physically different stimuli that we are absolutely incapable of discriminating.

I suggest that it is to the extent that our quality spaces are innate and unmodifiable that our perception of the world involves the perception of "secondary qualities." The perceptual system relativity of color similarity, and of other sorts of secondary quality similarity, is a reflection of the fact that what similarities and differences we see in the world depends in part on the nature of our sensory apparatus – i.e., on the nature of our quality spaces. One might put this by saying that one's perceptual experience necessarily projects onto the world the structure of one's quality space – or, more accurately, that experience in a certain sense modality projects onto the world the structure of the quality space for that modality. This amounts to projecting onto the world similarities and differences among our experiences. If these similarities and differences were merely intentional, the claim that we project them onto the world would come to nothing more than the truism that when we have experiences "as of" certain similarities and differences, we experience the world as manifesting those similarities and differences. But that truism leaves out the crucial fact that our quality space plays a constitutive role vis-à-vis the holding of these similarities and differences in the world.

V

But this brings us back to the projectivist view mentioned earlier. It may seem that if I allow that our perceptual experience projects onto the world similarities and differences between our experiences, I am committed to holding that our experience projects onto the world the features of our experience, the qualia, in virtue of which these similarities and differences hold. And there are other things I have said that may seem to commit me to this view. I have claimed that at least partial spectrum inversion is possible. This seems to mean that it is possible for it to be standardly the case that things of the same color look different to two different people under the same circumstances, owing to differences in the qualitative character of the experiences produced in them in those circumstances. If the qualitative character of an experience determines how the object of the experience looks, and if this qualitative character is something we are aware of in having the experience, it is natural to conclude that the object's looking a certain way consists in our perceiving it as having the qualitative character that in fact belongs to the experience. And that is certainly a projectivist view.

Notice that this projectivist view attributes to perceptual experiences a necessarily false representational content, over and above whatever true or possibly true representational content they have. Some projectivists hold that in the case of color this necessarily false representational content is all that there is; an experience's representing something as having a certain color just is its representing it as having a certain color quale.[14] But I have been assuming, and will continue to assume, that colors are

14 See, for example, Bohossian and Velleman 1989.

properties of external objects, and that in representing objects as red, green, blue, etc., our experiences can be, and normally are, representing them correctly. If we combine this assumption with the projectivist view, we must attribute two different sorts of intentional properties to experiences. The sort of intentional properties that figured in my previous discussion I will henceforth call possibly veridical, or *PV*, intentional properties. Being "as of red" will be such a *PV* intentional property. The other sort of intentional properties I will call necessarily illusory, or *NI*, intentional properties. If an experience having quale Q thereby represents its object as having Q, this will be an *NI*-intentional property of it. On the projectivist view, a case of spectrum inversion will be one in which, given the same circumstances, the color experiences of two different people are alike in their *PV*-intentional properties but differ in their *NI*-intentional properties.

One could hold that our color experiences have *NI*-intentional properties without holding that the properties these falsely represent things as having are ones that actually belong to the experiences themselves. One could hold that the represented properties are ones that in fact are never instantiated in anything, at least in this world. If I understand him correctly, this is how Barry Stroud understands the "theory of secondary qualities" in his book on Hume.[15] This too might be called a projectivist view. So let us distinguish *literal projectivism*, which says that our experience represent external things as having properties that in fact belong only to experiences, and *figurative projectivism*, which says that in virtue of properties they do have our experiences represent external objects as having properties that in fact belong to nothing.

If one accepts figurative projectivism, it seems that one should not hold that our experiences have *both* qualia *and* *NI*-intentional properties. On that view it is presumably the *NI*-intentional properties of experiences, rather than nonintentional properties in virtue of which the experiences have them, of which we are introspectively aware.[16] And if we don't have introspective access to the latter, they cannot count as qualia.

15 Stroud 1977, p. 87. 1995: Such a view seems to be ascribed to Locke, and endorsed in Mackie 1976.
16 In Essay 12 I construe figurative projectivism slightly differently – as holding that experiences do have qualia in virtue of which they have their *NI*-intentional properties. On such a view, our awareness of qualia would have the same status as it does on the view I favor in that essay; although in the first instance what we are aware of are the intentional properties of experiences, this awareness brings with it the ability to be aware of the similarities and differences that experiences have in virtue of the qualia they instantiate.

Moreover, the *NI*-intentional properties can do all the work that qualia are supposed to do. Cases of "qualia inversion" can be redescribed as cases in which the experiences of different creatures are systematically different in their *NI*-intentional properties despite being alike in their *PV*-intentional properties. It can be sameness with respect to these that permits Emily's *R*-produced experiences right after her operation to be "phenomenally" the same as her *R*-produced experiences several months later when she has completed her accommodation, despite a change in what I earlier called their intentional properties and what I now call their *PV*-intentional properties. And it can be what *NI*-intentional properties are produced under various circumstances that determines the structure of a creature's quality space. If one embraces figurative projectivism one should either deny that there are qualia or modify the definition of "qualia" to allow *NI*-intentional properties to count as qualia. If we do the latter, then instead of characterizing qualia as nonintentional we can characterize them as not *PV*-intentional. A believer in *NI*-intentional properties can save the letter, although not all of the spirit, of the intentionalist view that the only properties of experiences that we have any introspective access to are intentional ones. My earlier arguments against the intentionalist view had as their target the view that the only introspectively accessible features of experiences are *PV*-intentional properties; and of course any believer in *NI*-intentional properties, whether a literal projectivist or a figurative projectivist, will join me in rejecting this.

Both versions of the projectivist view have the unattractive consequence that our color experience is systematically illusory. Opinions will differ as to how much of an objection to them this is. But there are objections to them over and above this one. As for literal projectivism, I cannot myself make any sense of the idea that any property I perceive as belonging to the surface of the tomato, when I perceive its color, is in fact a property of the experience itself. As for figurative projectivism, it is a mystery, to say the least, how the content of our experience can include reference to properties whose actual instantiation we have never experienced or had any other epistemic access to – properties we know neither "by acquaintance" nor "by description," unless we have some sort of nonsensory acquaintance with a Platonic realm of uninstantiated properties.

It is worth mentioning a possible rejoinder to this objection to figurative projectivism. Perhaps the figurative projectivist need not hold that there actually *is* a property my experience falsely attributes to the surface of the tomato, and so need not explain how the content of my experience can include reference to such a property. We noted earlier that an intentionalist must hold that sensory experiences have something like sense as well as reference – that they have what I called "sense-individuated intentional properties." This suggests that there is more than one way in which such an experience might be illusory. It might be the case that the property-senses involved in its content do pick out genuine properties, but that these are not instantiated in the way the experience represents them as being. But it might instead be the case that at least one of these senses fails to refer – it in some sense purports to pick out a property that the experience attributes to the surface of the tomato, but it in fact fails to do so.

But it is not easy to see how this would work, partly because it is unclear what sort of thing an experiential property sense, or "sense-individuated intentional property," would be. One possible way of working this out would yield a view very similar to literal projectivism. The sense would involve a quale. What it would purport to refer to would be a property that can belong to physical objects but in a certain way resembles the quale. There being no such property, not even in Plato's heaven, this sense fails to refer. The illusion is not that a certain property belongs to the surface of the tomato, but that there is a property of a certain description that belongs to it. Obviously this version of figurative projectivism would be of no use to someone who wants to avoid commitment to qualia. I am unable to think of a version that would be of use to such a person.

I mentioned two features of my view that might seem to commit me to projectivism. One was that my view says that in some sense we project similarities and differences between experiences onto things in the world. This might seem to imply the literal projectivist view that our experiences project onto objects the features of them, qualia, in virtue of which these phenomenal similarities and differences hold. But all that it need be taken to imply is that what similarity and difference relations we perceive in the world is a function of what relations of phenomenal similarity and difference relations hold among our experiences, and that does not imply that we project the properties of experiences. This is not in itself even a figurative projectivist view about the properties we experience objects as having, although it might be said to be a figurative projectivist view about the similarity and difference relations we perceive as holding between them.[17]

17 But this would require a modification of my characterization of figurative projectivism. For what I want to say is not, of course, that the color similarities we perceive between objects do not in fact hold between them, but rather that they hold between them rel-

The other feature of my view that might seem to imply projectivism is the fact that it allows for the possibility that things might look different to two different people even when their experiences are exactly alike in their PV-intentional properties. It should now be apparent that what this threatens to commit me to is not literal projectivism, as such, but rather the view, which is shared by literal projectivism and figurative projectivism, that our perceptual experiences have NI-intentional properties. This doesn't exactly get me off the hook, for I find this view as nearly as abhorrent as I do literal projectivism. If one wants to reject this view, one must say, I think, that the possibility my view allows for has been misdescribed. Take the case of Jack and Jill, and suppose that Jack's experience is as Emily's was before her operation and Jill's is as Emily's was after her operation. It is natural to say that R things look different to Jack than they do to Jill. But that is what will commit us to NI-intentional properties. What we must do is say that Jack's experiences of R things are phenomenally different from Jill's experiences of them, and resist the temptation to cash this by talking about differences in how things "look."[18]

My main target in this essay has been the view that the only introspectively accessible features of experiences are what I am now calling PV-intentional properties. Initially I supposed that these are the only intentional properties there are. But reflection on projectivism made me realize that it is just a special case of a possible view according to which color experiences (and secondary quality experiences generally) have what I call NI-intentional properties. This view is supported by the common intuition that there is a conflict between the way we experience the world and the way science tells us it is. It is also supported by the intuitions Harman appeals to in arguing that the only properties of our experiences that we are introspectively aware of are intentional ones. And if we revise our definition of "qualia" so that it covers NI-intentional properties of experiences, this view enables us to reconcile the claim that we are introspectively aware of qualia with the claim that only the intentional properties of experiences are introspectively acces-

ative to observers like us. Let's take figurative projectivism about these relations as the view that in virtue of similarities and differences between experiences, they represent objects as standing in similarity relations that are not grounded solely in intrinsic relations between the objects that are perceived as so related.

18 We needn't resist this temptation if we accept the view suggested in Essay 12, which holds that what in the first instance our experiences represent are "phenomenal properties" as there conceived.

sible. I have already said what I have against this view. But the central argument of this essay is unaffected by whether we accept it or not. If it is true, then *NI*-intentional properties can play the role I have attributed to qualia. If it is false, there must be nonintentional properties that play that role. Either way, the *PV*-intentional properties of experiences are not enough.

6

Qualia and consciousness

I

Qualia, if there are such, are properties of sensations and perceptual states, namely the properties that give them their qualitative or phenomenal character – those that determine "what it is like" to have them. I combine the belief that there are qualia with adherence to a materialist and functionalist view of mind, and thus hold a "compatibilist" view that puts me in a crossfire between two sorts of "incompatibilists" – those who believe in qualia and think that this supports a rejection of functionalist or materialist views, and those who deny the existence of qualia, or "quine" them (as Daniel Dennett puts it), as part of their defense of functionalist or materialist views.[1]

My compatibilist position (see Shoemaker 1975a, 1975b, 1981, and 1982) can most conveniently be sketched by reference to the "inverted qualia argument" and the "absent qualia argument", both against functionalism, advanced some years ago by Ned Block and Jerry Fodor (1972). I agree with Block and Fodor that the inverted qualia argument shows that individual qualia are not functionally definable. This is my one concession to incompatibilism. But I maintain that there is a good sense in which the qualitative character of an experience can be accommodated in a functionalist account. A functionalist account can be given of what it is for a property to be a quale, of what it is for mental states to have qualitative character, and of what it is for mental states to be in greater or lesser degrees similar in qualitative character. In consequence of this, while there *can* be what Block and Fodor call cases of "inverted qualia," there *cannot* be cases of what they call "absent qualia." A creature

I am grateful to Earl Conee, Mark Crimmins, and Michael Tye for comments on the essay.
1 Those on the first side include Ned Block and Jerry Fodor, among those who see qualia as threatening to functionalism – see their 1972 – and Thomas Nagel and Frank Jackson among those who see them as threatening to physicalism – see Nagel 1974 and Jackson 1982. Those on the other side include Daniel Dennett and Gilbert Harman – See Dennett 1988 and Harman 1990.

functionally just like a creature having qualitative states would itself have to have qualitative states, for it would have to have states standing in relations of qualitative similarity and difference to one another that are isomorphic with the relations of qualitative similarity and difference holding between the states of the creature that is its functional duplicate. All that follows from the fact that individual qualia are not functionally definable is that such a functional duplicate would not necessarily have states that are the *same* in qualitative character as the corresponding states of the creature of which it is the duplicate, not that it might lack qualitative states altogether.

This position is clearly compatible with materialism. Even if individual qualia cannot be functionally defined, because of the possibility of qualia inversion, the fact that their similarity and identity conditions can be functionally defined makes it legitimate to speak of them as being physically realized in much the sense in which a functional state or property can be physically realized. And there seems no reason why a quale should not be identified with the disjunction of its possible realizations. The chief apparent obstacle to such an identification is Frank Jackson's "knowledge argument," and similar arguments in Nagel (see Jackson 1982 and Nagel 1974). I shall spare you yet another telling of the story of the super neurophysiologist Mary and her black and white room. The general point of the argument is that knowing all of the physical facts about color vision, or having all of the relevant physical information, is not sufficient for knowing what it is like to see red. I shall not add here to the now extensive literature on this argument; I shall only say that I think that a satisfactory answer to it can be fashioned out of points made in the existing literature (see Lewis 1983, Nemirow 1980, Horgan 1984, Tye 1986, and Loar 1990). In brief, someone who knows all of the relevant physical and functional facts about color perception will know, among other things, what physical property the red quale is (meaning by that the quale that experiences of red have under normal circumstances), and so in one sense will know what the red quale is; she may nevertheless lack, if she has never seen red things, the ability to recognize this property introspectively, and so in that sense may not know "what it is like" to have an experience having this quale; but there is no warrant for construing the lack of this recognitional capacity as the ignorance of any fact, unless facts are individuated in such a way that the substitution of coreferential terms changes what fact a sentence expresses, in which case there is no warrant for the claim that if physicalism is true, then knowing all of the truths expressible in physical terms will amount to knowing all of the facts.

My main focus in this essay will be on the relation of qualia to consciousness. I will approach this by addressing Thomas Nagel's now famous question "What is it like to be a bat?"

Kathleen Wilkes (1988, p. 224) asks, tongue perhaps in cheek, "How do we know that the bat's echolocation is not 'blindsighted'; i.e. that there is *nothing* that it is like for a bat to echolocate?" One might suppose that the supposition that there is nothing it is like for bats to echolocate is the same as the supposition that the states involved in echolocation are without qualia. But why shouldn't it be instead the supposition that these states do have qualia, but that these are inaccessible to the bat's consciousness? Of course, that will sound a bit crazy if it means that bats do have introspective consciousness of *some* things, but just happen to lack it of the states involved in echolocation. A more likely thought about bats is that they lack introspective consciousness altogether, and *so* lack it of the qualia, if any, of their sensory states.

But does it make sense to speak of *qualia* that are not accessible to introspective consciousness? Aren't qualia supposed to be what determine the introspectable character of sensations and the like? What about blindsighted humans – do we think that they have sensory states that have qualia, but that these are not introspectively accessible to them? Is it even coherent to think that? Can we say that there is something it is like for the blindsighted person to see what she claims not to see? Or can we somehow drive a wedge between the notion of the qualitative character of sensory states and the notion of what it is like to have them?

One claim about bats that should be relatively uncontroversial is that they have "quality spaces" *à la* Quine. There will be physically different stimuli they are unable to discriminate from one another. And among stimuli that they can discriminate, i.e., respond differentially to, some will be easier for them to discriminate than others. This imposes a kind of bat-relative similarity ordering on the stimuli available to bats. To the extent that bats are capable of learning and induction, the role of stimuli in this learning and induction will be a function of their position relative to each other in the similarity ordering. Rewarding a response to a given stimulus will tend to increase the likelihood of other stimuli eliciting that response to the extent that those other stimuli are similar – i.e., bat-similar – to that one. Perhaps the role of the stimuli relative to one another in learning and induction is partially constitutive of the similarity ordering.

To some extent this similarity ordering will be innate and not modifiable by learning. To what extent that is so is of course an empirical question. Perhaps one can conceive of creatures such that there are no physically different stimuli that they cannot discriminate, and also such that the ease or difficulty with which they can discriminate different stimuli is modifiable by experience. So, for example, once these creatures have learned that they dislike the taste of one sort of mushroom and like the taste of another, they henceforth have no difficulty discriminating these kinds of mushrooms visually, although previously they discriminated them only with extreme difficulty. The similarity ordering of stimuli changes as they acquire evidence about what the various stimuli indicate about their environment; it is a function of their beliefs about the objective similarity of the normal environmental causes of these stimuli. To some extent we are like that – we can learn to discriminate things we previously couldn't, and can learn to discriminate things with greater ease than we could initially. But we are like this only to a very limited extent, and I would assume that bats are like this to an even lesser extent.

It is, I think, to the extent that the similarity ordering of stimuli relative to a creature's perceptual system is innate and not modifiable by experience that there is a distinction between similarity of experiences, or sensory states, that is just a matter of similarity in representative content, or what I have called "intentional" similarity, and a different kind of similarity that might be called "phenomenal" or "qualitative" similarity. At a minimum, phenomenal similarity will include the exact similarity relative to the creature of physically different stimuli that the creature absolutely cannot discriminate. There will also be a structure of just noticeable differences that does not change appreciably with changes in beliefs about what the various stimuli portend.

Returning to bats, what I would like to say is that corresponding to the similarity ordering of stimuli relative to bats there is a similarity ordering of the sensory states produced in bats by these stimuli – the internal states that mediate the causal connections between these stimuli and the bat's behavior. And in virtue of there being this ordering, these states will have properties that play some part of the role of qualia. There may be various different respects in which stimuli can be similar or different, relative to bats. And the corresponding sensory states will be similar or different in respects corresponding to these, in virtue of what properties of this sort they have. I will call these "quasi-qualia."

Why "quasi"? Why am I reluctant to call these genuine qualia? Well, for one thing, I suspect that if I knew more about bats I would want to insert a "quasi" into most of my attributions to them of the mental states that figure in common sense psychology. Their "beliefs" are most likely "registrations" of information that fall short of being full-fledged beliefs. An important part of the functional role of qualia is their role in the production of beliefs, in particular perceptual beliefs; and if bats have only quasi-beliefs, that is a reason for saying that they have only quasi-qualia. One reason for "quasi"-ing one's attributions of mental states to such creatures as bats has to do with the fact, or what I am here assuming to be the fact, that such creatures have little or nothing in the way of introspective access to their internal states, largely because they have little or no capacity to conceive of themselves as having such states. The mental states in question are those that figure in "folk psychology"; and the folk psychological level of description is one that essentially involves states that are self-ascribable in a certain way, i.e., introspectively, by the creatures that have them. I will say something later on about why this is so. My claim here is that if bat "qualia" are only quasi, this is because they belong to a family of states (events, etc.), that are only quasi relative to the folk psychological states they somewhat resemble in functional role, in large part because the functional economy to which these states belong is not rich enough to yield anything that could be called introspective self-consciousness.

Could there be a case of *absent* quasi-qualia? We could have this if we could have a bat that is functionally indistinguishable (at the appropriate level) from an ordinary bat, but whose states lack quasi-qualia. But that is a self-contradictory description. I have explained the notion of quasi-qualia in functional terms. Some will think this the reason why quasi-qualia are only quasi. For it is often taken for granted that genuine qualia are not functionally characterizable. But here, it seems to me, there has been a persistent failure to appreciate the distinction made in my introductory remarks, between the functional characterization of individual qualia, on the one hand, and the functional characterization of the identity and similarity conditions of qualia, on the other. It is the former of these that is impossible if "qualia inversion" is a possibility. But it is the latter that has to be impossible if cases of "absent qualia" are to be possible. And my functional characterization of quasi-qualia was (in sketchy form) a characterization of their identity and similarity conditions.

Can there be cases of *inverted* quasi-qualia? I do not see any reason why not. Given this set of states and properties, and the similarity relations between them, there seems no reason in principle why there could not be a rewiring that changes their relation to stimuli in such a way as to preserve the discriminatory capacities of the creature. Here *intra*subjective inversion would reveal itself in the creature's behavior – behavior that had been conditioned to one stimulus would be elicited by the "inverse" stimulus. There might then be the same reason in the case of quasi-qualia as there is in the case of qualia for saying that individual ones of them are not functionally definable. But this should not prevent us from appreciating the sense in which quasi-qualia are functionally characterizable.

It may help to consider a device considerably more primitive than a bat, to which the same point applies. Here, then, is a functional specification of a color detecting device that is capable of something analogous to intrasubjective spectrum inversion.

The device has two pairs of states, (A1, A2) and (B1, B2) such that at any time it is in exactly one of the states in each pair. Which member of each pair it is in can differ from one time to another. It also has in its repertoire four other states, S1, S2, S3, and S4. Which of these it is in depends on what sort of light is falling on its sensor (I will assume that this light is always either predominately red, predominately green, predominately yellow, or predominately blue). The nature of the dependence is as follows:

> If the device is in state A1, then
>> red stimulation puts it in S1
>> green stimulation puts it in S2
>> yellow stimulation puts it in S3
>> blue stimulation puts it in S4.
> If the device is in state A2, then
>> red stimulation puts it in state S2
>> green stimulation puts it in state S1
>> yellow stimulation puts it in state S4
>> blue stimulation puts it in state S3.

The device has a display, on which exactly one of the words "red," "green," "yellow," and "blue" appears whenever its sensory is stimulated. This output is determined as follows:

> If the device is in state B1, then
>> Its being in S1 causes "red" to appear
>> Its being in S2 causes "green" to appear
>> Its being in S3 causes "yellow" to appear
>> Its being in S4 causes "blue" to appear.

If the device is in state B2, then

Its being in S1 causes "green" to appear

Its being in S2 causes "red" to appear

Its being in S3 causes "blue" to appear

Its being in S4 causes "yellow" to appear.

The device has an "error button" on it. If the error button is pressed, the device goes from B1 to B2, or vice versa. (One can think of the pressing of the error button as corresponding to a person's getting information indicating that she has undergone intrasubjective spectrum inversion.)

Constantly revolving insider the device is a tape, on which at one minute intervals are recorded (a) the time, (b) a symbol corresponding to the S-state it is currently in, and (c) a symbol corresponding to the B-state it is currently in. Traces are retained on the tape for 12 hours, which is the length of a complete revolution of the tape. There is also a mechanism that can scan the tape. The scanning mechanism enables the device to answer "yes" or "no" to two sorts of questions about pairs of times during the last 12 hours: whether it was in the same S-state at the two times, and whether it was stimulated by the same color at the two times. The answers to these questions will be the same except when the error button has been pressed between the two times in question.

Are any of these states (A1, A2, B1, B2, S1, S2, S3, S4) functionally definable? Not on the basis of this functional specification of the device. We could tell on the basis of the internal makeup of something that it was a realization of this functional specification. And we could find pairs of physical states that play the role of (A1, A2), (B1, B2), (S1, S2), and (S3, S4). In some particular device let these be, respectively, (P1, P2), (P3, P4), (P5, P6), and (P7, P8). We could also know that if we assign P1 to A1, we must assign P3 to B1, P5 to S1, and P7 to S3, while if we assign P2 to A1 we must assign P4 to B1, P6 to S1, and P8 to S3. But nothing would justify making one of these sets of assignments rather than the other.

Nothing in our description says what causes the device to go from one A state to the other. But let us suppose that in one realization of it there is a switch inside it such that reversing the position of the switch changes its A-state from A1 to A2 or vice versa. If our description were expanded so as to mention the switch and identify one of the switch positions, then of course we would have a way of assigning physical realizations to all of the other states. Again, our description says that our device records its S-states on the tape with symbols that correspond to them. If it were part of the specification that a certain symbol, say "X1", corresponds to S1, another, say "X2", to S2, and so on, then by examining the tape we could find out what S-state the thing was in at a given time, and, using that information, discover how all of its various states were realized. But either of these changes in our specification would sully its abstract functional character, and restrict in an arbitrary way what things would count as realizations of our description.

If the functional specification is the one I originally gave, and the expressions "A1", "S1", etc. have no meaning beyond what is given by their role in this description, then it will be meaningless to ask of a given realization of it whether it is in A1 or in A2, or whether when it "sees red" it is in S1 or S2. But of course it won't be meaningless to ask whether it is in the S-state corresponding to the symbol "X1" that appears on its tape. And we can, if we want to, use this symbol, or some other, to designate the S-state the device is in on a given occasion, and likewise introduce symbols for its other S-states and its A-states and B-states. Such names might be defined ostensively; e.g. "X1" might be defined as meaning "the S-state this device is in now." But these names, and the states they define, will not be functionally definable, at least not at the level of abstractness at which the functional specification of the device was given.

Letting our S-states be quasi-qualia (with heavy emphasis on the "quasi"), our device is plainly capable of intrasubjective quasi-qualia inversion. Can there be a case of "absent quasi-qualia" here? Obviously not. Such a case would have to be one in which a device is, at the appropriate level of abstractness, functionally identical to a device having quasi-qualia but itself lacking in quasi-qualia. And this makes no sense – anything functionally identical to a device having these quasi-qualia will be a device satisfying my functional specification, and any such device will have S-states, and so will have quasi-qualia.

Can there be *inter*subjective inversion relative to these quasi-qualia? I think so. It will not be true that for any two devices that are realizations of my functional description, either they have the same quasi-qualia (given the same stimulus) or they are quasi-qualia inverted relative to each other. This will be so only if the devices are physically alike to the extent of having the same physical states as realizations of their S-states, A-states, etc. Where they are alike in that way, then they can be said to be quasi-qualia inverted relative to each other if they differ systematically with respect to which S-state realization they are in when their sensor is stimulated by light of the different colors. This would be so, for example, if they were both the sort of device that has the A-state reversing switch, and one of them is in exactly the physical state the other would be in if the position of its switch were changed.

As I have already suggested, where quasi-qualia fall short of being qualia is, in part anyhow, their inaccessibility to consciousness – because there is no consciousness there, worthy of the name, for them to be accessible to. As I see it, the requirement of accessibility to consciousness is not due to a special link between the notion of qualitative character and consciousness, but rather to a general link between the notion of consciousness and the notions of the family of folk psychological states with which the notion of qualia is intimately bound up. It has become part of the received wisdom that much, indeed most, of what goes on in the mind is unconscious. It is one of my aims to keep this from obscuring the fact, which until recently was obvious to everyone, that there is an important sense in which it is of the essence of folk psychological states to be accessible to consciousness.

Seen as a Cartesian claim, this may seem to make folk psychological states prime candidates for elimination. But I think it can be given a Darwinian twist that can help to forestall acceptance of that absurdity. There seems good reason to think that folk psychology, *qua* tacit theory of the mind, is to a very considerable extent innate (see Clark 1987 and Fodor 1987, pp. 129-133). In evolutionary terms, this means that at the same time that we evolved to *have* a repertoire of folk psychological states, we evolved, as part of the same process, to be such as to be disposed to *conceive* of ourselves and our conspecifics in terms of these states, and, what goes with this, we evolved to be sensitive to the instantiation of these states and to be reliable detectors of them. In the case of others this means being sensitive to the behavioral signs and manifestations of the states, and in our own case it means being such that, normally, the consideration of whether we have a certain belief, sensation, etc., directly issues in knowledge that we do, or that we don't. In Dennettian terms, we evolved to be creatures that naturally and successfully take the "intentional stance" toward each other and toward themselves. It isn't that we first came to be a certain way and then thought up the theory that we were that way, which theory we are justified in believing because it fits our behavior. Rather, it is part of being the sort of creatures we are that we conceive of ourselves in these terms, and so we came to conceive of ourselves as such creatures *in* coming to *be* such creatures.

129

Much of this process of evolution must have been inseparable from the process whereby we evolved to be language-users, which must have occurred as part of the development of complex patterns of social interaction among our ancestors. There is, of course, a close correspondence between the main sorts of folk psychological states and the main sorts of speech acts – between believing and asserting, between wanting and requesting or ordering, and between intending and saying what one will do. Presumably language would not have evolved at all if it were not for the crucial role played by these speech acts, or primitive forms of them, in social interactions that had great survival value for our species. Now it is a very short step from being able to engage in such speech acts to being able to self-ascribe the mental states of which they are expressions. In our social interactions with others, the roles played by such self-ascriptions are closely related to, and sometimes the same as, those played by the associated "first-order" speech acts. For example, in a cooperative endeavor the role played by self-ascriptions of belief, saying "I believe that *P*", is a sophisticated version of the role played by straightforward assertions of the contents of the belief, i.e., saying "*P*." Both indicate to the hearer the assumptions on which the speaker is going to be acting. Only a radical design failure would give a creature the ability to assert without the ability to self-ascribe belief, or the ability to express wants in requests and orders without the ability to self-ascribe wants. It seems a good bet that our ability to self-ascribe these mental states evolved together with our ability to use language (see Essay 2).

It also seems a good bet that our ability to recognize such states in others evolved together with our ability to use and understand language. A rudimentary ability to detect folk psychological states in others is involved in the ability to get information from the utterances of others about how they are likely to behave in various circumstances – and presumably the survival value of language use consists in part in its being able to convey such information. Considerations of language aside, it seems plausible to suppose that human beings evolved in such a way as to be sensitive to aspects of one another's behavior that are revelatory of how they are likely to behave. Sensitivity of this sort to the behavior of conspecifics is common in the animal kingdom, and unlikely to be mainly the result of learning. What is special about humans is that this sensitivity meshes with a conceptual framework, folk psychology, in such a way that observed behavior suggests explanations of it in terms of that framework that make possible much more precise, extensive, and detailed expectations of future behavior. Where such explanations are most likely to be available is where the behavior in question is produced with the aim of providing others with such expectations – and a prime example of such behavior is the linguistic behavior that occurs in people involved in a cooperative enterprise. One can see here that our being prone to give folk psychological explanations of the behavior of others goes with our having "direct" access to folk psychological states in ourselves; for it is this direct access that makes it possible for us to provide others with the behavioral evidence they need if they are to come up with the right explanations and expectations, which in turn is what is needed if we are to form correct expectations of their behavior.

As is widely appreciated, explanations involving folk psychological concepts are typically and paradigmatically explanations in terms of *reasons*. And our ability to communicate usefully with others depends on our being able to convey not only what we intend to do (and will do, unless we are prevented or persuaded otherwise) but what our reasons are for doing it – what our objectives are, and what assumptions we are making about the world in pursuing those objectives. It is important, again partly for reasons having to do with our interactions with others, that we have access not only to our reasons for acting but to our reasons for believing. And here is where access to sense-experiences and the like comes in. In forming beliefs based on sense-perception, one will be handicapped if one does not have the ability to be aware of how things look, sound, feel, etc., to one, and so is not in a position to consider whether conditions are such that things looking (sounding, etc.) that way to one is a good reason for thinking that they are that way. Normally one does not explicitly consider the look or the feel of things. But if one were not implicitly aware of it, or capable of becoming aware of it when the need arises, one could not use one's tacit knowledge of principles of perspective, the effects of lighting conditions on the appearance of things, etc., to adjust one's perceptual beliefs in the light of information about one's situation or condition.

IV

This brings us back to qualia. The accessibility of qualia to consciousness is closely related to the accessibility to consciousness of how things look, sound, feel, etc., to one, i.e., to the accessibility of the representational, or intentional, content of one's experiences. But these are not the same thing. If I am aware that my experience is "as of" something red, I am aware of an intentional property of it. And that won't be a quale, for qualia are supposed to be nonintentional features of experiences that somehow underlie their intentional features. There are philosophers, Daniel Dennett and Gilbert Harman for two, who question whether there are any such features that are accessible to consciousness.

There is, indeed, a prima facie strong phenomenological case for questioning whether we are aware of any such features. As G.E. Moore (1922, p. 25) complained nearly a century ago, the sensation of blue is "as if it were diaphanous"; if one tries to introspect it one sees right through it, and sees only the blue. In general, the properties we are aware of in sense experience – colors, tastes, etc. – are experienced as belonging to things in the environment or parts of our bodies (e.g., the tartness is experienced as being in one's mouth), not as features of an experience, *qua* mental state or event. Gilbert Harman (1990) develops this point in a recent essay, arguing that the only properties of experiences to which we have conscious access are intentional ones.

However, I shall argue that the awareness we have of the intentional content of our experiences, of how things look, feel, etc., involves an awareness of qualia. My basic strategy is to argue that this awareness involves an awareness of a kind of similarity between experiences – call it phenomenal similarity – which cannot be equated with "intentional similarity," i.e., with having the same or similar intentional or representational features, and then to claim that this requires that experiences have nonintentional features, of which we are aware, in virtue of which they stand to one another in relations of phenomenal similarity and difference. These will be qualia.

Someone might think he can grant me the first step of this argument but refuse to grant the second. That is, it might be thought that while experiences are phenomenally similar or different in virtue of nonintentional features of them, there is no need to suppose that we must be capable of being aware of these features in order to be aware of the similarities and differences that hold in virtue of them. That seems to be the view of J.J.C. Smart in "Sensations and Brain Processes." Smart thinks that while sensations have plenty of properties, namely neurological ones, "in speaking of them as being like or unlike one another we need not know or mention these properties." This rests on "the possibility of our being able to report that one thing is like another without being able to state the respect in which it is like" (1962, pp. 167-168). But here Smart seems to overlook the familiar point that since any two things resemble one another in *some* respect or other, the assertion that two things are like one another is completely empty unless accompanied by an indication of the respect of likeness. Someone might suggest that we could have the capacity to detect a certain kind of likeness among things, likeness in a certain respect, without having the capacity to detect the presence or absence of the properties in virtue of which these likenesses hold. After all, there could be a device that tells us whether two things are the same size without telling us what the size of anything is. But suppose we have a device which given a pair of objects as input delivers as output a correct verdict about whether they are exactly alike with respect to F-ness, which given a triplet of objects as input delivers a correct verdict about their comparative similarity with respect to F-ness, and which can perform such tasks diachronically as well as synchronically, i.e., has a "memory" that enables it to compare objects presented to it at different times with respect to their degree of F-ness. Such a device could be used to sort objects into the same or different classes depending on whether they have the same or different F properties; in being an F similarity detector, it would also be an F property detector. Likewise, insofar as we are detectors of phenomenal similarity amongst experiences, we are detectors of the phenomenal qualities, the qualia, in virtue of which these hold. Of course, we might, as Smart says, know that experiences are alike without knowing what "neurological" properties they have in common; and we might do this even if it is in virtue of sharing these neurological properties that they are alike – even if the qualia in virtue of which they stand in their similarity and difference relationships are identical to neurological properties. But this would not be a matter of knowing the similarity relations without knowing in virtue of what properties they hold; it would be a matter of knowing the similarity relations without knowing those properties *under their neurophysiological descriptions*. So I think the point stands that if we are aware of "phenomenal" similarities and differences amongst experiences, which are not as such intentional similarities and differences, then we are in some sense aware of nonintentional features, qualia, in virtue of which they hold.[2]

There are a number of ways of bringing out the need to distinguish between intentional similarity and difference and phenomenal similarity

---

2 The argument here assumes that we are detectors of both synchronic and diachronic similarity between experiences. Mark Crimmins has pointed out to me that the applicability of this to our awareness of similarity of color experiences is complicated by the fact that we are much better at distinguishing adjacent shades than ones spaced an inch or two apart, or ones viewed at different times, and that there is reason to think that our synchronic distinguishing of adjacent shades involves an "edge-detecting" device that, as he puts it, does not "do" memories.

and difference. One is by considering putative cases of partial and total spectrum inversion, and in particular cases of *intra*subjective inversion. Briefly, it is conceivable that someone should undergo a change in her color experience and then accommodate to the change in a way that does not involve undoing it, in such a way that the intentional content of the experiences she has in a given sort of circumstances is the same after the accommodation as it was before the initial change. The case can be so constructed that it gives us phenomenal similarities and differences, between preinversion and postinversion experiences, that cannot be intentional similarities and differences. I have developed this line of thought at length elsewhere, and shall not pursue it further here (1982 and Essay 5)

Another way of bringing out the need for the distinction is by considering Twin Earth (or "Inverted Earth") cases. If I and my doppleganger on Twin Earth are physical duplicates, there is surely a good sense in which our experiences are phenomenally the same. But if we suppose that one or the other of us is fitted with spectrum-inverting lenses, it is compatible with this that the distribution of colors in our environments is systematically different, e.g., that on Twin Earth grass is red, ripe tomatoes are green, the sky is yellow, and so on. And if that is so, the intentional content of my doppleganger's experiences will be systematically different from that of their phenomenally identical counterparts in me (see Block 1990). The point is a special case of the "externalist" moral usually drawn from Twin Earth cases: intentional content, and so similarity with respect to intentional content, depends on external factors – relations to the environment – in a way qualitative character and phenomenal similarity do not.

A perhaps more debateable source of support is the consideration of "Molyneux" cases. It seems plausible, although it is hardly uncontroversial, that if someone blind from birth acquires the capacity of sight, and begins having visual experiences, then for a time there will be similarities and differences in the person's visual experiences that do not as yet have representational significance for the person, because the person has not yet learned what the experiences signify. So there will be phenomenal similarities and differences that are not intentional similarities and differences.

I think that all of these arguments have merit. But I think that we can see the need to distinguish phenomenal and intentional similarity and difference without considering out of the way examples.

Consider, as a limiting case, a situation in which two objects are indistinguishable to one. One would say that they look alike, and this might be construed as meaning that the experiences of them share the same intentional properties. They are both "of red." In virtue of this they stand in a relation of intentional similarity: they are "of," i.e., represent, the same shade of color. It is also true that they are phenomenally exactly alike. But here it seems clear that they both represent the same shade of color *because* they are phenomenally alike, in a way that could not be true if their being phenomenally alike just meant that they represent the same shade of color.

Or consider a case in which two objects are barely distinguishable by color (and otherwise indistinguishable). They look alike, and that can mean that the experiences of them are similar in their intentional properties, i.e., in their representational content. The experiences can also be said to be phenomenally similar. And it seems plain that the experiences have similar representational contents *because* they are phenomenally alike, in a way that could not be true if their being phenomenally alike just amounted to their being similar in representational content.

In these cases the experience similarities are synchronic. But we can have otherwise similar cases in which they are diachronic. If two stimuli are indistinguishable to me, then if one succeeds the other the way I am "appeared to" will remain unchanged. The experience produced by the later stimulus will be both intentionally the same and phenomenally the same as the experience produced by the earlier one; and these experiences will be intentionally the same *because* they are phenomenally the same. Similarly in the case where the stimuli are barely distinguishable.

There are in fact two different senses in which it can be said that experiences are intentionally similar because they are phenomenally similar. The phenomenal similarities and differences amongst our experiences reflect the structure of our quality space; the phenomenal similarity of experiences is a function of the proximity in our quality space of the stimuli that normally elicit them. And our quality spaces have the structure they do in part because we evolved to be sensitive to certain similarities in the world, ones that are relevant to our needs. In consequence of this, there is a correlation between there being certain phenomenal similarities between our experiences and there being certain objective similarities between the causes of these experiences. And in virtue of this correlation, certain phenomenal similarities come to represent the correlated objective similarities.

But where the represented similarities are with respect to secondary qualities such as color, the cashing out of the "because" brings in a constitutive as well as a causal and correlational element. The similarities between the experiences represent similarities in a certain respect (e.g., color) in the world because what it *is* for things in the world to be similar in that respect is for them to be apt to produce experiences that are similar in that way. Color similarity, and in general "secondary quality" similarity, is perceptual system relative. If we confronted creatures whose visual quality spaces were different from ours, and who made judgments of color similarity and difference that were systematically at odds with ours, it would be preposterous to claim that they are systematically wrong about the color similarities between things, and it would be equally preposterous to suggest that maybe they are generally right about this and that it is we who are systematically wrong. The sensible thing to say would be that things that are similar in color relative to us are dissimilar in color relative to them, and vice versa. This is not to deny that one of these quality spaces might be the better one to have for getting along in the environment we live in, or, what is probably not at all the same thing, that one of them may come closer than the other to "carving nature at its joints." But the discovery that our quality space is inferior in either of these respects to that of some other species of creatures, actual or possible, would be irrelevant to the truth or falsity of our ordinary judgments of color similarity and difference, and our ordinary assignments of colors to objects.

For surface properties of objects to be similar in color relative to a certain sort of perceptual system is presumably for it to be the case that objects with those properties standardly produce, in creatures having that sort of perceptual system, experiences that are similar in a certain way. This will be the sort of similarity that bears most directly on the creature's discriminatory and recognitional capacities, and which determines its quality space; it is such that exact similarity of this sort goes with indistinguishability, and the extent of this sort of similarity, or the corresponding sort of difference, varies with ease of discrimination. This is what I am calling phenomenal similarity. And if the similarity of objects with respect to color (relative to a certain sort of creature) consists in their aptness to produce color experiences that are phenomenally similar, then the phenomenal similarity of color experiences cannot consist in the fact that they represent their objects as similar with respect to color (relative to that sort of creature).

Once the distinction between intentional and phenomenal similarity is made, it becomes apparent that the relation between them is complex. There is a presumption that intentional similarities and differences are realized in phenomenal similarities and differences; this is, we might say, the default condition. But the presumption can be overridden. Presumably it is when we view objects that are partially in shadow, or on which there are highlights. For a more extreme case, consider Frank Jackson's (1982) Fred, who can easily discriminate red things the rest of us find impossible to discriminate. Fred might speak with us in his attribution of colors to things. Having learned our color language, and knowing no other, he might describe things as being of the same shade of red, and even *looking* the same shade of red, even though he can easily discriminate them. It is true that sometimes he will say that things look different when we say they look exactly alike. But if, as seems possible, his color concepts are the same as ours, he won't be able to say that the things look different *with respect to color*. Insofar as the intentional content of his experiences can be framed in terms of concept of color, the content of his phenomenally different experiences of things of the same color will be the same. Now of course he might invest for himself a different notion of color, call it color*, such that similarity with respect to color* is relative to his perceptual system rather than relative to ours. And then his experiences might be said to represent objects which he sees as similar with respect to color as being dissimilar with respect to color*. But while in that case the phenomenal difference between his experiences of certain pairs of objects that are color identical relative to us would realize an intentional difference, namely with respect to color*, it would also realize an intentional similarity, namely with respect to color.

V

While talk of things looking or tasting the same or different is the talk of ordinary folk, talk of "experiences" or "sensory states" being phenomenally the same or different is the talk of philosophers. Where talk of some alleged phenomenon or possibility or entity is philosopher's talk, and where that phenomenon or possibility or entity seems to make trouble for otherwise promising theories, it is natural to view such talk with suspicion, and to look kindly on the enterprise of "quining" the alleged phenomenon or possibility or entity. And it is natural for those on the other side, those who resist such quining, to hope that the philosopher's talk can be paraphrased away, and that the phenomenon (possibility, entity) can be described in ordinary terms. Thus in the present case it is natural for someone who takes my view to think, or at least hope, that talk of experiences being phenomenally the same or different can always be paraphrased into talk of things looking or tasting the same or different.

But there is an obvious difficulty with this. It is essential for me to distinguish "phenomenal" or "qualitative" similarity of experiences from "intentional" similarity of experiences. But the "looks," "feels," etc. terminology is made to order for describing the intentional content of experiences – and it is difficult, and I think in the end impossible, to keep this terminology to its ordinary meaning while using it to express what in philosopher's talk would be expressed by talking of phenomenal, in contrast to intentional, similarity. Of course, it is central to my position that there is a close connection between these. For it is central to the functional role of phenomenal similarity, as I conceive it, that ceteris paribus the holding of this relation between experiences leads to belief in there being a corresponding similarity between the things experienced, and this means that ceteris paribus the holding of phenomenal similarity between experiences results in an intentional similarity between them. Nevertheless, it is also central to my case that these relations must be distinguished, and here is where uncritical reliance on the "looks," "tastes," etc. terminology can cause difficulty. For the fact that the standard use of this terminology is to describe the intentional content of experience lends plausibility to the view that the only consciously accessible features of experiences are intentional ones. And if that is so, it would seem that no *other* features of experience can properly be termed "qualitative" or "phenomenal," for those terms seem to connote accessibility to consciousness.[3] And this is just the claim of the qualia skeptics (the "quiners" of qualia).

I agree with the qualia skeptics that none of the expressions and idioms available in ordinary speech have the express function of ascribing qualia or phenomenal similarity. Nor do I think that the ordinary person has the concept of either this sort of property or this relation. So I agree that there is a sense in which we are not consciously aware of qualia or of phenomenal similarities – we do not (ordinarily) have introspective awarenesses whose contents involve these notions. But in another sense we are conscious of them.

The concept of a quale, the concepts of particular qualia, and the concept of phenomenal similarity are theoretical concepts, in a way the concepts of folk psychology are not. Or, if one insists that the latter are theoretical, on the grounds that folk psychology is a theory, then the concept

---

3 In Essay 12 I deal with this difficulty by suggesting that the intentional features involved here are ones that represent what I call "phenomenal properties," these being properties that are individuated by causal relations to qualia.

of a quale, the concept of phenomenal similarity, etc. are theoretical concepts at one remove. But they are not to be compared with the concepts of cognitive psychology. What they do is bring out something that is implicit in folk psychology. We need them to make sense of the battery of concepts people do employ in their introspective judgments; their applicability is a necessary condition of the applicability of the concepts, like that of "looking the same," that people do employ.

So what does the "accessibility to consciousness" of qualia come to? In part it is that judgments we actually make are sensitive to relations of phenomenal similarity and difference amongst our experiences, although these judgments are not themselves judgments about qualia, as such, or about phenomenal similarity and difference, as such, but are rather judgments about the properties of things in the environment and about the intentional features of our experiences of those things. This does not of course require that we make judgments about qualia and phenomenal similarity, or even that we have concepts of them. But the *way* in which qualia affect the judgments we do make suggests that they themselves are potentially the objects of immediate, i.e., uninferred, knowledge.

Thomas Reid remarks that there are "habits of inattention" to our sensations that we acquire early in life because of their usefulness, i.e., because our attention is more profitably directed toward things in our environment, and that we must overcome these habits and "become as little children again, if we will be philosophers" (1801, Ch. 5, §2, p. 106). While I have sympathy with this, I have to disassociate myself from the suggestion here that at some point we were attentive to sensations, or qualia, and then ceased to be so. To be attentive to qualia *as such* would require concepts no one would have at an early age and few people have ever.[4] What is needed to produce explicit awareness of qualia as such is not a redirection of attention, and certainly not a shift of one's mental gaze from one sort of object to another, but rather a reconceptualization of what one was aware of all along.

I see that this piece of paper resembles that one. Reflecting, but with my gaze and attention still fixed on the pieces of paper, I "see" that this piece of paper looks similar to that one, and hence that my experience of the one is intentionally similar to my experience of the other. Reflecting

4 One view on which we are aware of qualia without being aware of them "as such" is the "projectivist" view according to which we are constitutionally subject to an illusion whereby we take qualia to be properties of external things. See Boghossian and Velleman 1989. There is some discussion of this in Essay 5. I am in the uncomfortable position of finding the view both plausible and unintelligible.

still further, and again with no shift in my gaze and attention, I "see" that while there are cases in which intentionally similar experiences are phenomenally different (remember the case of Fred), the present case is not of this sort – it is the standard case in which experiences are intentionally similar because they are phenomenally similar. All of these judgments stem causally from the qualitative character of my experience, but only the last is explicitly about it. It seems reasonable to me to say that if an experience issues in judgments of the first or second of these kinds, and fails to issue in a judgment of the third kind only because the subject did not bring to bear on it the appropriate concepts, then its qualitative character is accessible to the subject's consciousness, and is some sense an object of awareness, even though the subject is not aware of it "as such".[5]

---

5 Here is a variation on this case. I see that the piece of paper is the same color it was a few seconds ago. Reflecting, I "see" that the paper now looks the same, with respect to color, as it did a moment ago. Reflecting further, I "see" that this is a case in which my successive experiences of the paper are intentionally similar because they are phenomenally similar. I mention this case to bring out that sometimes our awareness of diachronic phenomenal similarity and difference is as direct as our awareness of synchronic phenomenal similarity and difference. But I make no claim about our awareness of diachronic similarities that extend beyond the "specious present." It may be, for all I know, that what is stored in long term memory is in the first instance information about the intentional content of experiences, and that such knowledge as we have about the qualitative character of our past experiences, and about phenomenal similarities between past experiences and present ones, is the product of inference. Where noninferential awareness of phenomenal similarity is implicit in awareness of intentional similarity is where we are actually perceiving, or seeming to perceive, similarities in the world.

7

Intrasubjective/intersubjective

I

One natural route to the view that intersubjective spectrum inversion is possible is via the plausible claim that we can imaging the occurrence of *intra*subjective inversion – a change whereby the different colors systematically look different to a person than they did before, although she is able to make all the same color discriminations as she did before, and sees things as having the same color similarity and difference relationships as before. Whereas the existence of complete intersubjective inversion would be behaviorally undetectable and might seem unverifiable, the occurrence of intrasubjective inversion seems straightforwardly verifiable, both from the first-person and the third-person perspective. Yet if intersubjective inversion is at least a logical possibility, it seems that intersubjective inversion should also be at least a logical possibility.

This line of argument I will call the intra-inner argument. It is an argument I have advanced in several places.[1] As might be expected, it has met with a variety of objections.

First, some maintain that insofar as intrasubjective spectrum inversion is conceivable, it would consist simply in its coming to be the case that the subject systematically misperceives the colors of things – sees red things as green, blue things as yellow, and so on. This sort of inversion is possible on the "intentionalist" view according to which the only introspectively accessible features of color experiences are their intentional or representational features, their being "as of" certain colors. And on most versions of the intentionalist view, such an intrasubjective inversion could not survive the subject's "accommodating" to the point that she spontaneously and without inference applies the right color words to things and makes the same judgments as other people about what colors things look to have. So the onus is on the proponent of the intra-inner argu-

My thanks to Bob Stalnaker for very helpful comments.
1 See Shoemaker 1975a, 1982, 1990, 1993a.

ment to show that we can conceive of cases of intrasubjective inversion that do not admit of such a deflationary intentionalist interpretation; for only the possibility of such cases will support the possibility of behaviorally undetectable intersubjective inversion, where experiences of different persons have the same intentional content but differ in phenomenal character. Section II of this essay will be devoted to arguing that such cases of intrasubjective inversion are conceivable.

Second, even if it is allowed that a robust form of intrasubjective spectrum inversion is possible, it may be questioned whether the inference to the possibility of intersubjective inversion is legitimate. Although the text of my essay "The Inverted Spectrum" (Shoemaker 1982) defends a version of the intra-inner argument, a postscript I added to a reprinting of the essay (in Shoemaker 1984a) presents an argument that seems to call that inference into question. That argument, if sound, would lend support to what I have called the "Frege-Schlick view," which holds that the relations of phenomenal similarity and difference between experiences that would constitute a case of intrasubjective inversion are relations that are well-defined only for the intrasubjective case. Section III of this essay will be devoted to arguing that that argument is not sound.

Third, there are various considerations that suggest that as a matter of fact the structure of our color experience – of our color "quality space" – is not symmetrical in ways it would have to be if behaviorally undetectable spectrum inversion were possible. Some of these have to do with the fact that there are fewer discriminable shades in some quadrants of the circle of hues than in others, where the quadrants are divided by the pure, unitary, colors. Others have to do with the fact that red, orange, etc. are perceived as "warm," "positive," "advancing," etc., while green and blue are perceived as "cool," "negative," "receding," etc., and that therefore an intersubjective inversion in which the experiences of red and green, yellow and blue, etc., were transposed would not be behaviorally undetectable. Clearly, such asymmetries in our color quality space also constrain what sorts of intrasubjective inversions we could undergo. In Section IV I shall argue that, assuming that these claims are correct, they do not seriously undermine the claims about color experience that the possibility of spectrum inversion has been alleged to support.

II

My aim here is to present a case of intrasubjective spectrum inversion that cannot be given an intentionalist interpretation. Like any case of in-

142

trasubjective inversion, it will initially involve what we might call color content inversion – changes in what colors objects appear to have. The claim, however, is that these changes involve, in addition to a change in the color content of experiences produced by certain causes (e.g., a change in ripe tomato produced experience from being "as of red" to being "as of green"), a change in the "phenomenal character" of the experiences that could persist even after the color content of the subject's experiences has reverted to normal. The challenge is to present a case whose most plausible description involves such a distinction between phenomenal character and intentional color content – a case appropriately described by saying that after the person has reverted to her former way of talking about the colors of things (including how they look as well as how they are) it remains true that the phenomenal character of her experience of them is different from how it was before.

I start with the possibility of a *partial* inversion. Someone reports, after the microsurgeons have been at work on her, that nearly everything looks the way it did before, but that the shades of color within a very small range have "switched places" with their complementaries, each shade now looking the way its complementary used to look. This would be a change in the structure of the subject's quality space, and would be reflected in behaviorally detectable changes in the subject's discriminatory abilities. (It could not be the result of memory tampering.)[2] We can suppose that the subject makes a *semantic* accommodation to this change, which for present purposes need only mean that, supposing chartreuse and crimson to be the shades that changed places, she comes to apply (spontaneously, and without inference) "chartreuse" and "crimson" in a way that accords with the usage of others and her own previous usage – except for what she says about the similarity relations between these and other shades. The reason for the exception is that the semantic accommodation does not undo the change in her quality space. At this point it seems right to say that things of most colors look to the subject the way they did previously but that, e.g., chartreuse things look the way crimson

---

2 According to Dennett, "this is simply not so. Shoemaker is taken in by the ordinary understanding of memory (a passive storehouse that materials enter *after* they have passed through the pre-processing stage and entered consciousness). We should remind ourselves that any transient informational effect in the course of perceptual processing is from one perspective a memory-effect" (Dennett 1993, p. 925). But this misses the point, which is just that it is not open to someone to suggest (as some have suggested about cases where total spectrum inversion is supposed to occur all at once) that the experiences are phenomenally the same as before and that the appearance of change is due to the person's systematically misremembering her past experiences.

things used to look, and vice versa, although the subject now says that the chartreuse things look chartreuse and that crimson things look crimson.

If one such partial inversion followed by semantic accommodation is possible, there is surely no impossibility of there being a series of such. And a series in which, one by one, all shades change places with their complementaries, and each change is followed by a semantic accommodation, would amount to a total spectrum inversion. The final partial inversion in the series would restore the structure of the subject's quality space to what it was before the series began; and we can suppose that together with the semantic accommodation to that change it would restore the person's "reactive dispositions" to what they were initially. But it would be ridiculous to suppose that these (final partial inversion plus semantic accommodation to it) would, at one fell swoop, restore the character of the person's experience to what it was originally – for what the subject reports, and what her behavior would confirm, is that the final change affected the appearance of only a tiny fraction of the shades of color.[3]

III

In my presentation of the intra-inner argument in my 1982, the inference from the possibility of intrasubjective inversion to the possibility of intersubjective inversion rested in part on the point that if intrasubjective inversion is possible, and if the relations of similarity and difference between experiences that are well-defined intrasubjectively are also well-defined intersubjectively (i.e., if the Frege-Schlick view is false), then on plausible assumptions every case of intrasubjective inversion will be a case of intersubjective inversion. If individual A undergoes inversion and individual B does not, and if both before the inversion and after A's accommodation to it A and B are alike in their use of color words and their ability to discriminate colors, then if at one of these times (before the inversion, or after the accommodation) the color experiences of A and B are the same (given the same stimulation), at the other time they are spectrum-inverted relative to each other.

But in addition I suggested an account, motivated by reflection on the

---

3 This case is taken from Shoemaker 1993a. It differs from the case in my 1982 in having each partial inversion be followed by a semantic accommodation which is completed before the next partial inversion occurs.

case of intrasubjective inversion, of what qualia are and how they are "realized," that would make cases of intersubjective inversion both possible and in principle detectable. Both the possibility of intrasubjective inversion and commonplace facts about the role of intrasubjective similarities and differences among experiences in influencing our beliefs and behavior suggest that these relations are functionally characterizable. That in turn suggests that the notion of a quale is functionally characterizable; qualia are the properties of experiences in virtue of which they stand in the functionally characterizable relations of qualitative similarity and difference, and their identity conditions can be stated in terms of these relations. Assuming physicalism, qualia must be realized physically. A physical property will be a realization of a quale if it is such that its being instantiated in different experiences of a single subject is sufficient for those experiences being qualitatively identical (in a certain respect), and different physical properties will be realizations of the same quale if, ceteris paribus, experiences instantiating the one are qualitatively identical to experiences instantiating the other. Here the qualitative identity relationship is defined by the role it plays in the intrasubjective case. But given that certain physical properties have the status of being qualia realizations, and certain equivalence classes of qualia realizations have the status of being classes of realizations of a single quale, relations of intersubjective qualitative similarity and difference are determined – experiences of different persons will be qualitatively similar to the extent that they instantiate the same qualia realizations or qualia realizations belonging to the same relevant equivalence classes, or to appropriately related equivalence classes. In principle, it would seem, we could investigate whether experiences of the same colors occurring in different persons are qualitatively the same or different, by finding out what qualia realizations they instantiate.[4]

It would seem that an account of qualia and qualitative similarity along these lines is needed if the intra-inner argument is to be cogent. And it is this account that is challenged by the argument, raised by my former self against my former self, which seems to support the Frege-Schlick view of qualitative similarity.

The argument rests on the following example. Let $S1$ be a brainlike system in which quale realization Pa can be instantiated, and $S2$ a brainlike system in which quale realization Pb can be instantiated. If $S1$ and $S2$ are joined in a certain way – call it "way C" – into a larger system $S3$,

4 For a more detailed account, see Shoemaker 1982.

then each of these system serves as a "backup system" to the other, and *Pa* and *Pb* are qualitatively identical, and so realize a common quale. Strictly speaking, it is not *Pa* and *Pb* simpliciter that realize this single quale, but rather the properties *Pa-and-C* and *Pb-and-C*, where *C* is the relational property a state has when it occurs in a system in which sub-systems like *S1* and *S2* are related in way *C*. *Pa* and *Pb* are "core realizations" of this single quale, and *Pa-and-C* and *Pb-and-C* are "total realizations." But it is also possible for *Pa* and *Pb* to be joined in a different way, call it *C**, such that when they are so joined *Pa* and *Pb*, or the total realizations of which they are "cores," are not qualitatively identical, and instead are qualitatively different to a considerable degree – as different as the character of seeing red is from that of seeing green. Here the total realizations are *Pa-and-C** and *Pb-and-C**.

But now consider the qualia that are realized by *Pa* and *Pb* in the unjoined systems *S1* and *S2*. Let the total realizations of these be *Pa-and-X* and *Pb-and-X*, where *X* is some property incompatible with *C* and *C**. Suppose that at t_1, when the systems have not yet been joined, a *Pa* experience occurs in *S1*. At t_2, after the systems have been joined in way *C*, another *Pa* experience occurs in *S1*. We can stipulate as part of the example that the effects of these successive qualia instantiations are precisely what, on our functional account, the effects of the successive instantiations of one and the same quale should be. It would seem that we should say that a single quale was realized at t_1 by *Pa-and-X* and at t_2 by *Pa-and-C*. Similar considerations will apparently show that a single quale was realized by *Pb-and-X*, occurring in *S2* at t_1, and *Pb-and-C*, occurring in *S3* at t_2. *Pa-and-C* and *Pb-and-C* are supposed to be qualitatively identical, so by transitivity of identity *Pa-and-X* and *Pb-and-X* should be qualitatively identical. Unfortunately, however, a parallel argument will show that *Pa-and-X* and *Pb-and-X* are qualitatively very different; for they will be identical, respectively, to *Pa-and-C** and *Pb-and-C**, which are qualitatively very different. So the functional account of intrasubjective qualitative identity seems to deliver contradictory verdicts about the intersubjective qualitative similarity and difference relationships between the t_1 experiences of *S1* and *S2*.[5]

That, in brief, was the argument. Where it goes wrong is in supposing that we cannot deny that *Pa-and-C* and *Pb-and-C* (likewise *Pa-and-C** and *Pb-and-C**) are, respectively, qualitatively identical to *Pa-and-X* and

5 See Shoemaker 1994a, pp. 353–357, where the argument is presented in somewhat more detail.

146

Pb-and-X, without abandoning the functionalist view of qualitative similarity and difference. It is of course supposed to be part of the example that after systems *S1* and *S2* are combined, in either way *C* or way *C**, the behavior of the resulting creature when it is in state *Pa-and-C* is related to the behavior of the earlier *S1* creature when it is in state *Pa-and-X* in just the ways the functionalist account says that the behaviors of a creature at different times should be related when the creature has at those times qualitatively identical experiences. (Likewise, *mutatis mutandis*, for the other pairs of similarity relations alleged to hold between the experiences of *S1* or *S2* and the experiences of *S3*). Among other things, *S3* will report that her experience at t_2 is like that she remembers (or quasi-remembers) having at t_1. But that much could be true if the t_2 memories of past experiences were the result of outside tampering. And the functionalist account should not say that in that case the holding of such relationships would constitute, or necessarily manifest, the holding of the relevant diachronic qualitative similarity relationships; it should not rule out the possibility of intervention from outside which simultaneously (i) inverts the qualitative character of the person's t_2 experiences, relative to her t_1 experiences, and (ii) instills in the person memories of her t_1 experiences that make their qualitative character seem to match that of the t_2 experiences. The causal chain linking *S1*'s t_1 experiences and *S3*'s states and behavior, including her memories, involves the episode in which *S1* became linked up with *S2*. And it is at least a question whether this can be construed as a normal case of mental states playing out their functional role over time, or whether it should be likened to memory tampering.

The functional role of a quale must surely include the ways in which its instantiation at one time combines with instantiations of the same or different qualia at later times to produce certain effects – e.g., recognition, or surprise. This means that the total realization of a quale will have to include the memory mechanisms by which qualia have the appropriate "downstream" effects. But we cannot combine different systems, such as *S1* and *S2*, without affecting memory mechanisms. After *S1* and *S2* are combined in way *C*, there will be a memory mechanism that didn't exist before, whereby a *Pa* event in one part of the system and a *Pb* event in another will leave memories of qualitatively similar experiences. If instead they are combined in way *C**, the memory mechanism will be different, and such events will leave memories of qualitatively different experiences.

Let's consider the memories and their physical realizations. Let *Ma* be

147

the physical realization in *S1* at t_2 of the memory of *Pa* (*Pa-and-X*) at t_1, and let *Mb* be the physical realization in *S2* of the memory of *Pb* (*Pb-and-X*) at t_1. The causal connections between each of these and the experience of which it is a memory are the same, we will suppose, whether or not the systems are joined at t_2, and whether they are joined in way *C* or way *C**. But these are only core realizations of the memories, not total realizations. The total realizations will be different depending on whether and how the systems are joined. This must be so, because if the systems are joined in way *C*, then *Ma* and *Mb* represent *Pa* and *Pb* at t_1 as alike, while if they are joined in way *C** they represent *Pa* and *Pb* as different. So by joining the systems, and joining them in one way rather than another, we influence what memories are caused by the earlier experiences – we influence what the contents of the memories are. It is true that whether or not we join them, and in whichever of these ways we join them, they will represent the t_1 *Pa* experience as similar to the t_2 *Pa* experience, and the t_1 *Pb* experience as similar to the t_2 *Pb* experience. But that cannot be given as a reason for saying that however we join them, they represent the t_1 experiences correctly. For in the different cases they will represent different (and incompatible) relations between the t_1 experiences. So we have reason for saying that in at least one case they represent at least one of the t_1 experiences incorrectly, and that therefore we do not have in all of these cases the functional relations constitutive of intrasubjective qualitative similarity between the t_1 and t_2 experiences. And it was on the assumption that we do have this that our problem arose.

It is useful to consider a variation on our example. Instead of considering two cases in one of which *S1* and *S2* are combined in way *C* and in the other of which they are combined in way *C**, consider a single case in which they are first combined in way *C* and then combined in way *C**. Now we get incoherent results in our single case – and ones that concern intrasubjective, and not just intersubjective, qualitative similarity relations. The t_1 *Pa* and *Pb* should be qualitatively alike in virtue of their qualitative identity to, respectively, the t_2 *Pa* and *Pb*, which are supposed to be qualitatively identical. But they should also be qualitatively different in virtue of their qualitative identity to, respectively, the t_3 *Pa* and *Pb*, which are supposed to be qualitatively different. But the same thing will be true of the t_2 *Pa* and *Pb*; they are supposed to be qualitatively identical, because the systems are joined in way *C*; but they should also be qualitatively different, because of their supposed identity to, respectively, the t_3 *Pa* and *Pb*. And at t_3 the person will have an incoherent set of memories and introspective judgments. She should remember the t_1 Pa as qualitatively similar to the t_2 Pa and to the t_3 Pa; and likewise with the t_1, t_2, and t_3 Pbs. She should remember the t_2 Pa and Pb as alike. Yet, since she remembers the t_2 Pa and Pb as similar, respectively, to the t_3 Pa and Pb, and introspects the latter as being different, she should remember the t_2 Pa and Pb as different. Likewise, it seems that she should remember the t_1 Pa and Pb both as similar (because of their remembered similarity to the t_2 Pa and Pb, which are remembered as similar) and as different (because of their remembered similarity to the t_3 Pa and Pb, which are introspected as different).

What is responsible for these incoherences is the assumption that intrasubjective qualitative similarity is well-defined over intervals during which there has been a change in the memory mechanisms involved. Consider the memory at t_3 of the t_2 experiences as similar. This is a memory of a state of the joined system. In going from the C connection to the $C^\star$ connection, we change the way synchronic qualitative similarity is realized in the system. But presumably a system for remembering qualitative similarities should be geared to the way the similarities are realized. If we change the latter, we must change the former. But we cannot both change it and keep it the same. We cannot both have the t_2 experiences jointly producing a veridical memory of them as qualitatively identical, a memory that persists till t_3, and also have them producing veridical memories of themselves which at t_3 represent them as different because qualitatively identical with t_3 experiences that are different.

Since the incoherences we have found involve intrasubjective as well as intersubjective qualitative similarity relations, they are not to be avoided by retreating to the Frege-Schlick view and giving up on intersubjective qualitative comparisons. Obviously the functionalist account of qualitative similarity must be formulated in such a way that such incoherences are ruled out. We must make it a requirement on diachronic intrasubjective qualitative similarity that insofar as the effects of this depend on memory, the same memory mechanisms must be preserved through the interval over which the qualitative similarity holds, and these must be such that when they are functioning properly it is not possible for the diachronic similarity relations represented as holding between experiences at t_1 and t_2 to be incompatible with the synchronic intrasubjective similarity relations holding between experiences at t_2 or those represented as holding between experiences at t_1. Given this, the functionalist account of qualitative similarity is not committed to – indeed, is committed to rejecting – the qualitative identity relations, e.g., between *Pa-and-C* and *Pa-and-X*, that generate the problem.

IV

Finally, I turn to the objection that, as a matter of empirical fact, the structure of our color quality space is such as to make spectrum inversion impossible. The sort of inversion that is held to be impossible for us is the sort that would be behaviorally undetectable if it occurred interpersonally. This sort of inversion requires that there be a mapping of shades of color onto different shades of color that maps unique hues (pure red, pure yellow, pure green, and pure blue) onto other unique hues, and binary hues onto other binary hues, maps any two discriminable shades on to two other discriminable shades, and preserves the similarity ordering of the hues. Such a mapping is said to be impossible for us, given our color quality space, because there are fewer discriminable shades between the unique hues pure green and pure blue than between the unique hues pure red and pure yellow. Further, for behaviorally undetectable spectrum inversion to be possible, it must be the case that there are no behaviorally detectable intrinsic differences between the experiences of the shades that are mapped onto one another. And this, it is said, rules out the mappings that typically figure in the "inverted spectrum hypothesis," since red, orange, and yellow are perceived as warm, positive, advancing, and stimulating, while green and blue ar perceived as cool, negative, receding, and soothing. This is said not to be a matter of learned associations (e.g., of red with fire and of green and blue with lakes and forests); so if someone experienced red things the way we experience green things, this should come out in the way she is disposed to describe her experience of them.[6]

I will assume that the empirical facts are as claimed – that there are these sorts of asymmetries in our color quality space – and therefore that for creatures like us both intrasubjective and intersubjective spectrum inversion are impossible. But it seems easy enough to imagine creatures who are psychologically just like us except that their color quality spaces are symmetrical in the ways ours are not. In their case the relevant sort of mapping is possible. And they lack wired-in associations of colors with other properties (e.g., warmth and coolness) or with emotional responses. Such creatures seem possible. And for such creatures spectrum inversion would be a possibility.

6 See Hardin 1988, Ch. 3.

Daniel Dennett rejects this argument:

> What *anchors* our naive sense that there are such properties as qualia are the multiple, asymmetrical, interdependent sets of reactive dispositions by which we acquaint ourselves with the sensible world. Our sense that the color red has, as it were, an identity, a "personality" all its own is *due* to the host of *different* associations that go with each color. Shoemaker's envisaged creatures, lacking all such reactive landmarks in their dispositional make-up, would not think that they had qualia at all – what it was like to have one sort of experience would not differ at all from what it was like to have a different one! (Dennett 1993a, 927).

But here Dennett seems to be simply refusing to heed the description of the case. *Ex hypothesis*, the envisaged creatures do have a quality space that enables them to distinguish red things and green things, and which is such that red things and green things are more dissimilar than red things are to orange things, or green things are to blue things. Given that, what it is like for them to have an experience of a red thing will differ from what it is like for them to have an experience of a green thing. Dennett gives no reason to think that such a quality space would have to be asymmetrical (that it would have to involve an "asymmetrical . . . set of reactive dispositions"), and the claim that this is so seems to me utterly implausible. His claim that the envisaged creatures "would not think they had qualia at all" is a red herring. The relevant question is not whether they would think they have qualia, but whether they would have qualia. And in any case, why shouldn't they come to realize that they have qualia by imagining the scenario described in Section II?

But it is worth asking what the possibility of such creatures says about us. One thing that the possibility of spectrum inversion has been taken to show is that qualia, the properties that determine the qualitative character of experiences, are not functionally definable properties of them.[7] Supposing that spectrum inversion is a possibility for my envisaged creatures, it would be true that the qualia of their experiences are not functionally definable. For two such creatures who are functionally exactly alike (at the appropriate level of description), and are both looking at a ripe tomato, could be spectrum-inverted relative to each other, and so differ in what qualia are instantiated in them. But, someone might suggest, it is compatible with this that in the case of creatures like us, whose color quality spaces are asymmetrical in a way that rules out spectrum inversion, color qualia are functionally definable.

7 See Block and Fodor 1972, and Shoemaker 1975a and 1982.

We can see what is wrong with this by reflecting further on my envisaged creatures. Let A and B be two such creatures who are spectrum-inverted relative to each other. A and B have the same color qualia in their repertoire of possible states; it is just that they differ as to what sorts of stimuli produce in them experiences having particular qualia of these sorts. These qualia will not be functional properties, in the sense of having topic neutral functional definitions. Nevertheless, so I claim, the similarity and identity conditions of these properties will be functionally definable; and the property of being a quale will be functionally definable. And assuming materialism, these properties must be realized in the physical properties of the experiences that have them. We can suppose that they are, like functional properties, "multiply realizable." Two physical qualia realizations will be different realizations of the same quale if (ceteris paribus) experiences instantiating the one are qualitatively identical with experiences instantiating the other. Each quale will be associated with a class of possible realizations, and can be thought of as the higher-order property of having some property or other belonging to that class. Returning to A and B, they share the same repertoire of higher-order properties of this sort. But now consider a third creature C, which is functionally just like A and B but differs radically from them in physical makeup. C's physical makeup differs enough from A's and B's that its experiences cannot share with them any of the physical properties that realize their qualia. So if the qualia instantiated in the experiences of A and B are the higher-order properties that belong to their repertoires and not to C's, then C's qualia are altogether different from A's and B's. What we have in C, relative to A and B, is not inverted qualia, but "alien qualia."

Someone might ask why the realizations of A's and B's qualia should be limited to properties that can be instantiated in experiences of A and B. Why shouldn't the class of possible realizations include the qualia realizations that characterize certain of C's experiences? But to suppose that this is so is to posit truths for which there are no plausible truth makers. By hypothesis, when A and B look at a ripe tomato, their experiences of it instantiate different color qualia. Now suppose that C is looking at the tomato as well. If we suppose that the same qualia, although not the same qualia realizations, that are instantiated in A's and B's experiences are also instantiated in C's, then we will be faced with the question of whether C's experience of the tomato is qualitatively like A's or qualitatively like B's. There seems to be absolutely no way of deciding this. Moreover, there seems to be nothing that could plausibly make it the case that one rather than the other of these states of affairs obtains. On a materialist view, a quale will be a higher-order property that an experience instanti-ates in virtue of having one or another of a set of physical properties be-longing to a certain equivalence class of physical properties. If we restrict the members of such an equivalence class to properties that are all with-in the repertoire of the creature in which the quale is instantiated, we can use a functional characterization of intrasubjective phenomenal sim-ilarity to determine what goes into such an equivalence class. If we try to suppose that membership in the equivalence class is not restricted in *some* such way, there seems no basis on which its membership can be deter-mined.

But the restriction just stated seems too severe.[8] If we restrict the members of the equivalence class of realizations of a quale to properties that are within the repertoire of the creature in which the quale is in-stantiated, we will rule out the possibility of a change in the way a partic-ular quale is realized in a single individual. But it seems plausible that brain damage, illness, or just normal aging might diminish the number of quale realizations in a person's repertoire without thereby changing what qualia that can be instantiated in that person's experience. And if that is possible, it is presumably possible as well that there should be an increase in the number of quale realizations in a person's repertoire without there thereby being a change in what qualia can be instantiated in that person's experience. But of course a change of the latter sort would be subject to the restriction stated at the end of Section III; it could not involve a change in memory mechanisms of the sort ruled out there. Assuming ap-propriate constraints on what sorts of changes there could be in the way a given quale can be realized in a single individual, the sort of equiva-lence class that would constitute the possible (total) realizations of a giv-en quale can be characterized as follows: properties $P1$ and $P2$ belong to such a class if and only if their instantiation in experiences of a single in-dividual, either at the same time or at different times, is sufficient for those experiences being qualitatively identical in a certain respect. This allows there to be differences in the way a quale can be instantiated in different individuals, but it restricts the ways in which the possible real-izations of a particular quale can differ intersubjectively to the ways they can differ intrasubjectively. Accordingly, let us broaden the notion of an individual's "repertoire" of quale realizations; let this include not only those quale realizations that can be instantiated in the individual's experi-ence at a particular time, but also all those quale realizations that could

8 Here I am indebted to comments of Bob Stalnaker.

come to be, or at any time could have been, instantiable in that person's experience. On this broadened conception, we can restrict the equivalence class of possible realizations of a quale to properties within the repertoire of the individual in which the quale is instantiated.

Now let's return to the case of creatures like us, whose color quality space (we are assuming) is asymmetrical in ways that rule out the possibility of spectrum inversion. If all possible quality spaces were asymmetrical in this way (as Dennett seems to believe), it would seem open to us to take qualia to be functionally definable properties. We could then hold that creatures who are functionally just like us, but who differ from us physically in such a way that the class of qualia realizations that can be instantiated in their experiences is disjoint from the class of qualia realizations that can be instantiated in our experiences, nevertheless share our qualia. But this option does not seem open to us if the envisaged creatures are a possibility. Consider a creature functionally like us whose physical makeup is as different from ours as C's is from A's and B's. It would be intolerable to allow (as I think we must) that C's qualia are alien relative to A's and B's, and yet hold that this creature's qualia are the same as ours. If in the case of creatures like A and B the realizations of a given quale are limited to physical properties that are within the repertoire (on the broadened conception sketched above) of the subject of the experience having the quale, then surely that should be true as well in the case of creatures like us. If that is so, then there can be creatures who are functionally like us, and whose perceptual experiences have the same color content as ours do, whose qualia are alien relative to ours. And in that case individual qualia are not functionally definable, and cannot be identified with such intentional properties as being as-of-red.

PART III

Mental unity and the nature of mind

8

The first-person perspective

Some would say that the philosophy of mind without the first-person perspective, or the first-person point of view, is like *Hamlet* without the Prince of Denmark. Others would say that it is like *Hamlet* without the *King* of Denmark, or like *Othello* without Iago. I say both. I think of myself as a friend of the first-person perspective. Some would say that I am too friendly to it, for I hold views about first-person access and first-person authority that many would regard as unacceptably "Cartesian." I certainly think that it is essential to a philosophical understanding of the mental that we appreciate that there *is* a first person perspective on it, a distinctive way mental states present themselves to the subjects whose states they are, and that an essential part of the philosophical task is to give an account of mind which makes intelligible the perspective mental subjects have on their own mental lives. And I do not think, as I think some do, that the right theory about all this will be primarily an "error theory." But I also think that the first-person perspective is sometimes rightly cast as the villain in the piece. It is not only the denigrators of introspection that assign it this role. Kant did so in the Paralogisms, seeing our vantage on our selves as the source of transcendental illusions about the substantiality of the self. And Wittgenstein's "private language argument" can be seen as another attempt to show how the first-person perspective can mislead us about the nature of mind.

My concern here is with the role of the first-person perspective in the distinctively philosophical activity of conducting thought experiments designed to test metaphysical and conceptual claims about the mind. In conducting such a thought experiment one envisages a putatively possible situation and inquires whether it really is possible and, if so, what its possibility shows about the nature of mind or the nature of mental concepts. Such envisaging can be done either from the "third-person point

My thanks to Ned Block, Mark Crimmins, Carl Ginet, Chris Hill, Norman Kretzmann, Dick Moran, and Bob Stalnaker for their very helpful comments on earlier versions of this essay.

of view" or the "first-person point of view." In the one case, one imagines seeing someone doing, saying, and undergoing certain things, and one asks whether this would be a case of something which has been thought to be philosophically problematic – e.g., someone's having an unconscious pain. In the other case, one imagines being oneself the subject of certain mental states – imagines feeling, thinking, etc., certain things – in a case in which certain other things are true, e.g., one's body is in a certain condition, and asks what this shows about some philosophical claim about the relation of mind to body. The question I want to pursue is whether there is anything that can be established by such first-person envisagings that cannot be revealed just as effectively by third-person envisagings.

It is not difficult to see why first-person thought experiments have often been thought to be more revealing than third-person thought experiments. In a broad range of cases, first-person ascriptions of mental states are not grounded on evidence of any sort. It is natural to move from this to the claim that they are grounded on the mental states themselves, or on "direct acquaintance" with the mental states themselves. One can, apparently, have this knowledge without presuming anything about the connections between the mental states and the bodily states of affairs, behavioral or physiological, which serve as the evidence for our ascription of these same mental states to other persons. Thus the first-person perspective apparently gives one a freer rein than the third-person perspective in investigating, empirically, the connections between mental states of affairs and bodily ones. And so if we are concerned with what the possibilities are, with respect to these connections, imagining what we could discover from the first-person perspective seems potentially more revealing than imagining what we could discover from the third-person perspective.

There are a number of areas in the philosophy of mind in which first-person imaginings have played an important role in philosophical reflection. These include the issue of whether the identity over time of a person involves the identity of a body or brain, the issue of whether disembodied existence of persons is a possibility, the issue of whether "spectrum inversion" is a possibility, and the issue of whether mental states can be identical with physical states of bodies or with functional states realized in physical states of bodies. In many of these cases I agree with the possibility claims that first-person imaginings have been used to support. I think that personal identity does not require bodily identity or brain identity, and I think that spectrum inversion is a possibility. But I think that in these cases the possible states of affairs in question are ones that could be known to obtain from the third-person perspective. In any event, it is not these cases I shall be discussing here. My focus in the remainder of this essay will be on the bearing of first-person and third-person imaginings on physicalist views of mind, in particular the identity theory and functionalism.

My thoughts about this were partly inspired, or perhaps I should say provoked, by a recent argument of John Searle's, and my discussion will be in large part about that. But I will lead up to this by considering briefly what is perhaps the best known piece of philosophical imagining in recent times, namely Saul Kripke's assault, over twenty years ago, on the psychophysical identity theory.[1] Kripke claimed that for any given brain state that is a candidate for being identical with pain, one can imagine both being in pain without one's brain being in that state, and also not being in pain when one's brain is in that state. What was novel about Kripke's argument was of course not the claim that these states of affairs are imaginable, or the claim that they are possible, but certain other claims that licensed the inference from these imaginability and possibility claims to the conclusion that pain cannot be identical with any such brain state – most importantly, the claim that "pain" is a rigid designator, and the point that identity judgments involving rigid designators are necessarily true if true at all. But it did seem central to his case, as he presented it, that the imagining was from the first-person point of view. When he speaks of the "epistemic situation" *vis à vis* pain, he is plainly speaking of the epistemic situation of the putative subject of pain. The claim that it is possible that there should be pain without C-fiber stimulation, or C-fiber stimulation without pain, seems to be grounded on the claim that one can imagine being in pain without there being any C-fiber stimulation occurring in one, and can imagine not being in pain when there is C-fiber stimulation occurring in one. Kripke was of course well aware that the inference from imaginability to possibility could be challenged, and he had very interesting things to say about this; but these do not bear on the issue of first-person versus third-person imagining that is our concern here.

Around the time Kripke presented this argument, other philosophers, most notably Hilary Putnam, were challenging the psychophysical identity theory in a way that also depended on the claim that for any given sort of brain state there could be pain in the absence of that brain state.[2]

1 Kripke 1972, pp. 144–155.
2 See, e.g., Putnam 1975b.

The arguments of these philosophers were in support of the view that pain is a functional state that is "multiply realizable." As originally presented, these arguments involved claims of nomological possibility rather than claims of metaphysical or logical possibility, and appealed to actual physiological differences between different species, e.g., humans and mollusks, rather than to imaginings of purely hypothetical situations. But it is easy enough to convert them into arguments from imaginings that differ from Kripke's only in that the imaginings are from the third-person rather than the first-person perspective. One imagines finding creatures that manifestly experience pain, as is shown by their behavior and circumstances, but lack whatever brain state is the candidate for being identical with pain. One goes from there to the claim that it is possible for there to be pain unaccompanied by that brain state, and uses Kripke's claims about the necessity of identity and the rigidity of the concept of pain to argue from this that pain cannot be identical with that brain state.

There is certainly a difference in spirit between Kripke's argument and its third-person counterpart. The arguments appeal to different groups of philosophers, and annoy different groups of philosophers. But it is far from obvious, to say the least, that the first-person imaginings carry any more evidential weight, vis à vis the issue of psychophysical identity, than the third-person imaginings.[3]

But now recall that there were two parts to Kripke's claim. For any brain state that is a candidate for being pain, one can imagine being in pain without being in that brain state, *and* one can imagine being in that brain state without being in pain. If the second half of the claim can be made out, and if the inference from imaginability to possibility is accepted, we will have more than an argument against the identity theory – we will have an argument against the view that pain can be realized in, or implemented by, brain states, and against the view that pain supervenes

---

3 Someone might try to ground a difference in the fact that judgments about the pains of others are inferential and subject to error in ways in which judgments about one's own pains are not. This might seem a reason for saying that in the first-person thought experiment, what one imagines knowing is that someone is *in pain* without there being any C-fiber stimulation going on, while in the third-person thought experiment what one imagines knowing is only that someone is *manifesting pain behavior* without there being any C-fiber stimulation going on. But if one insists that the only imaginable states of affairs are ones to which one has an access that is noninferential and not subject to error, then the first-person thought experiment is no better off than the third-person thought experiment; both require that one have access to whether there is C-fiber firing going on in one, and any access one has to that will be subject to error and, arguably, inferential in whatever sense one's access to the pains of others is inferential.

on states of the brain. For the latter views, while allowing that pain, being "multiply realizable," can occur without any *given* brain state occurring, will hold that there are brain states, perhaps a large number of them, each of which is such that its occurrence is necessarily sufficient, although not necessary, for the occurrence of pain. If *every* brain state is such that one can imagine it occurring without pain occurring, and if imaginability here implies possibility, then all such views topple.

Can the imagining that leads to this result be done from the third-person point of view? Well, it's easy enough to imagine a case in which C-fiber stimulation is going on in someone and that person is not in pain. But C-fiber stimulation never was a very good candidate for being pain. The question should be whether it is true of each and every brain state that it can be imagined to occur without the subject being in pain. This will have to include brain states that are good candidates for being pain. What will make a brain state a good candidate? Well, the ideal candidate would be one that satisfies some description which we have reason to think only pain satisfies. If the first part of the Kripkean argument is successful, and it is established that for any given brain state it is possible for pain to occur without that brain state occurring, then no brain state is an ideal candidate in this sense. No brain state is an ideal candidate for being *identical* with pain – and here nothing less than an ideal candidate will do. But it is compatible with this that there are brain states that are good candidates for "being pain" in the sense of being realizations of pain. And presumably what this requires is that they play the causal role of pain – that they make the contribution to causing other things, including other mental states as well as behavior, that we believe pain to make, and are caused by the things that we take pain to be caused by.

There are of course ways and ways in which causal or functional roles can be described. Some ways make explicit reference to particular mental states – e.g., part of the causal role of pain is causing the belief that one is in pain. A state having a causal role thus described cannot of course belong to something devoid of mental states. But I will assume here that the roles are described in "topic neutral" terms; this will permit us to consider the idea, rejected by functionalists but affirmed by philosophers such as John Searle, that for any causal or functional role there could be something that has a state playing that role without having any mental states at all.

Even if C-fiber stimulation did play the causal role of pain, it might do so only contingently. That is, it might do so in virtue of the fact that the brain is "wired" in a certain way, a way in which it could fail to be wired and still have *C*-fiber stimulation occur in it. It would then be only contingently an optimal candidate for being a realization of pain. In that case we could imagine discovering from the third-person perspective someone who was not in pain but in whom *C*-fiber stimulation was occurring – this would be a case in which the brain was wired up differently. But now consider the state, call it "*C*-fiber-stimulation-plus," which consists in the brain's having *C*-fiber stimulation occurring in it *and* its being wired in such a way that *C*-fiber stimulation plays the causal role of pain (or what we believe to be the causal role of pain). Let's say here that, on the supposition we are making, *C*-fiber stimulation is an optimal candidate for being a *core* realization of pain, and *C*-fiber-stimulation-plus is an optimal candidate for being a *total* realization of pain. One can easily enough imagine from the third-person perspective a case in which someone is not in pain despite having in his brain what is an optimal candidate for being a core-realization of pain. But can one imagine from the third-person perspective a case in which someone is not in pain despite having in his brain an optimal candidate for being a total realization of pain?

I think that the answer is no. The reason is that playing the causal role of pain, or at any rate playing what we have good reason to think is the causal role of pain, will essentially involve producing precisely the kinds of behavior that serve as our third-person basis for ascribing pain. We cannot be in a position to judge about someone *both* that she is not in pain *and* that she is in a state that influences her behavior in just the ways we think pain influences behavior. Of course, someone can be in pain when there is no behavioral evidence that she is, and when there is behavioral evidence that she is not – she may be successfully suppressing the manifestations of pain. And in such a case we will normally believe, mistakenly, that the person is not in pain. We might in such a case know that the person's brain is in the state *C*-fiber-stimulation-plus – and if we don't realize that this is an optimal candidate for being a total realization of pain, we may continue to believe that the person is not in pain while believing that she has in her brain what is in fact an optimal candidate for being a total realization of pain. But if we realize that it is an optimal candidate, we will have to believe that something, such as an effort to suppress tendencies to manifest pain behavior, is preventing it from having its normal effect; and then we can no longer believe on the basis of the behavior that the person is not in pain.

So it seems that nothing we can imagine from the third-person perspective would entitle us to say that someone is not in pain despite instantiating what we acknowledge to be an optimal candidate for being a total realization of pain. And now we may seem to have a case in which a first-person imagining can achieve something no third-person imagining can achieve. For can't I imagine feeling no pain and yet finding, with the help of an autocerebroscope, that I am in state C-fiber-stimulation-plus, a state I know to be an optimal candidate for being a realization of pain?

One physicalist response to this would be to say that faced with such a case I ought to conclude that while it *seems* to me that I do not feel pain, the evidence of the autocerebroscope should persuade me that after all I do. This is not my response, and I count it as not sufficiently respecting the first-person perspective. While I am willing to allow that there are circumstances in which a sincere self-ascription of pain can be mistaken, I am not willing to allow that someone might be in excruciating pain and yet that it might seem to him, when he reflects in a calm and unflustered way on his state, that he feels no pain at all, and that it might continue to seem that way to him throughout the extended period during which the excruciating pain is supposed to last. And yet that is what would have to be possible if the seeming evidence of the autocerebroscope were overriding in such a case.

But we need to appreciate how bizarre our latest version of Kripke's example is. You are to imagine feeling no pain while having very good evidence that you are in a state that plays the causal role of pain. If you have such a state, you ought to be behaving, or disposed to behave, like someone who is in pain. Suppose you are. Then you should reply affirmatively if asked whether you are in pain. Suppose you do. How does this seem to you, from the inside? Does it seem like your own action, something you are intentionally doing? Will it seem to you that you are lying? But if you can imagine what we have already envisaged, surely you can also imagine that in addition to feeling no pain you have your normal desire to tell the truth. So is it instead that you try to say that you feel no pain, but hear coming from your mouth an avowal of excruciating pain? But if you are alienated from your verbal behavior in this way, presumably you will be similarly alienated from other kinds of behavior as well. You will have no intention of taking aspirin; but you will see your hand reaching for the medicine cabinet and removing the aspirin bottle. You will have no intention of seeing the doctor; but you will see your hand reaching for the telephone, and hear your voice making an appointment. And so on.

Before I discuss the implications of this feature of the case, I want to switch to a somewhat different example – a first-person thought experiment that is presented by John Searle in his recent book *The Rediscovery of Mind*.[4] I think that Searle's thought experiment can usefully be viewed as a version of Kripke's, or rather, an elaboration of the extended version of the second half of Kripke's that we have just been considering. Searle is, of course, an outspoken and eloquent advocate of the first-person point of view.

Searle's example is a variation on the familiar one in which, in a series of operations, the parts of someone's brain are progressively replaced by silicon chips, until eventually the brain is entirely composed of silicon. The replacements are always such as to preserve the behavioral dispositions of the person, and the functional organization needed to sustain these. Searle's variation on the example is to invite the reader to imagine being the subject of this procedure, and to imagine the results from the inside. In his presentation of the case, the procedure starts as a treatment for blindness due to deterioration of the brain, and is successful as long as the replacements are limited to the visual cortex. For my own expository purposes, I prefer to have the subject be someone who has bravely volunteered to be the subject of a philosophical experiment – one designed to test the hypothesis that a creature with a brain having a certain functional organization, one that underwrites behavioral dispositions that enable it to pass the most stringent Turing Test, will be conscious, no matter what the material composition of that brain.

One possible outcome of the experiment is that one finds that each successive replacement of grey stuff with silicon makes no difference to one's conscious life: "You continue to have all of the sorts of thoughts, experiences, memories, etc., that you had previously; the sequence of your mental life remains unaffected" (p. 66). Searle thinks that in fact it is "empirically absurd to suppose that we could duplicate the causal powers of neurons entirely in silicon," but says that this cannot be ruled out a priori.

He goes on to describe two other ways the experiment might turn out. One is that "as the silicon is progressively implanted into your dwindling brain, you find that the area of your conscious experience is shrinking, but that this shows no effect on your external behavior. You find, to your total amazement, that you are indeed losing control of your external behavior. You find, for example, that when the doctors test your vision, you hear them say, 'We are holding up a red object in front of you; please tell me what you see.' You want to cry out, 'I can't see anything.

4 Searle 1992.

I'm going totally blind.' But you hear your voice saying in a way that is completely out of your control, 'I see a red object in front of me'" (pp. 66-67). Here, he says, "we are imaging a situation in which you are eventually mentally dead, where you have no conscious mental life whatever, but your externally observable behavior remains the same."

This second case is the main one I want to examine. But Searle also mentions a third possible outcome. This is that "the progressive implantation of the silicon chips produces no change in your mental life, but you are progressively more and more unable to put your thoughts, feelings, and intentions into action" (p. 67). Here your external behavior eventually ceases, and the doctors think you are dead. But you know better.

My focus, as I said, will be on the second case. Searle takes this to show how it could be known that a certain physical makeup, one consisting in assemblies of silicon chips, fails to support mentality and consciousness, even if it is the case that something having this makeup would be behaviorally and functionally indistinguishable from a normal human being. This is not explicitly presented as a possibility argument of the sort Kripke gives. But, plainly, if he can show what he thinks he shows, he thereby establishes at least the conceptual possibility of a mindless creature that passes the most stringent Turing test imaginable, and does so in virtue of having physical states that are from a functionalist point of view optimal candidates for being realizations of mental states.

Let the sad character in Searle's story, the one on the verge of extinction, be me. My situation, as imagined here, is much the same as it is if I imagine myself as the subject of the most recently considered version of the Kripke example. In both cases I am alienated from my behavior. In the Searle example I hear my voice engaged in conversations with others, conversations to which I am not myself a party, and – here I extend the example – I see my hand writing answers to questions on an IQ test, questions that I am, in my weakened state of mind, unable even to understand. The main difference between the two cases, besides the fact that in Searle's case my consciousness is waning, is that Searle's story contains an account of how I got into this mess – it is the result of my volunteering to be the subject of the philosophical experiment, and the infusions of silicon I subsequently underwent. From now on I will concentrate on Searle's version of the case, but my main points will apply to the earlier version as well.

Let me focus on the alienation from my behavior that this case involves. This amounts to a kind of alienation from my body. Indeed, its status as *my* body should seem problematic, from my point of view, for by hypothesis I have no voluntary control over it, and it moves about, and spouts utterances, in defiance of my will. I do seem to see through its eyes and hear through its ears. But given my alienation from it, or rather, given that I am alienated from it *if* my experiences are veridical, shouldn't I be wondering whether these experiences *are* veridical? Notice that I lack the normal ways of checking to see whether things are as they appear – I cannot initiate tests of any sort, and I cannot consult with others. My situation seems rather like a bad dream. And of course, if it is a bad dream, or if I am not entitled to think it isn't, then I am not establishing what Searle has me establishing – that the behavior of my body is independent of such consciousness there is in it, and that very soon, when my consciousness has vanished completely, this body will be behaving as it is, passing the most stringent Turing Tests, without there being any consciousness in it at all.

Admittedly, I would be rash to conclude, just on the basis of my alienation from my behavior, that I cannot trust my senses. What I am calling alienation from behavior occurs, although in a less dramatic way, in actual cases of paralysis, and we do not think that people in that condition should doubt their senses. But it would seem that I have reasons for doubting my senses over and above the fact that I have no voluntary control over the body I seem to be perceiving from. For if what my senses tell me is right, people are ascribing to me, on the basis of my behavior, mental states that I know I don't have. And these ascriptions are regularly being confirmed by my subsequent behavior. What is at stake here is the reliability of a well established practice of mental state ascription, one we rely on in all of our dealings with other people. Can I justifiably take it that my perceptual experiences are veridical in this instance? *If* they are then, it seems, *both* a well established practice is systematically issuing in mistaken mental state ascriptions in this case, *and* I am alienated from by behavior and body. That seems to me a reason for saying that I can't be justified in taking my perceptual experiences to be veridical. And if I can't, then in the imagined situation I do not establish what Searle thinks I do.

I am not going to rest my case on this point. But I think that it has some force. When first-person thought experiments seem to have philosophically interesting results, the content of the first-person imagining always has an "objective" as well as a "subjective" component. In the present case, the subjective component is my being in a certain mental condition, which includes my having certain sense-experiences – my seeming to see and hear certain things. The objective component is my body's being in a certain condition, and my being surrounded by people and instruments of which certain things are true. Normally, when the veridicality of sense experiences is in no way in question, it is unproblematic to move from saying that one imagines *seeming to see* such and such to saying that one imagines *seeing* such and such, and from there to saying that one imagines *such and such being the case.* But when what is in question is the relation between the mental states of a creature and the creature's bodily condition and situation, then the veridicality or otherwise of the creature's sense experiences is part of what is in question. Obviously, that my sense-experiences are veridical is not something I know "from the inside," in the way I know that I have them. This is not something about which I have "first-person authority." There is, to be sure, a presumption in favor of the assumption of veridicality. But there is also a presumption in favor of the assumption that our ordinary third-person ways of ascribing mental states are reliable. If, holding fixed the nature of my mental states over some interval, these two assumptions come into conflict, nothing that I know from the inside, nothing about which I have first-person authority, tips the balance in favor of the assumption that my perceptual experiences are veridical. Perhaps what we have is a standoff between the two assumptions. But I think that the fact that on the veridicality assumption I am alienated from the body from which I am supposed to be doing the perceiving could reasonably be held to tip the balance against the veridicality assumption.

To see that the veridicality of experiences *can* be an issue in such cases, consider a modification of Searle's example in which the brain operations are replaced by something less invasive. E.g., instead of a series of operations in which brain matter is replaced by silicon, they give me a series of *shampoos!* As before, we will try to suppose, each item in the series is followed by a diminution of consciousness, and I end up radically alienated from my body. But in this case, the behavior of my body in the final stages of the procedure stems from just the sorts of neural goings-on that such behavior stems from in normal cases. At any rate, this is how things seem to me. I doubt if anyone will want to maintain that this thought experiment shows, or even provides prima facie evidence, that the actual processes going on in our brains are not metaphysically sufficient for the mental states we take to be manifested by the behavior they produce. And I think that if things did seem to me as just imagined, it would be more reasonable for me to doubt my senses or memories than to conclude that a series of shampoos could destroy my mentality without affecting my brain or its influence on my behavior.

167

But let's return to Searle's example, with me again as the subject. As it happens, we do not have to choose between overriding the presumption that my sense experiences are veridical and overriding the presumption that our ordinary practice of third-person mental state ascription is reliable. For there is a way of honoring both presumptions. Assume that my sense experiences are veridical. Then I am radically alienated from the body I am perceiving from. Given its independence of my will, my claim that it is my body is a bit shaky. So maybe someone else has a less shaky claim on it. That is precisely what the third-person evidence indicates to others. The behavior of the body is such as to lead them to take it to be the body of a person having certain mental states, mental states that as a matter of fact are, except for the perceptual experiences among them, utterly different from my own. Nothing I know from the inside, nothing about which I have first-person authority, gives me any reason to reject this possibility.

Is this a possibility? Well, to begin with, there would seem to be no conceptual incoherence in the idea that two minds, or persons, or "consciousnesses," might simultaneously animate a single body, or at any rate have that body as the point of view from which they experience the world. This is what some have thought happens in split-brain cases, and what others have thought happens in cases of multiple personality; and while that view of those cases appears not to fit the actual facts, there are possible facts that it does fit. If we think about the features of these cases that make it tempting to speak of there being multiple persons, or multiple minds, in a single body, it is not difficult to envisage cases of which this would be the literally correct description.

But how do we apply this to Searle's example? As an example of an unsatisfactory application of it, let me quote my own response to Searle when he presented this example at a conference a year or two ago: "You seem to imply that . . . just after your consciousness fades out you have all the functional organization there without any mentality. Surely that's not warranted, because it's perfectly compatible with this that as you fade out someone else is coming in."[5] Daniel Dennett subsequently put the point in a similar way in his review of Searle's book.[6] Supposing that I am the subject of the series of operations, what this formulation suggests is that what the scientists were perhaps unwittingly doing in their series

---

5 See CIBA 1993, p. 73. Unaccountably, the transcript has the word "representation" where I have put "organization."
6 Dennett 1993b, p. 198.

of operations was building in my skull a new person, one with a silicon brain, while gradually destroying the brain and person, namely me, that was there originally. As appropriate connections were established between the silicon brain and the nervous and motor systems, the new brain took over control of the body. The trouble with this version of the story is that it is not compatible with a central feature of it, namely that throughout the series of replacements, the behavior of my body was such that from a third-person point of view it appeared to be animated by a *single* person with normal mental abilities and normal consciousness, and exhibiting normal mental continuity over time. Yoking a waning mind to a waxing mind could hardly be expected to produce this result. What it should produce, instead, is conflicted behavior, dominated in the early parts of the interval by behavior showing mental decline, dominated during the later parts of it by behavior showing the opposite, and perhaps manifesting at various times behavior analogous to that of the split-brain monkey, reported by Tom Nagel, whose right and left hands had a tug of war over a nut.[7]

But there is a version of the story that is compatible with what we are supposed to imagine about the behavior of the body. It says that a single person animated the body throughout the interval, and that during the interval that person's brain was gradually reconstituted – it began as a normal human brain, and ended as a functionally equivalent silicon brain. It follows that if at the end of the story there was "in" the body a feeble mind that was not in control of it, then that was not the mind that was there at the outset. Or, putting it in terms of persons, the person who near the end found himself a mentally enfeebled prisoner in the body is not, although he *thinks* he is, the same as the person who at the beginning volunteered to undergo the series of operations. Perhaps the case could be construed as a case of "fission," in which both of the inhabitants of the body, the mentally enfeebled prisoner as well as the person who controls the body's behavior, have veridical "quasi-memories" corresponding to the life of the original person. But if so, it is unequal fission, and the "closest continuer," the person with the best claim to be the original possessor of the body, is the one who controls the body's behavior, not the mentally enfeebled prisoner.

Someone might object that I have here fallen into skepticism about memory, and about personal identity. Surely, it will be said, if someone remembers being the person who did such and such, that person has

7 Nagel 1977.

every reason to think that he is the person who did such and such. And if I imagine remembering being the person who did such and such, I have every reason to describe the imagined situation as one in which I am the person who did such and such.

But the point here is much the same as the point made earlier about sense perception. Normally one has no reason to distrust one's senses, and normally one has no reason to distrust one's memories. But in the thought experiment now under consideration we have moved very far from normal circumstances. And the content of the memory, insofar as it is first-person content, actually conflicts with the judgments of personal identity others would make on the basis of third-person evidence. Assuming that our subject can trust his senses to the extent of being entitled to think that the people about him really are saying the things they seem to be saying, this provides him with positive reasons for distrusting his memory. Conversely, if he trusts his memory this gives him a reason for distrusting his senses. What he cannot have good reason for believing is that *both* he is the person who volunteered to be the subject of the series of operations *and* he is in the envisaged situation, i.e., is alienated from the behavior of "his" body in the way described. So the imaginability of being in the situation he knows he is in (certain things *seeming* to be the case) is not evidence for the possibility of someone's being in the situation whose possibility is in question (those things really *being* the case).

One upshot of this discussion is that some cases of imagining from the first-person perspective are problematic in a way that is not initially apparent. One imagines what purports to be a succession of events involving oneself. Each event in the succession is imagined "from the inside." If the imaginability of each event in the succession is unproblematic, it may seem that the imaginability of the series of events is unproblematic. And if each event in the series is described in the first-person, it may seem that one has imagined oneself undergoing such a series of events. But if imaginability is to bear on possibility, we need to go slow here. First of all, we need to distinguish two senses in which one can imagine something from the "first-person point of view." This might mean simply imagining it "from the inside" – imagining some aspect of the life of a person as it might be experienced by that person. Or it might mean imaging *oneself* doing or undergoing such and such, where the imagining is again from the inside. Imagining from the first-person point of view in the first sense needn't involve imagining from the first-person point of view in the second sense. If I imagine the battle of Cannae as it might have been experienced by Hannibal, I do not thereby imagine *being* Hannibal – not, at any rate, in a sense in which the imaginability of something is at least prima facie evidence of its possibility. And if I imagine a series of personal episodes, imagining each from the point of view of the person involved and so imagining each from the inside, I do not thereby imagine myself, or any single person, being the subject of all of those episodes. It is tempting to say that I can simply stipulate that the subject of one of my imaginings is myself. And so I can, up to a point. But there are limits to what one can coherently stipulate. If I successively imagine how the President's State of the Union Address is being received by the different members of the Congress, in each case imagining the reception from the inside, I cannot *both* regard this as an imagining of a single series of events *and* stipulate that in each case the person imagined from the inside is myself – not, at least, if imaginability is to be evidence of possibility. Returning to the Searle example, I can imagine from the inside first the agreeing to be the subject of the experiment, and then the somewhat diminished mental condition of someone after the first operation, and then the somewhat more diminished mental condition of someone after the second operation, and so on. It is natural to describe this by saying that I imagine agreeing to be the subject, and then experiencing diminished consciousness after the first operation, and then experiencing a further diminished consciousness after the second operation, and then . . . and so on. But this implies, illegitimately, that it is one and the same person who is the subject of all of these imagined episodes. If I stipulate that I am the imagined person who initially agrees to submit to the series of operations, then I cannot, without begging the question, stipulate also that I am the imagined person who experiences the final stages of the extinction of his consciousness while observing the external behavior of the body to go on as before. And if I stipulate that the latter person is myself, then I cannot stipulate that the former person is. That is, I cannot make these stipulations if the description of what is imagined is not to beg the question by assuming the truth of the possibility claim it is supposed to support.

But let me stipulate now that I am the person with radically diminished consciousness who is totally without control of the body from which he experiences the world. And suppose that I am right in claiming that I would not, in these circumstances, be entitled to say that there is no consciousness behind the silicon driven behavior of the body I am imprisoned in. So we agree that for all we know there is another mind in there who is running the show. If we let "Sydney" be the name of the person who agreed to undergo the series of operations, we agree that while it seems to me that I am Sydney, since I remember Sydney's life from the inside, there is good third-person evidence that Sydney is the man whose behavior is generated in the now largely silicon brain that now inhabits my skull. Still, it might be thought that I know at least that there is something wrong with the view that a person's mentality is determined by the functional organization of the person's brain or body. By hypothesis, the brain part replacements were all such as to preserve the relevant sorts of functional organization. And let's take this to mean that the functional organization throughout is such that *according to functionalism* there is just one mind realized in the brain. It is ruled out, in other words, that there are two functional organizations there, one superimposed on the other, corresponding to the total mental states of two different persons. So, assuming functionalism, the mentality associated with this body ought to be that which others ascribe, on the basis of behavior, to the man they call "Sydney." And while I am not in a position to know directly that there is not this sort of mentality associated with the body, I am in a position to know that there is another sort of mentality, quite different from this, which is associated with it – namely the diminished consciousness, frustration, and despair that I am now experiencing. This might seem to undermine the functionalist view, even if it does not undermine the reasons others have for thinking that Sydney, as they conceive him, exists. Like the third outcome Searle imagines for his thought experiment, this seems to support the claim, not that that there is no functional organization that is *sufficient* for the possession of the mental states in question (which is what the possibility of the second outcome was alleged to show), but that there is none that is *necessary* for this.

But I do not think that this argument fares any better than the earlier one. First of all, once we are this far into the realm of fantasy, multiple bodies for one mind are as much a possibility to be reckoned with as multiple minds for one body. Supposing that the autocerebroscope indicates that the functional states in question are not realized in the body from which I see, it remains a possibility that they are realized elsewhere. I do not think that there is anything I could observe that could assure me that *no*where, and in *no* way, are there instantiated functional states that could underwrite the mental states I know myself to have. Moreover – and here I revert to the "bad dream point" invoked earlier – if what I seem to observe did *seem* to assure me of this, I would have at least as much reason to doubt the veridicality of my sense experiences and/or memories as I did in the previous case in which a series of shampoos seemed to produce alienation from my own body. In fact, of course, it is unrealistic to suppose that I would have to choose between wholesale distrust of my senses and the rejection of functionalism; I might more reasonably conclude that the cerebroscope is on the blink.

But there is more to be said than this. For I submit that it is out and out incoherent, and not just highly implausible, to suppose that the testimony of my senses could establish the negative existential that nowhere, neither in the body I see from nor anywhere else, does there exist a realization of the appropriate functional states that could be a realization of my current mental states. For the testimony of my senses to establish that negative existential would be for me to come to know on the basis of my senses that my current mental states are not playing the functional roles that according to functionalism are constitutive of such states. But if I *know* something on the basis of my senses, this requires, surely, that my beliefs be modified by my sensory inputs, acting in concert with my background beliefs, in a way that conforms to certain principles of rationality. And that *is* for certain mental states, sense-experiences and beliefs, to play functional roles that according to functionalism are constitutive of them. To the extent that knowledge requires rationality, and that what are held to be the defining functional roles of mental states are the causal roles constitutive of rationality, it is incoherent to claim that one could know that one's own mental states are not playing the defining causal roles. Admittedly, this argument by itself shows only that one could not know that there is a total lack of realization of the relevant functional states, not that one could not know that there is a partial such lack. But we have seen other reasons for denying that one could know even that.

Let's take stock. Searle has claimed that it is an *empirical question* whether beings with a physical makeup different from ours, e.g., beings made of silicon, can have conscious mental lives of the sort we have.[8] I take it this means a question that could in principle be settled, empirically, in the negative. It is of course an empirical question whether creatures with such a physical makeup could be behaviorally like us, to the extent of being able to pass the most stringent Turing tests. And it seems entirely possible to me, as I am sure it does to Searle, that the answer to this question is no. To put the point in a functionalist way, it may well be that the evolutionary process that resulted in us came up with the only possible implementation of the functional organization that bestows our sorts of mental states, and the only possible physical organization that bestows

8 See Searle 1980.

173

our behavioral dispositions. But Searle thinks that even supposing that there are possible creatures whose physical makeup is very different from ours but who are behaviorally just like us, *and* have whatever functional makeup you like, it is an empirical question whether such creatures could have a conscious mental life like ours. Now it is very difficult to see how this empirical question, supposing that it is one, could be settled in the negative by an investigation from the third-person point of view. Obviously it is not to be settled by observing the behavior of the creatures, since the creatures whose mentality is in question are precisely those which can be counted on to pass every behavioral test with flying colors. Nor does it seem that it could be settled in the negative by investigating their internal makeup; the most that could be established in that way is that certain functional states are realized differently in them than in us, and not that those functional states do not bestow mentality. Searle thinks that for any functional organization, it is an empirical question whether creatures that have it have genuine mental states. It does appear that if *this* is an empirical question, and one that could in principle be settled in the negative, it is one that could only be so settled from the first-person point of view. No wonder, then, that Searle devised his first-person thought experiment. What I have shown, however, is that where the question cannot be settled in the negative from the third-person point of view, it also cannot be settled in the negative from the first-person point of view.

I suspect that some people will be unmoved by all this because they think that the third-person point of view is, right from the start, parasitic on the first-person point of view. This would be true if we know what the various mental states are "from our own case," and if our entitlement to ascribe them to others on the basis of behavior rests on something like the argument from analogy. This view, call it the analogical position, is one of the hardiest weeds in the philosophical garden. It has been sprayed, in this century, with everything from the verificationist theory of meaning to Wittgenstein's private language argument, and it keeps coming back, usually under assumed names. A wholesale assault on it would be a task for another occasion. But I think that the considerations I have raised provide part of the case against it. They bring out that the first-person point of view does not provide a perspective from which, starting with no assumptions about the relations between mental and physical states of affairs, and about the causal roles of mental states, one can proceed to investigate empirically what these relations and roles are, first discovering what they are in one's own case and then extrapolating inductively to the case of others. This is for three related reasons. First, one can discover nothing at all about bodies, or about physical states of affairs, without assuming the veridicality of one's sense experiences, and to assume that is to assume something about the relations between mental and physical states of affairs – relations that are constitutively bound up in what it is for a body to *be* the body of a particular person.[9] The truth of this assumption is certainly not something one can straightforwardly discover empirically from the first-person point of view. Second, some of the causal relations amongst mental states involved in rationality must hold as a condition of one's coming to know anything at all, and there is no sense to the idea that one might investigate empirically, by introspection, whether these hold in one's own case. Finally, the use of the first-person point of view to discover counterexamples to claims about the sufficiency of bodily (or functional) states of affairs for mental states of affairs depends on the assumption that one is the sole inhabitant of one's body, and that assumption is not one whose truth one can discover empirically from the first-person point of view without relying on other assumptions about how the mental and physical realms are related.

The epistemology of modality is a large topic, and I have barely scratched its surface. But here, for whatever it is worth, is the moral I am inclined to draw. Where it seems that one can imagine discovering the realization of a putative possibility from the first-person perspective, one should always ask whether this seeming discovery could be confirmed from the third-person point of view. If one finds that it is impossible in principle that it should be, one should look to see whether the first-person thought experiment can be faulted in the ways I have tried to fault the first-person thought experiments considered here. I have not proven that the latter will always be the case. But I suspect that it will be.

9 See Shoemaker 1976.

175

9

Unity of consciousness and consciousness of unity

I

To speak of unity of consciousness is among other things to speak of an aspect of our awareness of external things, and so of something falling within the province of epistemology; and to speak of consciousness of unity – whether unity in the world or unity in our minds – is likewise to speak of something epistemological. But unity of consciousness has also been held to be a determinant of – to be partly constitutive of – mental unity, the belonging-to-one-mind (what Russell called "copersonality") of different mental states, and self-consciousness has been held to be a component of the unity of consciousness that plays this constitutive role. And whether this is so, and if so how, is of course a metaphysical issue. This essay is an exploration of this mix of epistemological and metaphysical issues. These are, of course, Kantian themes – but I shall stay clear of any attempt to expound Kant's own thinking about them. Although my ultimate concern is with self-consciousness and mental unity, the consciousness I shall begin with is our perceptual consciousness of the world.

II

Let us begin with a case – any case – of visual perception. Any object one sees will have parts, and in seeing the object, one will see various of its parts. And in typical cases, in order to see *that* something is an object of a certain kind, one must not only see a number of its parts, and see what properties these have individually, but must see how they are relat-

My thanks to Carl Ginet, Dick Moran, Susanna Siegel, and Allen Wood for helpful comments.

ed to one another. For things are of visually identifiable kinds in virtue of relations between their parts – those that bestow shape and size, and others as well. I will see that something is an American flag by seeing a rectangular blue field on which there are rows of white stars, this forming the corner of a larger rectangle the remainder of which is filled with alternating red and white stripes. To see that it is an American flag I must see that the field of stars is properly related to the red and white stripes. To see that the field is of the right sort, I must perceive the relationships between the parts of it – the white stars and the bits of blue background. And to perceive that what are on the field are stars, I must perceive their parts and their relations to one another and to the background.

What is true in this example is true generally in cases of visual perception; we perceive a thing as being of a certain sort by perceiving relations between parts of the thing to one another and between parts of the thing and surrounding objects (as we must do when we perceive color boundaries). And this means that every case of seeing something to be of a certain sort is a case of "unity of consciousness." Our experiences of the different parts of the thing, and of other things that surround it or form the background against which it is seen, must be related in such a way as to form a unified experience of the thing, one that represents the relationships between the parts represented by the component experiences, the relationships in virtue of which a thing of a given sort exists. Here then is a homely example of "synthesis"; the visual experience of a spatially extended thing is a synthesis of visual experiences of parts of that thing, which are in turn syntheses of visual experiences of parts of them, and so on.[1]

The different senses of course differ in the ways in which they present the world. In some cases of touch, the situation is parallel to that in vision – namely, those cases in which at a given time we perceive a spatially extended thing, and perceive it as a thing of a certain sort, or as having

1 In speaking of experiences as having "parts," I do not mean to be endorsing a sense-datum conception of experience, or an atomistic conception according to which – to use an example from Dennett 1991 – my experience of a wall covered with hundreds of portraits of Marilyn Monroe, *a la* Andy Warhol, must consist of hundreds of parts, each of which is a high resolution representation of Marilyn Monroe. So my use of "synthesis" must be taken with a grain of salt; it is not to be supposed that the parts are prior to the whole, and that the latter is in some sense constructed out of them. But I think that one can, without commitment to such views, distinguish in a particular case experiences of different things (e.g., different portions of an American flag), these together making up the experience of a whole composed of those things.

a certain property, by perceiving parts of the thing and perceiving relations between them. I know that I am feeling a cup because I feel the handle with the heel of my hand while feeling the top and rim with my middle fingers and the sides with my thumb and little finger. My different tactile experiences – the resistance I feel with different parts of my hand as I press down – make up a larger tactile experience that provides information about the shape of the cup. Often, however, the relevant unity of consciousness in tactual perception is diachronic rather than synchronic. I explore an object with my hand, and my successive tactual experiences, together with my knowledge of my hand's movements, provide me with information about its shape, size, texture, and so on. Only because my successive experiences are so related as to constitute a single temporally extended experience do I obtain this sort of information about the world. Without either the synchronic or the diachronic kinds of synthesis, the sense of touch would not be a *sense* at all – it would not be one of our windows on the world. Similar considerations apply to hearing, where again it is diachronic synthesis that is most important. And of course diachronic unity is important in the case of vision as well, being involved whenever we perceive something to move or remain stationary.

The unity of consciousness I have been concerned with so far is not the unity of all of the conscious states of a mental subject, either at a time or over time. It is something much more modest – the integration of experiences into larger, more encompassing, experiences whose unity derives from their content, i.e., from their functioning as experiences of things in the world that themselves have (or would have if they existed, i.e., if the experiences were veridical) a relevant sort of unity. By a "relevant sort of unity" I mean to exclude the merely notional unity of arbitrary mereological sums of things or thing-stages. The "relevant" wholes of which we have experience, in virtue of synchronic and diachronic synthesis of the sorts I have been talking about, are ones that it is important, or at least useful, for us to treat as wholes. They are the kinds of things whose concepts enter into our desires and intentions, and must enter into our beliefs if the beliefs are to be effective in guiding us to the satisfaction of our desires. These include things we can grasp, control, and employ as tools. And they include things that belong to kinds that conform to laws and generalizations that can be used to predict their behavior and effects. Here we have, at a very modest level, the Kantian connection between unity of consciousness and unity in nature. The relevant unity in experiences is that which goes with representing unified things or processes in the world, where the unity of those things is in part a matter of causal connections between their parts, or between successive temporal stages of them, and so of conformance to the Kantian categories.

But in fact, of course, the unity in our perceptual experience goes beyond the "local" unity involved in the perception of individual spatially or temporally extended objects or processes. At any given time, the things one sees occupy a single field of vision, the contents of which stand in a variety of perceived or perceivable relations to one another. Any two objects in this field will be perceived, if one attends to them, to stand to one another in determinate spatial relations, and in determinate relations of color similarity or difference. Similarly, the objects one perceives by touch at a given time are perceived to stand to one another in determinate spatial relations and determinate relations of similarity with regard to such properties as temperature and texture. Simultaneously heard sounds are likewise heard as standing in determinate relations to one another – location, relative loudness, pitch, etc. There are also relations that are perceived intermodally – one is aware that the sound one hears comes from a place to the right of something one sees, and that something one feels by touch is below something one sees. In all of these cases one could say that experiences of different things belong to a single, unified consciousness, in virtue of the contribution they make to the perception of relations between those different things.

This "global" perceptual unity seems a natural extension of the "local" perceptual unity involved in the perception of any spatially extended thing. The same basic capacities seem to be involved in both. It would be strange, a peculiar pathology, if a creature were able to perceive medium-sized physical objects, in a way that involves perceiving relations between their parts, but were unable to perceive relations between such objects. For example, if it were able to perceive the color relationships needed to identify something as an American flag, but unable to perceive the color similarities between an American flag and a French tricolor; or if it were able to perceive the spatial relations between the different parts of an American flag, or of a dining room table, but unable to perceive any spatial relation between the flag and the flagpole, or between the table and a chair. Perhaps damage to some part of the brain could produce such an anomaly. But a creature so afflicted would be severely handicapped in its ability to get from perception usable information about the world. If the

179

creature's visual perception does not tell it anything about the spatial relationships between the table and the chair, it will not tell it whether there is a gap between the table and the chair big enough for it to walk through. The visual perception of such a creature would not do the minimal job of informing it of what paths through the world are open to it. Indeed, if we include openings, gaps, holes, etc., among the possible objects of visual perception, it becomes incoherent to suppose that a creature is capable of seeing *all* of the objects we see but unable to see relations between these objects – there is no such thing as perceiving A and B and the gap between them without perceiving a relation between A and B.

One reason why our ability to perceive things involves the ability to perceive relations between them, and so why "local" unity of perceptual consciousness involves "global" unity of perceptual consciousness, is that insofar as our perception of objects yields usable information at all, it yields information about the spatial relations of those objects to ourselves. We see objects as near or far, as to the right or left. Only so can perception play an action guiding role. Seeing an apple when one wants one to eat will be of no use if the experience does not tell one where to reach in order to get it. But given the intuitive grasp of basic geometrical principles that comes with the concepts of spatial relations, knowledge of the spatial relation of various objects to oneself is ipso facto knowledge of their spatial relations to one another. Here self-knowledge of a kind, knowledge expressible in "I"-judgments, plays a central role in the unity of consciousness. My perceptual knowledge of various objects is integrated into a unitary consciousness that includes awareness of the spatial relationships between those objects, at least in part because the perceptual knowledge of each of these objects includes awareness of their spatial relationships to a single thing, namely myself.

The self-knowledge involved here is not, in the first instance, knowledge of mental states. And it is knowledge of a kind that we can ascribe to lower animals. A dog stalking a squirrel knows that, for example, the squirrel just moved to *its*, the dog's, right, and adjusts its movements accordingly; this "its" is what H.N. Castaneda called a "quasi-indicator,"[2] and its role in the report of what the dog knows is to indicate that the content of the dog's knowledge is self-referential, in the way first-person contents are self-referential.

2 See Castaneda 1967.

What we have seen so far is, first, that perceptual awareness of spatially or temporally extended things requires "local" unity of consciousness, and, second, that partly because our perceptual awareness is ego-centered, i.e., involves being aware of relations between things and ourselves, there must normally be a more "global" unity of consciousness in a creature's perceptual awareness of the world. But the second of these claims rested in part on the role of perceptual awareness in guiding action – the point was that usable information provided in sense perception must include information about the relation of the thing perceived to the perceiver. And of course it is not only a creature's perceptual representations of the world that play a role in guiding action. Normally these play this role only in conjunction with nonperceptual beliefs (beliefs not grounded on what is currently perceived), and so as parts of a more comprehensive representation or conception of the world. We now need to look at the ways in which this more comprehensive representation must be unified.

It is a commonplace that if a rational creature believes that P and believes that Q, it will tend to believe the conjunction $P\&Q$. This has some analogy to the fact that if someone perceives A and perceives B, she will tend to perceive certain of the relations between A and B, and, if A and B together make up some thing, will perceive that thing. But it is a special case of a more general fact, namely that a rational creature will tend to believe the joint consequences of the various things it believes.

Here then is one important dimension of mental unity. Arguably, some degree of rationality is required for the very existence of beliefs and other intentional states. And the beliefs in a mind having this minimal degree of rationality will be unified in the sense that there will be a tendency for the body of beliefs to evolve in a certain way – for beliefs that do not cohere with the rest to be eliminated, and for new beliefs to be added, namely ones whose contents are evidentially supported by the contents of beliefs that are already there. In some cases, of course, the adding of beliefs will involve explicit reasoning. In others it will be more or less automatic. But in either case, the addition of new beliefs will not be indiscriminate. What we reason about are things that matter to us in one way or another. And presumably our automatic belief formation mechanisms are also governed (thanks to natural selection) by considerations of relevance. What the evolution of the belief system is towards, in a well regulated mind, is a unitary conception of the world which is well suited for the guiding of action – for the effective pursuit of whatever goals we have.[3]

There is, of course, more to mental unity than coherence in the belief system. A rational creature will not only tend to believe the obvious consequences of the things it believes; it will tend to do those things which, according to its beliefs, will satisfy its desires, and it will tend to modify its desires in the light of its other desires together with its beliefs about the consequences of various courses of action. What is required for rationality is coherence in the belief-desire system, not just coherence in the belief system alone. But insofar as we are concerned with unity of *consciousness*, and not just mental unity in general, there is a reason for focusing on coherence in the belief system. What is here meant by a coherent belief system is one that passes all of the internal tests for being a true, and relevant, representation of the world – where "relevance" is a matter of being an appropriate guide to action, given the sorts of goals and desires we have. The consciousness afforded by such a system, to the extent that the beliefs are true, is consciousness of the world.

What would be best, of course, would be a system that was complete, in the sense of including all of the information about the world relevant to any goal we might have. Internal coherence obviously cannot guarantee completeness. But the internal processes that strive towards coherence also strive towards completeness – the more we come to believe the (relevant) consequences of the things we already believe, the more complete our system of belief comes to be. However, internal rationality can carry us only so far. To fill in the gaps in our representation of the world, we must often initiate investigations – we must probe reality and observe the effects of our probing. And part of rationality is being apt to make the appropriate investigations and observations. One must perceive what the gaps in one's representation of the world are, and what one must do

3 The way I have put this may be to some extent misleading. It suggests that there is a natural division of our representation of the world into individual beliefs, which then must somehow be unified into a single unified representation. This is the way of thinking of things that seems natural if one thinks of beliefs as corresponding to sentences. It is not so natural if one thinks of other ways of representing the world, e.g., maps. To the extent that one's beliefs about one's environment are realized in something like a map, it will be a unified representation (say a map of England) that is primary, and individual beliefs (such as that London is south of Edinburgh) will be an abstraction from this (see Stalnaker 1984). Of course, the unity of a map-like representation may be only local. One can have several maps of different parts of the world, and it can be a questions how what is represented by one of these is related to what is represented by the others.

in order to fill them – and of course in doing this, one will be relying on the rest of one's representation of the world.

IV

How does one know that there are gaps in one's representation of the world? In a simple case, this might be a matter of knowing that there is a mountain in one place, off to one's right, and a river in another, off to one's left, but not knowing what there is between them. The knowledge that there must be something between them (if only empty space) is part and parcel of knowing the spatial relation between them – that they are some distance apart. Again, one might know that an explosion occurred at one time and that a flood occurred at a later time without knowing what happened in between; knowing the temporal relation between the events, one knows that there must be some answer, even if only "an un-eventful interval," to the question "What happened in between?" Our ability to perceive gaps in our representation is a consequence of our knowledge of spatial and temporal relations between things we know about. In knowing those things to stand in spatial or temporal relations, we know them to belong to a single spatio-temporal system. Such a system defines a set of spatio-temporal locations, about each of which there must be an answer (even if only "nothing") to the question of what exists or is happening there. We know that there are gaps in our representation of reality by knowing that there are questions of this sort to which it does not contain answers.

But this ability to perceive a gap in one's representation presupposes awareness of one's representation – and so self-knowledge. I have argued elsewhere that, in creatures with cognitive and conceptual capacities comparable with ours, having a belief normally gives rise to the belief that one has it, or at any rate does so if one considers whether one has it.[4] And one of the arguments for this was, in brief, that being minimally rational involves constantly revising the contents of one's belief-desire system in such a way as to make and keep the system coherent, and that this requires that one be aware of the contents of the system, at least in those cases where preserving or restoring coherence involves initiating investigations aimed at determining whether a threatened belief should be retained or given up. The point here is similar. The rational subject must aim not only at making his or her belief system internally coherent,

---

4 See Essays 2 and 11.

183

but also at making it relevantly complete, where this means that it includes all of the information relevant to decisions about how to act. Relevant completeness is of course an ideal that is never fully attained. But the rational subject will be striving to approach this ideal as closely as possible. And this involves knowing what it is she does *not* know, and what she does *not* believe – which in turn involves knowing what she does know and believe.

Here then is one link between the notion of unity of consciousness and the notion of self-consciousness. Unity of consciousness is in part a matter of one's various beliefs forming, collectively, a unified conception of the world. And having a unified conception of the world requires being aware of gaps in one's world conception. We have already seen one way in which this involves self-knowledge. For it is only insofar as one is aware of the spatial relations *to oneself* of things one knows about that one is aware of their spatial relations to one another, and only insofar as one is aware of these that one is able to conceive of specific spatiotemporal locations of whose contents one is ignorant. That self-knowledge is not of mental states. But the knowledge of the gaps does involve knowledge of one's own mental states. In part it is knowledge that one does *not* know (and does *not* have beliefs about) something that is there to be known – e.g., what there is at a certain spatiotemporal location. But what gives significance to this lack of knowledge and belief is the background of knowledge and belief that makes it a "gap." It is because of what I know, or think I know, about what surrounds a given spatiotemporal location that it is important for me to know what is at that location. If, for example, the location is a portion of the sea obscured by a small island, then knowing what is there will settle the question whether what I see on either side of the island are the two ends of a single large ship or ends of two different smaller ships. And it will make all the difference in understanding two periods of civil turmoil known to have occurred in the past whether I find that the period between them was filled with similar turmoil or whether I find that it was characterized by relative tranquility.

It is clear enough that if I am aware of a gap in my knowledge I am aware of a negative fact about my belief system, namely that it does *not* include a belief about the matter in question. It is less obvious that the background of positive knowledge that makes this knowledge of a gap has to be, or include, knowledge of positive facts about one's belief system, i.e., knowledge that it does include certain other beliefs. Why shouldn't it be simply knowledge of the world? So, in the ship example above, I know that there is a ship part, a prow, to the right of the island

and a ship part, a stern, to the left of the island, and this is what makes my realization that I do not know what is behind the island a realization that there is a relevant gap in my knowledge. But let us consider this more closely. I know, let us suppose, the following propositions:

(1) There is a ship prow to the right of the island.
(2) There is a ship stern to the left of the island.
(3) I have no knowledge, or belief, about what is behind the island.

Suppose for the moment that I know these *without* knowing:

(1′) I believe (1).

and

(2′) I believe (2).

It must be agreed that knowledge of (3), by itself, is not knowledge of a relevant gap in my knowledge, or my conception of the world – or at any rate, not the gap addressed by the question "Is there one ship or two?" (1) and (2) are about the world, and not at all about my state of mind. So how can knowledge of these, in conjunction with knowledge of (3), constitute knowledge of such a relevant gap? It does, indeed, seem incongruous that someone should know (1)–(3) without realizing that there is a relevant gap in his knowledge. But I think that this is because it seems incongruous that someone should know (1) and (2) without knowing (1′) and (2′); for clearly anyone who knows (1′), (2′), and (3) does know that there is a gap in his conception of the world. If, *per impossible*, someone did know (1)–(3) without knowing, even implicitly, (1′) and (2′), it should be unclear to her what (3) has to do with (1) and (2), or vice versa. The relation of (1) and (2) to (3) should be like their relation to

(4) Smith (some other person) has no knowledge (or belief) about what is behind the island.

Knowledge of conditions (1), (2), and (4) does not amount to knowledge that there is a relevant gap in Smith's conception of the world, for the good reason that they are compatible with Smith having no knowledge of (1) and (2), or any other relevant background knowledge. If knowledge of (1)–(3) does amount to knowledge that there is a relevant gap in my own conception of the world, this is because knowledge of (1) and (2) implicitly involves knowledge of (1′) and (2′). This supports the claim that awareness of such gaps requires positive as well as negative knowledge of the contents of one's system of beliefs.

What makes this point of special interest, given our present concerns, is that it indicates that our awareness of our own mental states is a necessary condition of the unity of our consciousness of the world. Thus we have a link between unity of consciousness and self-consciousness. I now turn to a consideration of the unity of self-consciousness.

V

If it is true generally that in a rational creature different beliefs tend to give rise to further beliefs that they jointly imply or give evidential support to, this will be true in the special case where the beliefs are about one's own mental states. And obviously the "monitoring" role of self-knowledge, its role in enabling one to update and revise one's belief system, requires not only that one have knowledge of individual beliefs taken separately, but that one have knowledge of the relations of different beliefs to one another – e.g., that one supports the other, or is in prima facie conflict with it. Likewise, being aware of the contents of one's belief-system in the way required for being aware of gaps in one's conception of the world requires that one be aware, not just of the beliefs separately, but of the representation of the world that they collectively constitute.

Perfect unity of consciousness, then, would consist of a unified representation of the world accompanied by a unified representation of that representation, the latter including not only information about what the former represents, but also information about the grounds on which the beliefs that make up the former are based, and about what the evidential relations between the parts of that representation are. The unity consists not only in the integration of the two representations considered separately, but in the relation between them. The contents of the second not only correspond to, but are sensitive to and so change with, the contents of the first – as one's beliefs change, so do one's beliefs about what one believes. But there is also influence in the opposite direction; insofar as one's higher-order beliefs constitute awareness of incoherences in one's system of first-order beliefs, or of gaps in the representation of the world they constitute, they lead to investigations that modify the content of that system, normally by making it a more coherent and complete representation of the world.

But the awareness we have of our first-order beliefs is of course not all there is to the unity of self-consciousness. There is also awareness of sensations and feelings. And, importantly, there is awareness of desires, intentions, and goals. The latter plays an important role in deliberation. And it plays a role in the criticism and refinement of one's system of values that is similar to that played by awareness of beliefs in the criticism, revision, and refinement of one's system of beliefs about the world. Here, as there, it is essential that there be not only "vertical" unity, individual first-order states producing awarenesses of (beliefs about) themselves, but also "horizontal" unity, the higher-order beliefs being so related to each other that there is awareness not only of the first-order states taken one by one, but of relations between them. Without this, there would not be the detection of incoherences and gaps that it is part of the function of introspective consciousness to provide.

VI

That unity of consciousness as I have characterized it is essential if we are to have knowledge of the world is fairly evident. A stronger and more controversial claim is that such unity is constitutive of mental unity, or of what Bertrand Russell called "copersonality." As a first approximation, the claim is that what it is for a set of mental states to be the states of a single mental subject is, at least in part, for them to be related to one another in ways that constitute their having this sort of unity – i.e., that the first-order beliefs among them collectively constitute a unified representation of the world, that the contents of such higher-order beliefs as there are among them are counterfactually dependent on the contents of the first-order beliefs, and that the higher-order beliefs, in turn, play a role in promoting, over time, increased coherence, accuracy, and completeness in the representation constituted by the first-order beliefs.

One reason why this is only a first approximation to the claim I want to defend is that it misleadingly suggests that the nature of the various mental states, e.g., as beliefs having certain contents, is fixed antecedently to any consideration of their relations to other mental states – by which I mean, not what their actual causes and effects are, but how they are apt to influence, and be influenced by, other mental states. But it is part of the view I want to defend that part of what makes a state a state of a given mental kind, e.g., a belief with a certain content, is precisely its membership in a system of states having the sort of unity we are concerned with. There are cases in which one can know enough about the overall causal roles of two token states, including the relations of each to various other mental states, to know that they are mental states of certain kinds with certain contents, without knowing whether they are states of one and the same subject – and in such cases one may use unity of consciousness as a criterion of personal identity or mental unity. But this should not obscure the fact that the identities of mental states are holistically determined. So a better way of putting the claim I want to defend is this. Given a set of states, not saying yet whether they are mental states, what would constitute their being the set of mental states of a single subject, including first-order beliefs about the world and higher-order beliefs about first-order states, would be their having causal properties, and standing in causal relations, which collectively constitute their being a system of mental states of these various kinds united by unity of consciousness.

Another reason why my first formulation of my claim is only a first approximation is that what I really want to claim is that mental unity (or copersonality) is constituted by a functional unity of which unity of consciousness is only a special case. An example of functional unity that is not unity of consciousness is the relation between a belief that it is raining and a desire to keep dry in virtue of which they jointly contribute to rain-avoidance behavior, e.g., taking an umbrella if one decides to go outside. While the joint awareness of this belief and desire will be an instance of unity of consciousness, the aptness of the two states jointly to produce behavior that they rationalize will not be. Yet, arguably, the latter is partly constitutive of these being states of a single subject. Suppose that the belief is realized in one hemisphere of a brain, and the desire is realized in the other hemisphere, and that because all of the neural connections between the two hemispheres have been severed, and no other connections have taken their place, there is no disposition of the two states to contribute jointly to behaviors that they jointly rationalize. Of course, in supposing that the one is a belief with a certain content and the other a desire with a certain content, one must suppose, according to me, that each does stand in appropriate relationships of mental unity to *some* other states – presumably, in each case, states realized in the same hemisphere that it is. But the fact that the two states are causally insulated from each other in this way would be a reason for denying that they are states of a single subject, despite their being instantiated in the same body and the same brain.[5]

We could, of course, have an example like this in which the two states are both beliefs, and in which the lack of functional unity is also a lack of

5 I should make clear that I am not saying that this is how things are in the case of actual split-brain patients.

unity of consciousness. So, for example, the belief in the one hemisphere is a belief that if it is raining then the streets are wet, and the belief in the other is a belief that it is raining – but because of the lack of neural connections between the hemispheres, there is no tendency of these jointly to produce, in either hemisphere, the belief that the streets are wet. The reason this counts as a lack of unity of consciousness is that there is no tendency of the beliefs jointly to contribute, as "copersonal" beliefs should, to a unified representation of the world. Here again we have reason for denying that the states are states of a single subject, despite their being implemented in the same body and the same brain.

But the claim that unity of consciousness plays a constitutive role vis à vis mental unity seems to conflict with claims that philosophers have made. In the following sections I shall consider two challenges to it. One is the claim, made by Derek Parfit, that we can envision cases in which there is "divided consciousness" – i.e., two streams of consciousness running concurrently, such that there is no "co-consciousness" between events in the one and events in the other. (I should emphasize that Parfit does not present this case as an objection to the view that unity of consciousness plays a constitutive role vis à vis mental unity; in fact, he endorses a version of that view.) The other is the claim made by David Armstrong that it is only a contingent fact that the special access to mental states characteristic of introspective awareness is limited to states of the subject of awareness. This is a challenge to my claim because, as I am understanding unity of consciousness, the relation between a state and the introspective awareness of it is an instance of unity of consciousness. Parfit's claim seems a challenge to the claim that unity of consciousness is a necessary condition of mental unity, while Armstrong's claim seems a challenge to the claim that unity of consciousness is a sufficient condition of mental unity.

VII

Parfit asks us to suppose that he has been equipped with some device that can block communication between his hemispheres. "Since this device is connected to my eyebrows, it is under my control. By raising an eyebrow I can divide my mind. In each half of my divided mind I can then, by lowering an eyebrow, reunite my mind."[6] He then imagines that he is taking a physics exam, and, undecided as to which is the best of two

6 Parfit 1984, p. 246.

strategies for dealing with a problem, decides to divide his mind for ten minutes so as "to work in each half of my mind on one of the two calculations, and then to reunite my mind to write a fair copy of the best result" (p. 247). After the division, "each of my two streams of consciousness seems to have been straightforwardly continuous with my one stream of consciousness up to the moment of division. The only changes in each stream are the disappearance of half my visual field and the loss of sensation in, and control over, one of my arms." During the period of division, he will be oblivious in each stream to what is occurring in the other, except insofar as he can infer it from observed behavior, e.g., what he sees written down by the hand he does not control (in that stream). After his mind is reunited, "I shall suddenly seem to remember just having worked at two calculations, in working at each of which I was not aware of working at the other" (p. 247).

Allowing this case to be logically possible, one might wonder whether it is really a case of a person existing for a period of time with a divided mind. Why isn't it instead a case in which a person undergoes "fission," dividing into two people, who then in turn undergo "fusion," uniting into a single person (who, there would then be reason to think, cannot be identical with the original person or with either of the products of the fission). One might also wonder whether there is even a fact of the matter as to whether the case satisfies Parfit's preferred description or the one just given – and Parfit himself holds that it is not a "real question" whether there is one person here or two. However, I shall assume, for the sake of discussion, that Parfit's initial description is apt.

Two things are obvious here. First, *within* each of the streams there is unity of consciousness of the sort I have characterized. That is what makes each of them *a* stream. What we have within each stream is more than just an instance of the sort of "local" unity involved in a visual experience of the American flag; presumably there is within each stream a "global" unity of perceptual consciousness comparable with that there is in a person under normal circumstances. And going with this there would be a unified introspective consciousness of the perceptual states making up that perceptual consciousness and, more generally, of the first-order states making up the stream.

Second, while during the period of division no integration of the contents of the two streams takes place, eventually, after the streams are united, integration does take place. There is, internal to the system that incorporates the two streams, a mechanism for bringing about such integration. Of course, if two people are close friends, one could say that there is a "system" that incorporates a "mechanism" for bringing about integration of their mental states, namely their regularly conversing with each other. The mechanism for bringing about integration in Parfit's case is different from what we have in the case of the two friends, and it is also different from what we have in a normal mind. If one is inclined to favor Parfit's description of the case over the description of it as fission-followed-by-fusion, this may be because one sees the mechanism as being *more* different from that in the case of the two friends than it is from that in the normal case. But it is clear that in the absence of *any* such mechanism, there would be no good case for regarding the two streams of consciousness as belonging to a single person. If, perhaps *per impossibile*, there were streams of consciousness realized in the two hemispheres of a brain in such a way that the two were causally insulated from each other, and there were no possibility of integrating their contents (other than the way in which the contents of the minds of two friends are integrated), what we would have is two minds, and two persons, in one body. So Parfit's example is no threat (nor, I should emphasize, does he present it as a threat) to the view that unity of consciousness is constitutive of mental unity and the copersonality of mental states and events; at most it shows that the ways in which it is constitutive of this are more complex than one might suppose.

But one interesting point does emerge from the example. Suppose that Parfit's description of his case is right, i.e., that both streams of consciousness belong to one person, and suppose that a particular experience, say a pain, occurs in one stream but not in the other. Was that experience conscious? One might suppose that this translates into the question "Was the person conscious of it?" But the answer to that question seems to be: "Yes and no. He was conscious of it in the right hemisphere, but not conscious of it in the left hemisphere." This suggests that the property of *being conscious* is really a relational one, and that our example should be described as one in which the experience is conscious relative to one stream and not conscious relative to the other.

This may have application to more ordinary cases. The possibility represented in extreme form in Parfit's example, of "copersonal" mental states that are not integrated with each other, is regularly realized in less extreme form in ordinary people. It is a commonplace that people's minds become "compartmentalized," and that people engage in self-deception and denial. It is also widely accepted that mental states can be unconscious in ways described by Freud; that wishes, desires, intentions, and beliefs can be repressed. But this raises a question. If wishes and beliefs can be repressed, it does not seem out of the question that there should be a case in which the states repressed include both a wish (say, to kill one's father) and the higher-order belief that one has that wish. And this poses a prima facie problem. If the wish is repressed, it should be unconscious. If the person has the belief that he has that wish, and that belief is caused and sustained by the wish, then it would seem he should count as conscious of the wish, and it should count as conscious. But how can it be both unconscious and conscious? The relativization of the notion of consciousness provides a solution. Let us say that in the normal case, unlike in Parfit's case, there is a "dominant" stream of consciousness; a temporally extended set of states and events that is highly integrated, i.e., characterized by a high degree of unity of consciousness, and includes most of the subject's mental states, or at any rate significantly more of them than any other such set. When we say that a state or event is conscious, *tout court*, we mean that it is conscious relative to the dominant stream (or belongs to the dominant stream), and when we say that a state or event is unconscious, *tout court*, we mean that it is unconscious relative to the dominant stream. Both our repressed wish and the repressed higher-order belief about it are presumably unconscious relative to the subject's dominant stream. But the subject's mind harbors a mini-stream consisting of the wish and the belief about it, and perhaps other states and events as well. And the wish is conscious relative to that.

This suggests a general strategy for dealing with these issues. Much of what philosophers have said about unity of consciousness and about personal identity applies in the first instance to what I am here calling streams of consciousness. For example, some conceptions (but by no means all conceptions) of "psychological continuity" are really conceptions of the kinds of continuity there must be between successive stages of a single stream of consciousness. And the functionalist claim that mental states and events are defined by their relations to other mental states and events could be understood as meaning that they are to be defined by their relations to the other states and events belonging to the same stream. I have suggested elsewhere that the functionalist account of mental states and the psychological continuity account of personal identity are really two sides of the same coin; that psychological continuity over time is simply the playing out over time of the defining functional roles of mental states.[7] Perhaps the psychological continuity this is true of is not (quite) that which constitutes the identity over time of a person, but that which constitutes the identity over time of a stream of conscious-

7 See Shoemaker 1984b.

192

ness. If this is right, then the first thing we have to understand is the mental unity that characterizes the contents of individual streams, and, what is inseparable from this, the functional natures of the states and events that make up such streams. Given the notion of a stream of consciousness, we can then go on to inquire into (a) what it is that makes different streams of consciousness "copersonal," i.e., streams of consciousness belonging to a single subject, and (b) what it is that makes a given stream of consciousness the "dominant stream" of a given subject. As I have already indicated, the notion of unity of consciousness will come in again, although in a somewhat different way, in answering these questions. What makes streams copersonal will be, at least in part, some sort of accessibility of the contents of the one to awareness in the other – an accessibility that may not be direct or immediate, but which at any rate is more direct than the accessibility of one person's mental states to the awareness of another. And presumably the dominant stream will be the one that is most encompassing and that contributes the most sustained and coherent control of the subject's behavior.

VIII

I turn now to the other challenge to the claim that unity of consciousness is constitutive of mental unity and copersonality. In his "Consciousness and Causality" David Armstrong maintains that the confinement of introspective awareness to the subject's own mind is, like the confinement of proprioceptive awareness to the subject's own body, a contingent confinement: "We can conceive being directly hooked-up, say by a transmission of waves in some medium, to the body of another. In such a case we might become aware e.g. of the movement of another's limbs, in much the same sort of way we become aware of the motion of our own limbs. In the same way, it seems an intelligible hypothesis (a logical possibility) that we should enjoy the same sort of awareness of what goes on in the mind of another as the awareness we have of what is going on in our own mind. *A* might be 'introspectively' aware of *B*'s pain, although *A* does not observe *B*'s behavior."[8] If this is right, then one important dimension of unity of consciousness, namely the connection between a mental state and the introspective awareness of it, is not sufficient for mental unity and copersonality – the mental state might belong to one mind, and the awareness of it to another.

8 Armstrong 1984, p. 113.

193

Let me begin by getting a red herring out of the way. Armstrong defends the possibility of there being "Siamese minds," which, since he is a materialist, he thinks of as "Siamese brains." These are cases in which the brains of two people overlap, and Armstrong thinks that in such a case the two people could share a pain. For reasons I will not go into, I think he is mistaken in thinking this – not, perhaps, in thinking that brains of different persons could overlap, but in thinking that this would make it possible for the very same sensation, the very same token mental state or event, to belong to two different people.[9] But the point I want to make is that even if he were right about this, this would not support the view that it is at most a contingent fact that the special access one has to one's mental states is one that one can have only to one's own mental states. For, after all, if I share a pain with you, then while my access to the pain is an access to your pain, it is still an access to mine as well. What the possibility of sharing sensations would make contingent is the fact that one cannot have this special access to a pain that belongs to another person. But that would not jeopardize the claim that this special access is constitutive of mental unity. To put that in jeopardy, we would need a case in which someone has this sort of access to a mental state that belongs to someone else and *not* to the person who has the access.

Let me describe a conception of self-knowledge on which this is a possibility. According to this, there are what I shall call "channels of information" connecting minds and minds, and the existence of one of these channels involves some sort of causal mechanism whereby the existence of a mental state in a mind at one end of the channel, call it the transmitter mind, produces a belief in the existence of such a mental state in the

9 Briefly, my reason for rejecting this possibility turns on the distinction I have made (see my 1981 and 1994 [Chapter 11]) between "core realizations" and "total realizations" of mental states. Suppose we have a case of Siamese brains in which brains A and B overlap. (For ease of exposition, I will assume that brains A and B can be identified with their owners.) The portion of overlap might contain a physical state, P, which is the core realization of a pain – or, better, of a state of being in pain. But the occurrence of this state is not by itself sufficient for either A or B being in pain, so P is neither A's pain-state nor B's pain-state. A is in pain only if the overall organization of A, including the portion that does not overlap with B, is such as to enable P to play the role of pain in A, and B is in pain only if the overall organization of B is such as to enable P to play the role of pain in B. Assuming that A and B are both in pain, the total realization of A's pain-state is P plus A's having such and such an overall organization, while the total realization of B's pain-state is P plus B's having such and such an overall organization. So the total realizations are different, and the pain-states are different. If we reject the act-object conception of pain, as I assume Armstrong joins me in doing, the only entities answering to the expressions "A's pain" and "B's pain" are A's and B's pain-states, and these are different.

mind, call it the receiver mind, at the other end. In fact, in all probability, the only such channels are in fact loops, whose transmitter minds and receiver minds are one and the same. It is such loopy channels that account for our introspective knowledge. But it is at most a contingent fact that there are not also channels of this sort whose transmitter minds and receiver minds are different. If mental telepathy actually occurs, there actually are such channels. In the first instance, the belief produced in a receiver mind by such a transmission is the belief that someone, or someone of some general description, has the mental state in question. If the mental state is ascribed to some particular person, this ascription would have to be based in part on collateral information. This has to be so if the access we in fact have to our own mental states is the same in nature as the access we would have to the minds of others if there were channels of this sort connecting different minds. Obviously, if I were tapping into President Clinton's mind, it would have to be a fallible inference on my part that it is into *his* mind that I am tapping. Here the basis for the inference might be the contents of the quasi-introspective meta-beliefs, in conjunction with what I know on other grounds about Clinton. Who else would have thoughts that flit back and forth amongst the forthcoming Cabinet meeting, Whitewater, Hilary's latest speech, Chelsea's report card, and the musty smell in the Oval Office? In other cases the collateral information might include general information about the channels of information, e.g., that they are limited in length, or are blocked by lead shields. And in our actual situation, one's identification of oneself as the subject of the states would be based on the information that loopy channels are the only sort, or at any rate almost the only sort, there are.

I do not object to the view that there could, in principle, be channels of information of the sort envisaged, both of the loopy and the nonloopy kinds. Telepathic access to the minds of others is a logical possibility, and it is logically possible that there should be that sort of access to our own minds. But the view that our normal introspective access to our own mental states is just a matter of our each being equipped with a loopy such channel seems to me radically mistaken.

First, and perhaps most controversially, I have argued elsewhere that in the case of many sorts of mental states, there is an internal connection between being in a mental state of that kind and having, or at any rate being disposed to have, the introspective belief that one has it.[10] For example, I have argued that it is constitutive of belief that if someone has

10 See Essays 2 and 11.

normal human intelligence, rationality, and conceptual capacity, then if she has the belief that P, and considers whether she has it, she will believe that she has it. But presumably, if it is just a matter of contingent fact that there are *not* non-loopy channels connecting our minds to other minds, it is likewise a matter of contingent fact that there *are* loopy channels connecting our minds to themselves. The view I have sketched has no room for the view that any sort of mental state is, in virtue of its own inherent nature, self-intimating.

Second, I have argued elsewhere that an important class of first-person assertions and beliefs, those Wittgenstein had in mind in speaking of the use of 'I' "as subject," are immune to a certain kind of error, namely error through misidentification.[11] Gareth Evans makes the same point by saying that many first-person utterances and beliefs are "identification free."[12] One refers to oneself, and ascribes properties to oneself, without having to identify *as* oneself anything that is presented to one. And while sometimes, e.g., when looking in a mirror, one identifies someone as oneself, this depends on one's already having some first-person knowledge, e.g., that one is thumbing one's nose or sticking out one's tongue, and on pain of a vicious infinite regress one must allow that ultimately it requires having first-person knowledge that does not rest on an identification. There is no plausible account of what our identification-free first-person knowledge consists in that does not include self-ascriptions of mental states as among the things we know in this way. But plainly, loopy information channels of the sort described earlier could not be a source of such indentification-free first-person knowledge. As pointed out earlier, if a meta-belief gotten through such a channel refers to some specific person, it must be grounded in part on collateral information that makes it possible to identify that person as the person the channel-transmitted information is about.

Consider the idea, mentioned earlier, that one is able to convert the input from an information channel into a first-person judgment by making use of a general fact about the world, namely that all, or almost all, of the information channels that exist are loopy ones. (Let's put aside the awkward question of how one is supposed to know that general fact about the world.) On this view, when I say "I have an itch," this would be grounded on the channel-provided information that someone has an itch together with the general fact that only loopy channels are available.

11 See Shoemaker 1968 and Essay 1.
12 See Evans 1982, Chapters 6 and 7.

But let's spell the inference out. It would have as one premise the assertion of that general fact, and as another the claim that I have the channel transmitted belief that someone has an itch. The latter is of course a first-person claim. So is it in turn based on yet another such inference from yet another channel transmitted belief? That way lies the vicious regress. And if one allows that it is instead a piece of identification-free first-person belief that does not come via a loopy channel, one should see that one should give up on loopy channels altogether, and allow that one's belief that one has an itch is likewise information free. The loopy channel view of introspection is what its name suggests, loopy.

Perhaps there is a way of developing the view that our "special access" to our own mental states is only contingently limited to our own mental states that does not involve the information-channel view I have just rejected. But if so, I do not know what it is. And I do not see how any such view can deal with the fact that at least some of our first-person knowledge must be identification free. So I know of no good reason to challenge the view that the connection between first-person mental states and introspective beliefs between them is one form of unity of consciousness that is partly constitutive of mental unity, or copersonality.

197

PART IV

The Royce lectures:
Self-knowledge and "inner sense"

10

Self-knowledge and "inner sense"
Lecture I: The object perception model

I

The general topic of these lectures is the nature of our "introspective" knowledge of our own mental states, and, in particular, the question of whether this knowledge should be thought of as involving a kind of perception, an "inner sense" – whether it is appropriately conceived on a perceptual or observational model. The knowledge I have in mind is not, as you perhaps hoped, the difficult-to-get knowledge that arises from successfully following the Socratic injunction "Know thyself"; it is the humdrum kind of knowledge that is expressed in such remarks as "It itches," "I'm hungry," "I don't want to," and "I'm bored." In calling this knowledge "introspective," I of course do not mean to be prejudging the question of whether it is perceptual or quasi-perceptual in nature; as will become apparent, my own view is at odds with the answer to that question which the etymology of that term rather naturally suggests.

Faced with the question of how someone knows something, the most satisfying answer we can be given is "She saw it." Seeing is believing, the expression goes, and seeing is the paradigmatic explanation of knowing. No wonder, then, that many have been attracted by the idea that something like seeing explains that knowledge we have of our own minds. But while many philosophers have embraced an inner-sense model of

These three lectures were presented at Brown University in October of 1993. They constitute the third set of Josiah Royce lectures, established through a bequest by Curt and Mabel Ducasse; the lectures are given every four years at Brown. Early drafts of the material in Lecture I were read at a conference at Emory University and at MIT in the Fall of 1991. A much briefer version of some of the material in Lecture III were given at CIBA Foundation Symposium 174 in London in July, 1992, and published as "Functionalism and Consciousness" in CIBA 1993. Parts of Lecture III coincide with parts of my paper "Phenomenal Content," published in *Nous*, March 1994. I have had helpful comments from Simon Blackburn, Ned Block, Mark Crimmins, Daniel Dennett, Jaegwon Kim, Bill Lycan, Ulric Neisser, Dave Robb, and Ernest Sosa on various parts of this material.

self-knowledge, many others have found such a model profoundly misleading or mistaken.

Let me try to evoke some of the intuitions on which the issue turns. First, focus on some current sensation of yours – an itch or tingle or pain. Or, better still, generate a visual after-image and focus on it. Putting aside, if you can, any theoretical commitments you may have on such matters, does it seem natural to regard your access to the sensation or image as similar to the access you have to objects in your environment in sense perception? Second, consider whether you believe that Sacramento is the capital of California, and, assuming that you find that you do, consider the epistemological access you have to that belief and to the fact that you have it. Still putting aside theoretical commitments, do you find it natural to compare *this* access to your perceptual access to things and states of affairs in your environment? Finally, take note of the fact that in each of these cases what one knows is something about *oneself*, and consider the epistemological access one thereby has to the "self" about which we know these various things. Continuing to bracket any theoretical commitments, do you find it natural to think of *this* access as like your perceptual access to things you observe in your environment?

I have just been inviting you to consult your pretheoretical intuitions about whether your epistemic access to certain things is like the access you have to things in your environment when perceiving them. I have my suspicions, which for now I will keep to myself, about how you may be inclined to answer my questions. But you may well be suspicious of the questions. Everything is similar to everything else, in one way or another, so it is far from clear what these intuitions are supposed to be about. For similar reasons you may be suspicious of the question "Is introspection perception?" The words "perceive" and "perception" cover a variety of things. We can put aside the use of "perceive" in which one can perceive, or "see," anything one can come to know, even including truths of logic – our issue is whether introspection is appropriately thought of as a kind of, or as revealingly analogous to, *sense*-perception. But the kinds of sense-perception are themselves a diverse lot. It is not obvious that the modes of knowledge acquisition that have been classified as kinds of perception have any one feature or set of features in virtue of which they all count as kinds of perception; maybe the concept of sense-perception is a "family resemblance concept," or a "cluster concept," and there is no "real essence" of sense perception. And it could be that our concept of perception is vague in ways that leave it indeterminate whether introspection should count as perception.

Here a glance back into the history of philosophy may be instructive. David Armstrong, a recent champion of the inner sense view, cites John Locke as one of the classical proponents of this view (see Armstrong 1984). Now when Locke uses the term "perceive," what he usually has us perceiving are either "ideas" or the operations of our minds. But I assume that it was true in his time, as it is in ours, that one can be said to perceive whatever one sees, hears, feels, etc., and it was certainly true that one can be said to see, feel, etc., items in one's environment – trees, mountains, buildings, etc. So was Locke, in speaking of perception of ideas and operations of the mind, embracing the perceptual model? Was he thinking of our epistemic access to these mental entities as like our epistemic access to the standard objects of sense perception, i.e., trees, and the like? Well, he certainly wasn't thinking of it as being like that access *as he took it actually to be*. For, of course, he thought that in fact our perceptual access to external bodies is a rather complex affair that involves these bodies producing, via their effects on our sense organs, ideas in our minds that are representations of those bodies. And he certainly didn't think of our perception of our own ideas as like *that*. So if Locke embraced the perceptual model, his stereotype of perception was not sense-perception *as he took it actually to be*. Perhaps it was instead sense-perception *as we naively think of it as being*. This would involve, at least, thinking of it as an *immediate* access to its objects. And for Locke, as for Berkeley and Hume, immediacy was taken to involve not only lack of inference but also the lack of any distinction between appearance and reality – the objects of immediate perception necessarily are as they appear and appear as they are.

Now it is clear that *this* is not part of the stereotype of perception that is operating in recent advocacy of the perceptual model. In claiming that introspection is perception, philosophers like David Armstrong are not claiming that the access we have to our own minds in introspection is like the access we naively but mistakenly think of ourselves as having to external objects in sense-perception; they are claiming that it is like the access we *actually do have* to external objects in sense perception. And, like Locke, they think of the latter as mediated, causally if not inferentially, and as fallible.

There are, then, different versions of the perceptual model. We can think of each of these as associated with a "stereotype" of perception. I suggested earlier that in Locke's case the stereotype was not sense-perception as he took it actually to be but sense-perception as we naively take it to be. And I think that we can finesse the issue of whether there is a defining essence of perception, something that all and only cases of perception have in common. Even if there is not, there are certain widespread stereotypes of perception, based on actual or presumed features of certain central cases of sense perception, and it can be a genuine issue whether our introspective access to our own mental states conforms to one or another of these. Of course, to the extent that advocates and opponents of "the perceptual model" have different stereotypes in mind, they will be talking past one another.

In what follows I will be discussing two versions of the perceptual model. The first of these is what I think is most often the target of those who inveigh against the notion of introspection as inner sense. Its stereotype of perception is based on cases of perception, primarily cases of visual perception, in which one or more particular things are *objects* of the perception, and in which in it can be said that it is *by* perceiving these objects that the perceiver obtains whatever factual information she does from the perceiving. I will call this the *object perception model.* Here the word "object" covers only particular things, and excludes facts. If I perceive that the book is on the table, the book and the table will be objects of my perception, but the fact that the book is on the table will not be. The second model differs from the first in allowing for cases of perception in which there are no objects in this sense – in which the only "objects" are *facts* or states of affairs. But in common with the first model, it ascribes to perception the following feature:In perception we have access to things or states of affairs that exist independently of their being perceived and independently of there being any means of perceiving them. I will call this the *broad perceptual model.* I believe that both of these versions of the perceptual model are open to serious objections. But they are open to different objections.

II

I am now going to list and briefly characterize some features of certain ordinary cases of sense perception – or, as I shall sometimes speak of them, conditions satisfied by ordinary kinds of sense perception. These are not offered as features that all genuine cases of sense perception have in common. Rather, they collectively constitute the stereotype of sense-perception underlying what I am calling the "object perception model"; and a subset of them constitute the stereotype of sense-perception underlying what I am calling the "broad perceptual model."

(1) Sense perception involves the operation of an organ of perception whose disposition is to some extent under the voluntary control of the

204

subject. Acquiring perceptual knowledge involves getting the appropriate organs into an appropriate relation to the object of perception.

(2) Sense perception involves the occurrence of sense-experiences, or *Representation* sense-impressions, that are distinct from the object of perception, and also distinct from the perceptual belief (if any) that is formed. The occurrence of these constitutes the subject's being "appeared to" in some way – a way that may or may not correspond to the way the object actually is.

(3) While sense perception provides one with awareness of facts, i.e., awareness *that* so and so is the case, it does this by means of awareness of objects. One's awareness of the facts is explained by one's awareness of the objects involved in these facts. So, for example, I am aware (I perceive) that there is a book before me *by* perceiving the book – here the book is the (nonfactual) object. In such a case there is always the potentiality of a factual awareness whose propositional content involves *demonstrative* reference to the object or objects of which one is perceptually aware – e.g., that *this* book is to the right of *that* one.

(4) Sense perception affords "identification information" about the object of perception. When one perceives one is able to pick out one object from others, distinguishing it from the others by information, provided by the perception, about both its relational and its nonrelational properties. The provision of such information is involved in the "tracking" of the object over time, and its reidentification from one time to another.

(5) The perception of objects standardly involves perception of their intrinsic, nonrelational properties. We can perceive relations between things we perceive; but we wouldn't perceive these things at all, and so couldn't perceive relations between them, if they didn't present themselves as having intrinsic, nonrelational properties. To perceive that this book is to the right of that one I must perceive, or at least seem to perceive, intrinsic properties of the two books, e.g., their colors and shapes.[1]

---

1 The phrase "or at least seem to perceive" was added in response to a comment by Ernest Sosa, who pointed out that there are possible cases in which one is sure that one sees something, and is in a position to perceive relations between that thing and other things, even though the color, shape, etc. of the object are somewhat other than one perceives them as being. Here one does not actually perceive (veridically) intrinsic properties of the thing; but one does at least seem to perceive them. Sosa also pointed out that the salient property of an object perceived by touch might be its "heft," which on reflection turns out to be a relational property. And it is one of my own central contentions in Lecture III that the perceived properties of things include what I call "phenomenal properties," which I take to be properties that in fact involve a relation to the perceiver, although they are not perceived as doing so. It may be that many properties we naturally think of as intrinsic are in fact relational in this way (e.g., color is, on many views).

(6) Objects of perception are potential objects of attention. Without changing what one perceives, one can shift one's attention from one perceived object to another, thereby enhancing one's ability to gain information about it.

(7) Perceptual beliefs are causally produced by the objects or states of affairs perceived, via a causal mechanism (that normally produces beliefs ? that are true.) Given (2) above, this process involves the production of sense-experiences, which together with background beliefs give rise to the perceptual beliefs. Given (1), the specification of the causal mechanism makes reference to the organ of perception, and the reliability of the mechanism consists in there being a correspondence between the contents of the beliefs and what the sense-organs are directed towards.

Finally, (8) the objects and states of affairs which the perception is of, and which it provides knowledge about, exist independently of the perceiving of them, and, with certain exceptions,[2] independently of there being things with the capacity for perceiving them or being aware of them. Thus trees, mountains, etc. can exist without there being creatures with the capacity to perceive them, and it is in principle possible for houses, automobiles, and human bodies to exist in this way.

While all of these features belong to the stereotype that constitutes the object-perception model, the distinctive features of it are conditions (3)–(6). And I think that it is the appropriateness of a model for introspection based on cases having these features that is often at issue when philosophers discuss whether introspection should be thought of as inner sense. In the remainder of this lecture I shall be considering whether, or to what extent, our introspective access to ourselves fits this model.

III

The candidates for being (nonfactual) objects of inner perception are, first of all, the self itself, that which it calls "I," and then mental entities of

Should this turn out to be true of all or most perceived properties classified as intrinsic, the stereotype of perception I am describing would be wrong at this point – which is compatible with its being a stereotype that does figure prominently in ordinary thinking. But I cannot believe that it is wrong in this way. I doubt, for example, whether one can feel the heft of an object without feeling *something* about its shape (e.g., the curvature or lack thereof of the part of its surface one is touching), and shape is an intrinsic property if anything is. The minimal claim I want to make here is that an object of perception must be the sort of thing that one can perceive, and normally would perceive, by perceiving intrinsic properties of it.

2 The things we perceive include perceivers, i.e., other people or animals. Even here one might say that what "in the first instance" one perceives, namely a body of a certain shape and coloration, is something that could exist in a world devoid of perceivers.

various kinds – sensations, feelings, thoughts, beliefs, desires, and so on. These will be discussed separately in the sections that follow. But it will be convenient to treat them together in discussing conditions (1) and (2).

It is generally conceded that our introspective access does not satisfy condition (1). There is no organ of introspection that the self directs either to itself or to mental entities of any kind. David Armstrong thinks that this is not damaging to the perceptual model because there is a *bona fide* kind of sense perception, our "proprioceptive" awareness of states of our own bodies, that also does not involve the operation of an organ. Since the satisfaction of (1) clearly is essential to vision, which is the object-perception model's paradigm of sense perception, Armstrong's point works better as a defense of the broad perceptual model than as a defense of the object-perception model. But nothing in my subsequent discussion will turn on the failure of introspective access to satisfy (1).

Let's move on to (2), the point that perceiving something involves there being a sense-experience, an appearance, of it. It seems widely agreed that introspection does not have this feature, and this is perhaps the most commonly given reason for denying that it should count as perception. No one thinks that in being aware of a sensation or sensory experience, one has yet another sensation or experience that is "of" the first one, and constitutes its appearing to one in a particular way. No one thinks that one is aware of beliefs and thoughts by having sensations or quasi-sense-experiences of them. And no one thinks that there is such a thing as an introspective sense-experience of oneself, an introspective appearance of oneself that relates to one's beliefs about oneself as the visual experiences of things one sees relate to one's beliefs about those things. Certainly this is an important difference between introspection and sense-perception as it actually is. But I shall refrain from declaring it fatal to the perceptual model.[3]

3 After these lectures were delivered, I came to think that the point here can be deepened by bringing to bear points about the content of perceptual experience that have figured in recent discussions. It has been persuasively argued that the contents of perceptual experiences, as contrasted with the contents of the perceptual judgments to which these experiences give rise, are "analog" rather than "digital" (see Dretske 1981, and Peacocke 1989), and at least in part nonconceptual (see Evans 1982, and Peacocke 1989 and 1991). My denial that there are "introspective experiences" is in part the denial that our introspective judgments are grounded on states having this sort of content, in the way perceptual judgments are based on perceptual experiences. Of course, since our introspective judgments include ones about our perceptual experiences, the content of these will partake of the analog and nonconceptual character of the experiences they are about. I know that things look *this way*, and an adequate representation of *this way* would be analog and partly nonconceptual. But introspective contents will have this

It is when we come to condition (3), and the closely related conditions (4)–(6), that it is useful to separate the question whether the *self* is the object of quasi-perceptual introspective awareness, and the question of whether mental entities of various kinds are. I begin with the question about the self.

This is of course the subject of a famous episode in the history of philosophy: Hume's denial that when he enters into what he calls himself he finds anything other than individual perceptions, and, in particular, that he finds any *self* that is the subject of these perceptions (Hume, *Treatise*, I,iv,6). This denial (for short, the Humean denial) has won the assent of most subsequent philosophers who have addressed the issue. Nor is the denial original with Hume: Berkeley explicitly, and Locke implicitly, denied that there is any perception of the "spirit" or immaterial substance they took a self to be. But it was left to Hume to make vivid that what is denied is the introspective perceivability of anything that could be called the referent of the word "I."

What lies behind this denial? A bad reason for making it would be the muddled, though common, way of thinking about substance that represents a substance as something behind or beneath the properties it "has," and so as something we don't perceive in perceiving its properties. This of course would be as good a reason for denying the perceivability of a cup, *qua* material substance, as it is for denying the perceivability of the self. I have suggested elsewhere that a somewhat less disreputable version of this way of thinking may have been at work in Hume (see Essay 1). There are indications that Hume took it for granted that if there were a self, *qua* mental subject, all mental states of affairs would have to be *rela-*

character only in virtue of embedding perceptual contents that are not introspective, i.e., are about the environment rather than the subject's mind. And in such cases it is the introspective judgments themselves that have this character, and these judgments do not arise from yet other introspective states, quasi-sensory ones, whose content is analog and partly nonconceptual. Typically the introspective judgments will arise from states whose contents are analog and partly nonconceptual; but these will be perceptual experiences whose contents concern the environment.

Another feature of the contents of perceptual experiences is their perspectival character. But there are not different introspective perspectives on the same mental entities, in the way there are different perceptual perspectives on the same physical ones. This is a further reason for denying that introspective awareness satisfies condition (2). And perhaps a reason for denying that it satisfies condition (3), for it seems plausible that a nonfactual object of a perception-like epistemic access should be something on which different perspectives are possible.

tional – each would amount to a self perceiving a "perception" of one sort or another. This comes from assuming an "act-object" conception of sensation, imagination, thought, etc. In Hume's terminology the object would be a perception, an idea or impression, and the act would be an apprehension of it by the self. Given the act-object conception, and given Hume's dualist assumptions, the idea that if there is a self then all mental states of affairs are relational is a natural one; it is hard to see, on those assumptions, what an *intrinsic* property of a self would be – given dualism, it would have no physical properties, and all of its mental properties would be relational. But it seems a direct consequence of this way of thinking that a self, devoid of intrinsic properties, would be unperceivable. It would in fact fail one of the tests of perceivability that is central to the object perception model; condition (5) says that perception of a thing involves perception of *intrinsic* properties of the thing. Hume, of course, concluded that there is no self, over and above the individual perceptions.

But even if we put aside the act-object conception and the commitment to dualism, it seems clear that our introspective awareness of ourselves lacks a number of the features that make up the object perception model. I begin with (3), the requirement that awareness of facts is by means of awareness of objects. Selves are certainly objects in the required sense, and it is easy enough to define a notion of object awareness that takes selves as objects and would have introspective awareness as a special case. One is aware of an object, in this sense (call it the broad sense), just in case one is so related to it that, for some range of properties, its having a property in that range is apt to result in one's having the belief that it has that property. In the case of selves, the relation can be just identity, and the range of properties can be certain mental ones; if one *is* a certain self, its having certain mental properties will normally go with one's believing that it, i.e., oneself, has them.[4] But compare this with the case of visual perception. There the relation to the objects of perception involves the eyes being directed toward them under appropriate lighting conditions. This, call it the "in view relation," is a relation one can have to any of an indefinitely large number of different objects. And there is a straightforward sense in which someone's having knowledge about a particular object is *explained* by her standing in this relation to it. One can come to know facts about an object *by* getting oneself into this relation

---

4 Or perhaps the relation should be *is identical to and conscious*. It is when I stand in this relation to myself that I acquire true beliefs about its (my) properties.

to it. By contrast, one obviously cannot come to know facts about a self by getting oneself into the relation of identity with it. And one's being in that relation to a self does not enter into a causal explanation of one's having knowledge of it in anything like the way that having the "in view" relation to a tree enters into a causal explanation of one's having knowledge of it. If we expand condition (3) by saying that perception involves "object-awareness" and that object-awareness of a thing involves having to it a kind of relation such that, first, it is possible for one to have this relation to any of a range of different objects, and, second, having this relation to an object enters into the causal explanation of one's knowing facts of a certain kind about it, then it is clear that introspective awareness of the self does not satisfy it.

The failure of introspective awareness to satisfy this condition goes with its failure to satisfy several of the others, in particular (1) and (4). The obvious fact that there is no organ of introspection is in part the fact that there is no such thing as getting oneself in a position – a position one might not have been in – for making oneself the object of one's awareness. So the failure of introspective self-awareness to satisfy condition (1) is in part its failure to satisfy condition (3).[5]

As for (4), the requirement that perception yield identification information, one case in which awareness of an object enters into the explanation of awareness of a fact is where the fact is about the object, perhaps among other things, and where one comes to know the fact by perceiving the object, perceiving it to have certain properties or stand in certain relations, and *identifying* it as the object it is. For example, I become aware that George has shaved his beard by seeing George, seeing that he is beardless, and identifying the man I see as George, the man I know to have previously been bearded. So the provision of identification information is an important part of the role played by awareness of objects in giving us awareness of facts. But in introspective self-knowledge there is no room for an identification of oneself, and no need for information on which to base such an identification (see Shoemaker, 1968 and 1986). There are indeed cases of genuine perceptual knowledge in which awareness of oneself provides identification information, as when noting the features of the man I see in the mirror or on the television monitor

5 A kind of perception, or what is often classified as such, that does not satisfy (1) or (3) is proprioception – our awareness of the position of our limbs, and the like. As emphasized in Section VIII, not everything that is classified as perception conforms to the object perception model.

tells me that he is myself. But there is no such role for awareness of one-self as an object to play in explaining my introspective knowledge that I am hungry, angry, or alarmed. This comes out in the fact that there is no possibility here of a *mis*identification; if I have my usual access to my hunger, there is no room for the thought "Someone is hungry all right, but is it me?"

Perhaps the most decisive point here is that where the use of "I" *does* involve an identification, the making of the identification will always presuppose the prior possession of other first-person information. Recall the episode in the Marx Brothers movie "Duck Soup" in which Grou-cho begins to suspect, correctly as it turns out, that instead of seeing himself in a mirror he is seeing, through an empty mirror frame, a double (Harpo, in fact) who is agilely aping his actions. Groucho goes through all sorts of antics in an attempt to fake out and expose the suspected double. Suppose, contrary to the film script, that it really was himself Groucho was seeing in the mirror, and that he became satisfied of this by seeing that the man in the mirror was performing the very same shenanigans that he himself was performing. Plainly, in order to identify the man in the mirror as himself in this way, Groucho had to know that *he himself* was performing those movements, i.e., had to know what he could express by saying "*I* am moving in the ways I see that man mov-ing." To avoid an infinite regress, we must allow that at some point Grou-cho had first-person knowledge that did not rest on an identification. In general, identification-based first-person knowledge must be grounded in first-person knowledge that is not identification-based; and the mak-ing of introspective judgments is one of the main cases in which this oc-curs.

It also seems apparent that the fact that our introspective access to our-selves lacks feature (2), i.e., does not involve an introspective sense-expe-rience of oneself, goes with the fact that this access lacks features (3) and (4). For it is one's sense experiences of a thing that, when veridical, pro-vide one with the identification information which, as just noted, helps make possible knowledge of facts about that thing.

At the beginning of this lecture I said that it is natural to suppose that we need something like vision to *explain* our introspective self-knowl-edge. But we now see that the knowledge one has of oneself requires an access to facts about oneself that does not conform to the object percep-tion model, in particular to the requirement having to do with the provi-sion of identification information. So, far from its being the case that in order to explain our self-knowledge we have to assume that we have a vision-like access to ourselves, it appears that in order to explain it we have to have an epistemological access to ourselves that in very fundamental ways is *not* like vision.

V

I turn now to the other candidates for being the nonfactual objects of introspective perception, namely the various sort of mental entities of which we have knowledge in introspection – sensations, feelings, thoughts, beliefs, desires, and so on. I begin with intentional states such as beliefs, desires, intentions, hopes, suspicions, etc.

I will start with a consideration reason that has only recently come to the fore. Condition (5) says that the information about objects we get in perception crucially involves their intrinsic, nonrelational properties. But intentional states are standardly individuated by their contents, and when one knows about one's intentional states introspectively what one knows is, standardly, just that one has a state of a certain kind with a certain intentional content, i.e., that one has a belief that so and so, a desire for such and such, or the like. And recent discussion of mental content seems to have established that a person's having a state with a certain content consists in part in "external" facts about the person's environment – in the person's standing, or having stood, in perceptual relations to external objects of certain kinds, in his belonging to a linguistic community in which certain practices exist, and so on. I have in mind the arguments of Hilary Putnam and Tyler Burge.[6] So having a state with a certain intentional content is not an intrinsic feature of a person, and having a certain content will not be an intrinsic feature of a belief or desire.[7] As Paul Boghossian puts the difficulty, "How could anyone be in a position to

---

6 See Putnam 1975 and 1981, and Burge 1979.

7 When I delivered these lectures at Brown, a member of the audience suggested that it is open to an externalist about content to hold that having a certain content can count as an intrinsic feature of a belief or desire. For instead of thinking of a belief as something internal to the person, and its content as constituted by its relations to other things, one could think of it as "reaching out into the world," and having as constituents whatever entities enter into the determination of content. I do not think that this version of externalism makes it more intelligible to suppose that we know the contents of our belief by "inner sense" – for how could inner sense reach out into the environment? I also think that the causal role of beliefs, their influence on behavior and other mental states, is better accounted for by taking them to be entities that are internal to the person, and whose content properties are relational, than by taking them to reach out into the world. But I think we should be wary of assuming that there must be a fact of the matter about which view is right.

know his thoughts merely by observing them, if facts about their content are determined by their relational properties" (Boghossian 1989, p. 11).

Further, it does not seem promising to suppose that for each belief or desire we can isolate something that is "inside the head," such that it is *by* being introspectively aware of that thing's intrinsic, nonintentional properties that one is aware of the belief or the desire. For example, it does not seem plausible to model one's introspective awareness of such intentional states on one's perceptual awareness of drawings, maps, and sentences, where one perceives something having representational content by perceiving its non-intentional feature – colors, shapes, etc. There simply are no promising candidates for the non-intentional features of beliefs, etc., that this would require.[8]

But there are other reasons for denying that beliefs and such can be the nonfactual objects of a kind of perception. I am aware that I believe that Boris Yeltsin is President of Russia. It seems clear that it would be utterly wrong to characterize this awareness by saying that at some point I became aware of an entity and identified it, that entity, as a belief that Boris Yeltsin holds that office. To say that would suggest that it ought to be possible for someone to become aware of a belief and misidentify it as something other than a belief, or as a belief with a content other than the one it has; or that it ought to be possible for someone to become aware of something that is not a belief, say a wish that Adlai Stevenson had been elected President of the United States, and misidentify it as a belief

---

8 It may seem that the claim that the content of mental states is fixed in part by states of affairs outside the head of the subject of the mental states poses a problem for *any* theory of introspective self-knowledge, and not only for those that invoke the inner sense model. If what makes it the case that my thoughts are about *water*, and not about the different stuff *twater* that abounds on Putnam's Twin Earth, is the fact that if it is water rather than twater that abounds in my environment, then how can I know that I am thinking about water without investigating my environment? The short answer to this is that the contents of mental states are fixed holistically, and that whatever fixes the content of the first-order belief I express by saying "There is water in the glass" also fixes in the same way the embedded content in the second-order belief I express by saying "I believe there is water in the glass" – assuming that "water" would be used by me univocally in those reports. Given that the first is about water rather than twater, the second will ascribe a belief about water rather than a belief about twater. So to explain how I can know what I believe without investigating my environment, all we need to suppose is that I am such that having a first-order belief with a certain content typically gives rise to a second-order belief that one has a belief with that content. In such an account the inner sense model has not so far been invoked, and so far there is no mystery. The mystery arises when we say that the first-order belief gives rise to the second-order belief by means of a process involving a perception of intrinsic, nonrelational features of the first-order belief – for we have no idea what such features could be.

that Boris Yeltsin is President of Russia on the basis of the intrinsic features one observes it to have. And while mistakes about one's propositional attitudes are no doubt possible, *these* kinds of mistakes seem clearly not to be. Closely related to this is the point that our access to our own beliefs does not issue in judgments involving anything that could be called demonstrative reference to beliefs – one is not aware of any "this" that one can go on to identify as a belief with a certain content.

There seem, then, to be good reasons for denying that introspective awareness of intentional states satisfies conditions (3) and (5) – i.e., denying that it is an awareness of facts mediated by awareness of nonfactual objects and their intrinsic features. It goes with this that it does not satisfy condition (4), that it is not a relation to objects that supplies identification information about them.

VI

Let us move to the case of sensations and sense experiences. I think that it is here that the perceptual model of introspective self knowledge has its greatest intuitive plausibility. In particular, it is here that we meet the mental entities that seem most "object-like," and it is here that it is most plausible to say that we are introspectively aware of mental facts *by* being aware of nonfactual entities that are constituents of those facts.

In part, at least, this is due to the intuitive attractiveness of something alluded to earlier, the "act-object conception" of sensations and sensory states. Accepting this conception amounts to taking the surface grammar of sensation statements at face value – which is no doubt one source of its intuitive attractiveness. So, for example, the statement "I see a red, round after-image" is construed as asserting a relation between the subject and a particular thing, an image, that is in some sense red and round, and the statement "I feel a sharp pain in the elbow" is construed as asserting a relation between the subject and a particular thing, a pain, that is in some sense sharp and in the elbow. After-images and pains are perhaps the mental entities that seem most robustly object-like. And if we take our ordinary talk about such entities at face value, our awareness of them clearly satisfies my condition (4). I am aware that my red after-image is to the right of my yellow one by being aware of these and seeing the relation between them. And I am aware that the pain in my foot is more intense than the pain in my elbow by being aware of these two pains and their intrinsic features. It also seems natural to suppose that one's introspective access to such entities puts one in a position to designate them demonstratively – that an apt expression of my knowledge of the two after-images is "That after-image is to the right of that one." It also seems that our introspective awareness of such entities satisfies conditions (3) and (5). The awareness provides identification information, which enables one to pick out such objects, discriminate them from one another, and track them over time. And it is natural to think of the properties by which one does this picking out, etc., as being, in the first instance, intrinsic features of the objects. It remains true that our awareness of such entities does not satisfy conditions (1) and (2). There is no organ of introspection. And we are not aware of such entities by having sense-experiences of them; we don't have sensations of our sensations. But if we have introspective awareness of such entities that satisfies conditions (3)–(5), that may seen enough to justify the use of an object-perception model of such awareness.

Traditional sense datum theory, and the theory of ideas of classical empiricism, applies the act-object conception more widely. Every case in which a person has any sort of sensory experience is construed as a case in which the person is presented with an object whose ontological status is thought of as being the same as that of after-images and pains, and of which the subject is supposed to have the same sort of awareness as we have, according to the act-object conception, of our after-images and pains. So, for example, when it looks to me as if there were an orange and a lemon on the table, the first to the right of the second, this is supposed to involve there *actually being* before my mind a round orange image and an oval yellow one, the first of which I see to be to the right of the second.

Sense-datum theory has been out of favor for thirty or forty years, for reasons I cannot undertake to rehearse here. But I think that it is not sufficiently appreciated that the reasons for rejecting the sense-datum theory are at the same time reasons for rejecting the act-object conception as applied to pains and after-images. Conversely, if one does continue to accept the act-object conception for pains and after-images, one ought in consistency to be a sense-datum theorist across the board. The traditional "argument from illusion" is surely right to this extent: if one thinks that in a case where one is "appeared to redly" and there is no red physical object in front of one, one must be seeing a purely mental object that is red, then one ought to think that in a case where one is "appeared to redly" and there *is* a red physical object in front of one, one must be seeing a purely mental object that is red. The account of what is involved in being appeared to redly, i.e., having the sort of experience that constitutes its looking to one as if one were seeing something red, should be the same for the case in which the experience is veridical as for the case in which it is illusory. Consider the case of double vision. It is natural to say that when my finger is near my nose I see two finger-shaped and finger-colored images. Suppose we take this literally, and hold that in such cases I am perceiving two mental entities, call them images, having the properties in question. What happens when I move my finger away, or focus my eyes, so that, as one might say, the two images coalesce into one? Surely it is intolerable to say that in this case two *mental images* coalesced into one *flesh and blood finger. If* we say that when seeing double I saw two fingershaped mental images, then we had better say that what these coalesced into is one finger-shaped mental image, and that, as the sense-datum theory says, veridically perceiving a physical thing always involves "immediately" perceiving a mental image. And if we find the latter view unacceptable, as most recent philosophers do, then one should resist the temptation, which I think is considerable, to reify double images. And I think we should also resist the temptation, which is almost irresistible, to reify after-images. In other words, we should reject the act-object conception as applied to these.

A classic statement of the rejection of the act-object conception as applied to after-images was J. J. C. Smart's claim, in "Sensations and Brain Processes," that "There is, in a sense, no such thing as an after-image, or sense-datum, though there is such a thing as the experience of having an image" (Smart 1962). One way of playing this out is by saying that the act-object conception depends on taking the *intentional* object of a sensory state to be an actually existing object. So, e.g., my statement that I have an experience of an orange, round object, which is true if interpreted as meaning that I have an experience that represents there being an orange, round object, is misconstrued as asserting that I have an experience that puts me into a relation to an object that is actually orange and round. Thus David Armstrong says that "To have an after-image is to seem to see a physical phenomenon of a certain sort: the after-image itself, I maintain, is a purely intentional object, like the thing believed in the case of a false belief" (Armstrong 1984). That Armstrong says this in a section headed "In Defense of Inner Sense" is evidence that *his* version of the inner sense model is not the object-perception version.

At the beginning of this lecture I invited you to focus on a current sensation or after-image of yours and consider whether it seems natural to you to regard your access to it as similar to the perceptual access you have to objects in your environment. This does seem natural to me, and I suspect that it seemed natural to you. If I am right, this may be because you share with me the deplorable tendency to think in terms of the act-object conception – and of course I framed my invitation in terms that might be said to presuppose that conception.

But there is another possible reason for this response. Having a red after-image *is* like seeing something red. That is, the experience of having a red after-image is phenomenally like (*somewhat* like) the experience one has when one sees something red in one's environment. Likewise, the experience of having a pain in one's foot is somewhat like the experience one has when one perceives, tactually, that one has a stone in one's shoe, or a cut in one's foot.[9] To a much lesser extent, having a visual image ("seeing in the mind's eye") is phenomenally like the experience one would have if one were actually seeing the thing imaged. And, at the opposite extreme, having a completely realistic hallucination is phenomenally very like, perhaps exactly like, the experience one would have if one were actually seeing a situation of the sort hallucinated. It is of course one thing to say that there is a similarity between certain mental states (imagings, etc.) and the experiences involved in veridical sense-perception, and quite another to say that there is a similarity between our access to those mental states and our access to the objects we perceive in cases of veridical sense-perception. But it is all too easy to make an unnoticed slide from the one similarity claim to the other.[10]

If, as my recent discussion suggests, <u>what we are aware of in being</u>

---

9 There are those, indeed, who hold that pains are simply sense perceptions of certain bodily conditions, so that in having a pain one normally is perceiving something (although not a pain). See Armstrong 1968 and Pitcher 1970.

10 This will be especially easy if one construes the first similarity as amounting to there being a similarity between something presented to one in the having of the mental state – say an image – and the object of the veridical perceiving. If indeed one thinks that having an orange image involves being presented with something like what one sees when one sees an orange on the table, it will be natural to think that one's access to that something must somehow be like one's perceptual access to the orange one sees on the table. This yields a version of the view, which seems to me incoherent, that conceives of imaging and the like in terms of the act-object conception (requiring that these have actual objects, and not merely intentional objects) but refuses to give an act-object account of veridical experience, and so rejects sense-data. It may be objected that this view does give an act-object conception of veridical experience – the external thing that is veridically perceived can serve as the object. But the objects posited by the act-object conception are supposed to be constitutive of, and internal to, experiences (or imagings, or whatever) in a way an external object cannot be. In any case, it is apparent that while there is a straightforward sense in which one sensory or experiential state can be phenomenally similar to another, there is none in which a sensory or experiential state can be phenomenally similar to, say, an orange on a table.

aware of sensory states are their intentional objects, or intentional contents, then the first of my reasons for rejecting the application of the object-perception model to the case of awareness of beliefs is also a reason for rejecting its application to the case of awareness of sensory states. It would seem that the intentional content of sensory states, like that of beliefs and other intentional states, is determined in part by factors "outside the head" of the subject of such states. So what we are aware of in being aware of such states will not be "intrinsic" features of them, and this awareness will not satisfy condition (5) of the stereotype underlying the object-perception model.

But this raises a major issue. There are philosophers who hold that the only features of sensory states of which we are introspectively aware are intentional or representational ones (see Harman 1990). It would simplify my case against the object-perception model if I could accept this. But I am a champion of "qualia," features of sensations or other sensory phenomena that give them their qualitative or phenomenal character, or determine "what it is like" to have them; and on the face of it these are not intentional properties, although they do in some way ground the intentional properties of perceptual experiences. The usual way of thinking about our awareness of qualia can easily seem to imply a perceptual model. I will return to this in my third lecture, where I will discuss the status of the "phenomenal character" of experience and our knowledge of it.

VII

Qualia aside, there remains one consideration that makes it more natural to think of our awareness of sensory states in perceptual terms than it is to think of our awareness of beliefs, desires, etc., in such terms. That is the role of *attention* in the two domains. It would seem that one can shift one's attention from one sensation to another, or from one sensory experience to another, in the same way one can shift one's attention from one object of perception to another. But the notion of attention is not really at home in the domain of the nonsensory intentional states such as belief. If it means anything to speak of my attending to my belief that Boris Yeltsin is President of Russia, it means either to think about the proposition and presumed fact that is the content of my belief, i.e., to think about Boris Yeltsin's being President of Russia, or to think about the fact that I have that belief. So all that answers to talk of shifting one's attention from one belief to another is shifting from thinking of one thing to thinking of another thing. It seems different in the case of sensations. Just as I put myself in a better position to get information about a perceived object by attending to it. I seem to put myself in a better position to get information about a pain by attending to it.[11] Thus our introspective access to sensory states, unlike that to intentional states, seems to satisfy condition (6).

But I think that there is less to this than there seems. If we put aside for a moment the case of bodily sensations, and put aside the rather special case of afterimaging, it becomes doubtful whether anything answers to talk of attending to sensory experiences, as opposed to attending to the objects of those experiences. Here is a little experiment to conduct. Raise both of your hands before you, about a foot apart and a foot in front of your face. Now perform the following two attention shifts. First, shift your attention from one hand to the other. Second, shift your attention from your *visual experience* of the one hand to your *visual experience* of the other. Do you do anything different in the second case than in the first? Perhaps you are more likely in the first case than in the second to change the *focus* of your vision – to fixate first on one hand and then on the other. But since we are talking about shift of attention, not shift of focus, we should make it part of the instructions that throughout the experiment your focus is on some point midway between the two hands. That may make the instructions hard to follow. But I suspect that insofar as one does anything different in performing the second attention shift than in performing the first, it will consist in your first *thinking about* your experience of the one hand and then *thinking about* your experience of the other. In other words, it will be like what happens in a "shift of attention" from one belief to another.

The case of after-images is trickier. If I simultaneously see two after-images, I can shift my attention from one to the other. It doesn't seem right to say that this is merely a matter of shifting from thinking about the one to thinking about the other. And, so one might suppose, it also cannot be just a matter of shifting one's attention from one *external* object of perception to another, i.e., from one object of *vision* (as opposed

11 Paul Boghossian cites as a reason for rejecting the view that self-knowledge is "cognitively insubstantial," which he seems to see as the only alternative to the observational model of self-knowledge, that "self-knowledge can be directed: one can decide how much attention to direct to one's thoughts or images, just as one can decide how much attention to pay to objects in one's visual field" (Boghossian 1989, p. 19), and cites D.M. Mellor as having made the same point. Notice that Boghossian does not restrict this to the case of sensations and the like, where I have said that it seems most plausible.

to introspection) to another, since here, unlike the case of the hands, there are no external objects. Or take the case of double vision – if I hold up one finger which I "see double," I can apparently shift my attention from the finger image on the right to the one on the left, and this won't be shifting my attention from one finger to another, since there is only one finger being seen. Notice, however, that to get objects of introspective attention I have slipped back into the act-object conception, and acquiesced in the reification of images. The attendings here were not attendings to experiencings. And if we reject the act-object conception, why shouldn't we say that the attendings are, not to existent objects of "inner sense," but to nonexistent *intentional* objects of outer sense? In the after-image case both of these objects are nonexistent, and in the double vision case at lease one of them is. Where, as in the two hands case, things are as they appear, we can say that the intentional objects actually exist – and then attending to these is just attending to actual objects of vision. Nowhere in this, I think, do we find an attending to mental entities that is a distinctively perceptual attending – i.e., that is over and above the thinking about which we can have in the case of purely intentional mental states such as belief.

Similar remarks apply in to the case of bodily sensations, such as pains. If, as some have suggested, these should be thought of sense-experiences of bodily conditions, the attendings to these can be thought of as proprioceptive attendings to their intentional objects, which may or may not exist, and not as introspective attendings to mental entities. If, as others have suggested, pains are themselves bodily conditions that are nonmental, then perceptual attending to pains does not require *inner* sense. And the attending to sensations that cannot be handled in either of these ways can be held to consist simply in thinking about, and so not to be perceptual at all.

I have suggested that what advocates of the object-perception model take to be attending to mental objects is really attending to the possibly nonexistent intentional objects of perceptual states. I think it is likewise true that what passes for demonstrative reference to mental states is typically demonstrative reference – or rather ostensible demonstrative reference – to intentional objects of mental states. When Macbeth asks "Is this a dagger which I see before me?", the ostensible reference is to something seen, not something introspected – and the actual reference is to nothing. Demonstratives can be used in this way even when one knows that the experience is illusory or hallucinatory. It is, in such cases, *as if* one were referring demonstratively to perceived objects, but in fact one is referring demonstratively to nothing.

VIII

I have been arguing that introspective awareness does not conform to the object-perception model. But why does it matter whether it does?

One reason for this should be already apparent. To the extent that this model incorporates the act-object conception of sensation and sensory states, it populates the realm of the mental with what many, myself included, regard as philosophically objectionable entities – sense-data, reified images, etc. Among other things, these *entia non grata* – to use Quine's phrase – are difficult if not impossible to incorporate into a naturalist account of the mind.

But there is another way in which how one thinks of the nature of mental phenomena can be influenced by whether one accepts the object-perception model. For acceptance of this model encourages one to think of mental concepts, or at least those that can be self-ascribed introspectively, as analogous to such observational concepts as those of particular colors, i.e., those that have traditionally been regarded as simple and undefinable. This seems incompatible with any view according to which it is constitutive of mental concepts that the states, events, etc. they are of occupy certain causal or functional roles, i.e., are causally or counterfactually related in certain ways to other mental states and to behavior. For we have been "taught by Hume" (I do not say that we have been *correctly* taught this) that any report that carries causal implications goes beyond what we can, strictly speaking, perceive to be the case.

Suppose that it were true that all introspective reports were grounded on observations of "intrinsic" features of mental entities, where in the first instance these features are conceived under "simple" observational concepts. There would then be at least some mental concepts, namely these simple observational ones, that are not functionally definable. Further, the judgment that the states introspectably observed in fact occupy certain causal or functional roles, and so fall under functionally defined mental concepts, would be inferential judgments. And it is not easy to see what the basis of the inference could be, especially if these judgments are to have the kind of authority that introspective judgments about many kinds of mental states appear to have. How is one supposed to know, and know with a high degree of certainty, that when one is in a certain introspectively observable state one is in a state that plays a highly complex causal role or has a number of causal and counterfactual features? At best it seems that one could know this only after having made an extensive investigation, in which one correlates what one knows by direct introspective observation with causal information gotten in other ways. But it seems clear that the authoritative introspective self-ascription of the various sorts of sensory and intentional states does not have to be preceded by such an investigation. The natural conclusion is that if the self-ascription of such mental states is grounded on inner sense, à la the object-perception model, then the concepts of those mental states cannot be causal or functional concepts. By the same token, if one thinks that these concepts *are* causal or functional concepts, one has a reason for denying that the self-ascription of mental states under these concepts is grounded on inner sense, à la the object-perception model, and has a reason for welcoming independent reasons for opposing that model.[12]

Of course, saying that self-ascription of functionally defined mental states is not grounded on object-perception does not explain how it *is* grounded. How *can* we make, noninferentially, judgments that have complex causal implications? Here is a sketch of an answer. Our minds are so constituted, or our brains are so wired, that, for a wide range of mental states, one's being in a certain mental state produces in one, under certain conditions, the belief that one is in that mental state. This is what our introspective access to our own mental states consists in. The "certain conditions" may include one's considering whether one is in that mental state, and will certainly include what is a precondition of this, namely that one has the concept of oneself and the concept of the mental state. The beliefs thus produced will count as knowledge, not because of the quantity or quality of the evidence on which they are based (for they are based on no evidence), but because of the reliability of the mechanism by which they are produced. And now we add that the concepts under which these states are conceived in these beliefs are causal or functional ones.

The account just sketched is very close to what I believe. But it also close to what has been maintained by philosophers – here I particularly have in mind David Armstrong – who are enthusiastic supporters of the idea that introspection is a kind of perception. Certainly the view sketched does not involve the object-perception model that I have been criticizing. But it is important to see that much of what we call perception does not conform to that model. The sense of smell, for example, does not ordinarily put one in an epistemic relation to particular objects

12 See Goldman 1993 and Shoemaker 1993b. In the latter, I suggest that Goldman's criticism of functionalism assumes a perceptual model of self-knowledge; Goldman indicates in his "Author's Response" that he is not persuaded that this is so.

about which it gives identification information. Smelling a skunk does not put one in a position to make demonstrative reference to a particular skunk, and there is no good sense in which it is *by* smelling a particular skunk that one gets the information that there is, or has been, a skunk around (for one thing, nothing in what one smells tells one that one skunk rather than several is responsible for the smell). Even in the case of normal human vision, my conditions (3)–(6), those that are distinctive of the object perception model, do not always hold. I may see motion in the periphery of my field of vision without perceiving any of the intrinsic features of the moving object, and without gaining any "identification information" about it. Moreover, in applying the notion of perception to animals of other species we seem willing to count as perception a means of obtaining information about the environment that is not keyed to particular items in the environment – e.g., a detector in fish that is sensitive to the oxygen level in the water, or the ability to sense that there are predators of some sort about.[13]

So there is room for a conception of perception that does not incorporate the object-perception model, and allows for perception of facts that is not based on perception of objects. It is this I have called the "broad perceptual model," and it is the conformance of introspective self-knowledge to this that I take David Armstrong to be maintaining in his defense of "inner sense." Its central features are items (7) and (8) on my list – the causal condition and the independence condition. The view that introspection conforms to these, and so is in that minimal sense analogous to sense-perception, can seem a truism. But my next lecture will be devoted to arguing that this view is mistaken, largely because introspectable mental states and our awarenesses of them are not independent in the way they would have to be if this view were correct.

13 Some of these points were forcibly presented to me by Daniel Dennett and Ulrich Neisser when I read a precursor of this lecture at a conference at Emory University in October of 1991.

11

Self-knowledge and "inner sense"
Lecture II: The broad perceptual model

I

Let me begin by presenting two opposed conceptions of the relationship between the realm of the mental and our knowledge of this realm, neither of which is the conception I shall be supporting.

One I will call, with no pretension to scholarly accuracy, the Cartesian conception. According to this, the mind is transparent to itself. It is of the essence of mental entities, of whatever kind, to be conscious, where a mental entity's being conscious involves its revealing its existence and nature to its possessor in an immediate way. This conception involves a strong form of the doctrine that mental entities are "self-intimating," and usually goes with a strong form of the view that judgments about one's own mental states are incorrigible or infallible, expressing a super-certain kind of knowledge which is suited for being the epistemological foundation for the rest of what we know.

The other is the view that the existence of mental entities and mental facts is, logically speaking, as independent of our knowing about them introspectively, and of there being whatever means or mechanisms enable us to know about them introspectively, as the existence of physical entities and physical facts is of our knowing about them perceptually, or of there being the means or mechanisms that enable us to have perceptual knowledge of them. This is the view that implies that our introspective self-knowledge should be construed in terms of what in my first lecture I called the broad perceptual model. The core of the stereotype of perception underlying that model consisted of two conditions, one of them (call it the *causal condition*) saying that our beliefs about our mental states are caused by those mental states, via a reliable belief-producing mechanism, thereby qualifying as knowledge of those states and events, and the other (call it the *independence condition*) saying that the existence of these states and events is independent of their being known in this way, and even of there existing the mechanisms that make such knowledge possible.

I do not hold either of the two views I have sketched. My aim is to develop a view that rejects the second, and so rejects the claim that introspection conforms to the broad perceptual model, without falling back into the first. The view I support holds that there is a conceptual, constitutive connection between the existence of certain sorts of mental entities and their introspective accessibility, while denying the transparency of the mental. It is a version of the view that certain mental facts are "self-intimating" or "self-presenting," but a much weaker version than the transparency thesis.

Although I am equally opposed to Cartesianism and the broad perceptual model, it is only the latter that I shall be arguing against here. This is because it is only the latter that nowadays commands widespread support. But some of the reasons for rejecting Cartesianism may seem to count equally against the weak version of the self-intimation thesis that I am supporting, and in favor of the independence thesis.

Even before Freud it was well known to novelists and ordinary folk, if not to philosophers, that there is such a thing as self-deception about one's motives and attitudes. And recent work in psychology has revealed that in certain circumstances people are systematically wrong in the claims they make about their reasons for actions, and that such claims are sometimes the result of "confabulation" (see Nisbett and Wilson 1977). Of a different sort, but equally damaging to the Cartesian conception, are various phenomena that have been observed in people who have suffered brain damage. One of the most striking is "blindsight." Here a person will emphatically deny that she can see anything in some portion of her visual field; yet when she is forced to make "guesses" about what is there, the ratio of correct to incorrect guesses will be much better than change. Finally, there are philosophical considerations of the sort that figure in David Armstrong's "distinct existences argument" – the argument that introspective beliefs, or introspective awarenesses, must be thought of as causal effects of the mental states that are objects of awareness, that causes and effects must be "distinct existences," and that distinct existences, as Hume taught us, can be only contingently connected (see Armstrong 1963, 1968).

None of this implies, of course, that there are not plenty of circumstances in which people do have reliable introspective access to what is going on in their minds, or that it is not often the case that one can make introspective claims with a high degree of certainty. But what it all suggests is that to the extent that we do have reliable introspective access to mental states and processes, this is a conceptually contingent fact about us. In blindsight the person is blind to facts about his own mental condition of which he would be aware if he were normal. What the considerations I have mentioned suggest is that it is at least conceptually possible that such blindness should be much more widespread – that there could be people who are blind to a wide variety of the mental facts to which normal people have introspective access. Of course, it will generally be agreed that introspective self-knowledge serves many useful purposes, and that creatures that are introspectively blind, or, as I shall say "self-blind," with respect to some kind of mental phenomena would tend to lose out, in the struggle for survival, to otherwise similar creatures who are not. So from an evolutionary standpoint, widespread self-blindness is not a real possibility. But it will be held that for each kind of mental fact to which we have introspective access, it is at least logically possible that there should be creatures in which such facts obtain, and who have the ability to conceive of them, but who are self-blind with respect to them. This I take to be a consequence of the independence condition that is built into the broad perceptual model of self-knowledge.

I should make it clear how I am understanding the notion of introspective self-blindness. To be self-blind with respect to a certain kind of mental fact or phenomenon, a creature must have the ability to conceive of those facts and phenomena (just as the person who is literally blind will be able to conceive of those states of affairs she is unable to learn about visually). So lower animals who are precluded by their conceptual poverty from having first-person access do not count as self-blind. And it is only introspective access to those phenomena that the creature is supposed to lack; it is not precluded that she should learn of them in the way others might learn of them, i.e., by observing her own behavior, or by discovering facts about her own neurophysiological states.

II

Judging from the frequency of its occurrence in philosophical examples, pain is the favorite mental state of philosophers. I think that there are in fact many ways in which pain is an atypical and misleading example of a mental state. But, following tradition, I shall start with it. Is self-blindness possible in the case of pain? Here, perhaps more than in any other case, intuition supports the answer I favor, namely "no." But the distinct existences argument, and the other considerations I have mentioned, may suggest that this intuition should not be trusted.

Examples abound of cases in which, allegedly, a person is in pain without being aware of the pain: the wounded soldier who in the heat of battle is oblivious to his pain, the injured athlete who doesn't notice his pain until he is put on the bench, and so on. These may seem to support the possibility of self-blindness with respect to pain; if there are cases in which there is pain but no introspective awareness of pain, why shouldn't there be creatures in which pain is never accompanied, and cannot be accompanied, by introspective awareness of it? But we should be wary of inferences from what can happen occasionally to what can happen as a matter of course: it may be true in Lake Wobegon that all of the children are above average, but it can't be true everywhere.

So let us try to imagine creatures who have intellectual, conceptual, etc. capacities comparable with ours, and who also have pain, but who are introspectively blind to their pains. Their only access to their pains is a third-person access – i.e., observing their own behavior, or their own inner physiology.

It must not be supposed that these creatures do not *feel* their pains. Pain is a feeling, and what they are self-blind to are, precisely, their feelings of pain. And surely it must not be supposed that their pains are not unpleasant. But can they be unpleasant to these creatures, who have no introspective awareness of them? Well, let's try to suppose that when a pain is occurring in one of these creatures, the creature actively dislikes it and wishes that it would end. It is just that the creature is unaware of this active disliking and wishing. Does the disliking and wishing have any of its normal consequences? Let's try to suppose that it does. When in pain the creature heads for the medicine cabinet, or calls the doctor's office for an appointment. But what does the creature itself make of this behavior? It now appears that its self-blindness has expanded to cover much more than just its pain – it must be blind to its finding the pain unpleasant, to its wishing that it would end, and to the reasons for its behavior. To such a creature it should seem as if someone else had taken possession of its body. And, indeed, if we saw someone engaging in normal pain behavior, including visits to the medicine cabinet and calls to the doctor, all of this interspersed with wonderings out loud about what this behavior is all about, one possibility we might consider is that there are two persons, or two "selves," or "personalities," inhabiting one and the same body – one of which is in pain, aware of the pain, and acting accordingly, and the other of which is a prisoner in the body and a passive observer of what is going on. That would be a *very* strange state of affairs indeed, but it would not be self-blindness – for what the passive observer is "blind" to would not be his or her own pain, but that of the other inhabitant of the body.

One thing that seems clear is that at least some kinds of "pain behavior" – taking aspirin and calling the doctor are good examples – are intelligible *as* pain behavior only on the assumption that the subject is aware of pain; for to see them as pain behavior *is* to see them as motivated by such states of the creature as the belief that it is in pain, the desire to be rid of the pain, and the belief that such and such a course of behavior will achieve that result. Indeed, to say that a creature wants to be rid of pain presupposes that it believes that it is in pain. One can want not to have something while being agnostic about whether one has it; but one can't want to be rid of something, to *cease* having it, without believing that one currently does have it.

So it seems that we cannot suppose that our self-blind creature has a desire to be rid of its pain, or engages in the kinds of pain-behavior that would be motivated by such a desire. Can we nevertheless suppose that it finds its pain unpleasant? Can it *find* the pain unpleasant, if it is in no way aware of the pain?

Perhaps it will be said: it isn't that the creature *finds* the pain unpleasant; it is just that it *is* unpleasant. It has an intrinsic phenomenal character that constitutes its being unpleasant, and so makes it such that anyone who was introspectively aware of it would find it unpleasant. One feature of this view is that it makes the connection between a state's being unpleasant and its subject's wanting to be rid of it a purely contingent connection. This suggests some apparently alarming possibilities. Maybe all of what we take to be innocent pastimes produce in us states that are extremely unpleasant, but of which we are totally unaware. Wouldn't that be terrible? Well, maybe not. Maybe this is a case of what you don't know can't hurt you. And likewise with our self-blind man: he is in extreme pain, his pains are extremely unpleasant, but there is nothing bad about this because he is unaware of his pains and, in this sort of case anyhow, what you don't know can't hurt you. His pains hurt, but they don't hurt *him*. But this of course is nonsense.

We have seen that if you take away the link with introspective beliefs from the total causal role of pain, you take away a lot else – namely the role of pain in explaining the behavior we take as indicating distress and the desire to feel better. But you don't take away everything. Part of the causal role of pain consists in its being caused by certain kinds of things –

bodily damage of various sorts – and its causing behaviors, such as winces, grimaces, and moans, that can be involuntary and do not have to be seen as motivated or "rationalized" by beliefs and desires. Certainly a state could play this role without its subject having introspective awareness of it. And such a state would be, if not bad in and of itself, at least indicative of something bad, namely bodily damage. This it would share with pain. But it seems obvious that a state that played this causal role, but did not play any more of the standard causal role of pain than this, would not be pain. Indeed, it would not be a mental state at all.

III

So self-blindness with respect to pain seems to be an impossibility. What goes for pain would seem to go as well for itches, tingles, and the like. And it would also seem to go for such phenomena as having a ringing in one's ears. Many people are plagued by ringing in the ears. It would sound more than a little ludicrous to suggest that countless others have the same condition but, mercifully, are totally unaware of it, being self-blind with respect to that particular mental phenomenon.[1]

I now want to turn our attention to the sorts of experiences that occur in normal perception, and consider whether one could be self-blind with respect to these. Having such an experience will be a matter of things appearing (looking, sounding, feeling, etc.) certain ways, or of one's being "appeared to" in certain ways. We will suppose that our putatively self-blind person has normal perceptual access to things in her environment, and to the fact that she is perceiving these things in this or that sense-modality, and that she has normal access to her beliefs (the question of whether there can be self-blindness with respect to beliefs will be addressed latter). She makes judgments like "I see a tree," "I taste something salty," and "I feel something with silky texture." So she is not self-blind with respect to her seeing, tasting, etc. But she is, we are to try to suppose, self-blind with respect to the perceptual experiences involved in these kinds of perception.

Someone with normal perceptual access to things in the environment must at least be sensitive to the nature of her perceptual experiences, in the following sense: the perceptual judgments she makes about things in

---

1 I am not talking about the possibility, which I do not deny, that some people have it but do not notice it. What would constitute self-blindness is not not-noticing but the impossibility of noticing.

the environment must be a function of the nature of her perceptual experiences, of how she is "appeared to," together with her beliefs, in particular her beliefs about perceptual conditions. This is not to say that her perceptual judgments are *inferred* from the nature of the perceptual experiences. If they were, there would have to be knowledge of the perceptual experiences, and self-blindness with respect to them would be ruled out from the start. But normally the perceptual judgments are not inferred. Normally it is the having of the experience, not the belief that one has it, that issues in the perceptual judgment. Normally, too, the beliefs about perceptual conditions that contribute to the judgment are only tacit, except where there are indications that the perceptual conditions are not normal. Still, the person must be sensitive to a vast number of combinations of experiences and beliefs about perceptual conditions. If she has an experience "as of" red and believes that conditions are normal, she will judge that the wall is red; if she has that same experience and believes that the wall is being illuminated by red light, she may judge that it is white; and so on. The question is whether the person could have the appropriate sensitivity to combinations of experiences and beliefs without having the capacity to be aware of the experiences.

I think that if we are out to conceive of a case of self-blindness with respect to perceptual experiences, the best we can do is to suppose that our putative self-blind person is "hard-wired" to respond to various experience-belief combinations by making the appropriate perceptual judgments. Such a person would in many cases be in a position to infer that she was having a certain kind of experience. Knowing what perceptual judgment she had made, and knowing what her belief about perceptual conditions is, she infers what her perceptual experience must be. So, for example, noting that she has judged that the wall is white, and noting also that she believes that the wall is being illuminated by red light, she infers that she must be having an experience as of something red. If the making of such inferences were automatic, she might seem like a normal person, making the right judgments about how things appear to her in a wide variety of circumstances. But she would give away her self-blindness by her inability to say what her visual experience is like if she is deprived of information about perceptual conditions. We rig things so that she cannot see whether perceptual conditions are normal, and tell her that we have done this, and then ask her about the color of the wall. Like a normal person, she is unwilling to make any judgment about what color the wall is. But unlike a normal person, she is unable to make any judgment about what color the wall *appears* to her.

I do not deny that this case is possible, but I do deny that it should count as a case of self-blindness – for I deny that the person, as described, has perceptual experiences in the sense we do. By hypothesis, she has states that play *some* of the functional role of perceptual experiences. In combination with certain beliefs about perceptual conditions, these states give rise to the same perceptual judgments about the world that certain of our perceptual experiences give rise to when combined with those same beliefs. But their role is not rich enough to give the subject normal perceptual access to the environment. And it is not rich enough to make them perceptual experiences of the sort to which we have introspective access.

I have been speaking as if beliefs about perceptual conditions were simply given to us. But such beliefs are themselves often grounded on our perceptual experiences. Sometimes, thrown into an unfamiliar setting, we simultaneously reason to conclusions about what sorts of things we are perceiving and to conclusions about what the perceptual conditions are. And the beliefs that influence our judgments are not limited to beliefs about perceptual conditions. Any of one's beliefs about how perceptible things behave under various conditions, about how the appearance of things of certain kinds should change as one changes one's situation with respect to them, and so on, can play a role in determining one's perceptual judgments about how things are in one's vicinity. Think, for example, of how one might move from a belief that one is perceiving some ordinary objects to the belief that one must be the victim of some hologram-produced or drug-produced illusion – or how one might move from a suspicion that the latter is true to a firm belief that things are after all as they appear. In such cases one is engaged in a certain kind of low level theorizing. And the data for the theorizing include facts about how one is appeared to, i.e., about the nature of one's experiences. So while often perceptual judgments are not inferred from facts about experiences, often they are. And having normal perceptual access to things in one's environment requires having the capacity to engage in this sort of theorizing, and therefore requires having access to the facts about current experience that provide the data for it.

We tried to suppose that our putatively self-blind person was "hard-wired" to respond appropriately to experience-belief combinations, in a way that did not involve having introspective access to the experiences. But it is not credible that the low grade theorizing I have just been talking about, in which an interplay between one's current perceptual experiences and one's entire body of background beliefs gives rise to perceptual judgments about the world, could be the product of *such* hard-wiring. Perhaps one could say, stretching the notion, that we are "hard-wired" to respond rationally to facts about our experience in the light of our background beliefs; but if so, that has to mean that we are hard-wired to have introspective access to those facts about our experience.

Suppose that neurosurgeons set to work on someone who is blind in the ordinary sense, i.e., totally unable to see, and manage to get her into the state I imagined the putatively self-blind person to be in. They wire her brain and optical system in such a way that certain external situations produce certain internal states, and by an astounding breakthrough, they wire her brain in such a way that these internal states together with certain beliefs about perceptual conditions give rise to perceptual judgments about her environment – judgements that are normally true when her beliefs about perceptual conditions are true. But when she has no relevant beliefs about perceptual conditions, she is totally unable to say which of these states she is in, and at other times she can do so only be *inferring* what state she is in from what perceptual judgment she is making and from what she believes about what perceptual conditions she is in. If thrown into a situation in which the sort of low grade theorizing discussed above is called for if one is to know what the perceptual conditions are, she is as helpless as she was before the scientists got to work on her. My question is, would it be reasonable to suppose that the scientists had bestowed on her visual experiences that are phenomenally just like those we have, but to which she lacks introspective access? And it seems to me that the answer is: obviously, no.[2]

---

2 After this was written it occurred to me that what the argument of this section implicitly invokes is the application of something like Stephen Stich's notion of inferential promiscuity (see Stich 1978) to perceptual experiences. It would be wrong to say that perceptual experiences are inferentially promiscuous *vis a vis* their actual contents. For it is by no means the case that contents of perceptual experiences are invariably believed by the subject, and contents that are not believed will not be available as premises of inferences. What is inferentially promiscuous is not the putative information that is the content of the experience (e.g., that there is a red wall in front of one), but the information that one has an experience with this content. It is the availability to one's system of this information that determines, in conjunction with one's background beliefs, whether one believes the content of the experience and, if one doesn't, what if anything one believes instead. And this information is inferentially promiscuous in the sense that it will combine with *any* relevant beliefs that one has. Of course, to speak of it as *inferentially* promiscuous is already to imply that the information is believed – only information that is believed can figure as a premise in inferences issuing in new beliefs. My claim is that it is of the essence of having perceptual experiences that the system behaves *as if* such information is believed, and that this is sufficient for its *being* believed. This is not to imply that over and above the perceptual experience there is a separate state that is the belief

IV

I want now to consider the possibility of self-blindness with respect to another aspect of our mental lives, namely the exercise of our wills. We have an introspective access, or at any rate a distinctive first-person access, to what we are doing or trying to do, and to the intentions with which we are doing or trying to do whatever it is. To what extent could we lack this?

If self-blindness is possible with respect to a given mental phenomenon, one would think that there should be something that would show, or at any rate provide good evidence, that someone was afflicted with such self-blindness, and that this should include that person denying, with apparent sincerity, that she was aware of the phenomenon in question in herself. There is an obvious difficulty in the supposition that someone might show in this way that she is self-blind with respect to *all* exercises of her will, i.e., with respect to the mental side of all of her voluntary actions. For either the behavior that seems to constitute her telling us that this is so is really an action on her part, or it is not. If it is not, it cannot be the required sort of evidence that she is self-blind. But if it is, then she is telling us that she is self-blind with respect to the very activity she is engaged in, which means that for all she knows "from the inside," and perhaps for all she knows *simpliciter*, this may not be an action on her part at all. And it hardly seems coherent to suppose that there could be a sincere assertion that says *of itself* that for all the speaker knows it is not an assertion of hers. "I am not saying this" seems to be a pragmatic contradiction on a par with "I do not exist"; and "For all I know I am not saying this" seems on a par with "For all I know, I do not exist."

To finesse this difficulty, let the suggestion be, not that someone could be self-blind with respect to *all* exercises of her will, but that someone could be self-blind with respect to some large class of such exercises – say all of those involved in actions other than certain speech acts. So a putative case of self-blindness will be one in which we observe what looks like someone engaged in some kind of action, and hear coming from the person's mouth statements to the effect that she has no introspective awareness of what she is doing, and that she can only gather this, as we do, by observing what she does.

that one has a perceptual experience with such and such content; it may be that the perceptual experience doubles as a belief about itself (just as, I suggest later, a first-order belief can double as a second-order belief to the effect that one has that first-order belief).

But the coherence of the case is still in doubt. As I have defined it, self-blindness is not supposed to involve any cognitive deficiency. Nor is our person supposed to be deprived of information about the environment relevant to the execution of her action plans. So our self-blind person ought to be capable of having and carrying out action plans as complex as those within the repertoire of an ordinary person. But many action plans involve combinations of verbal and nonverbal behaviors, all aimed at the same goal. In such a case, if the agent is self-blind with respect to the total execution of the action plan, she will have to be self-blind with respect to the verbal behaviors it involves. So what we apparently have to imagine is that we have someone engaged in what looks like the execution of a rational action plan, with verbal behavior integrated with the nonverbal behavior, and that the only thing out of the ordinary is that the utterances that are integrated with the rest of the behavior are interspersed with ones that profess introspective ignorance of what is going on.

No doubt it is conceivable that we should observe such a thing. But it does not seem that if we did we should conclude that we had come across a case of self-blindness. Various alternative possibilities suggest themselves. One is similar to one that came up earlier in our discussion of pain. Maybe the body in question houses two persons, or two "selves" or "personalities," one of which controls all of its nonverbal behavior and *some* of its verbal behavior, and the other of which controls that part of the verbal behavior that consists in professions of introspective ignorance of what is going on. In that case, of course, the blindness is not *self*-blindness, and not *introspective* blindness; it is a matter of one of the occupants of the body being blind to what the other occupant is up to – which is compatible with the other occupant having normal introspective access to what he or she or it is doing and to the intentions with which it is done.

Let us refer to the person performing the bulk of the actions realized in the movements of this body as "the agent," and let us refer to the person who professes introspective ignorance as to what is going on as "the agnostic." If anything would make it reasonable to say that the agent and the agnostic are one and the same person, it would be the fact that what the agent is doing fits with, and is "rationalized" by, beliefs and desire that can independently be ascribed to the agnostic. Now unless we *already* know that the agent and the agnostic are one, we cannot take the overall behavior of the agent/agnostic body as evidence of the agnostic's beliefs and desires – that will give us evidence of the *agent's* beliefs and desires, but whether these are the *agnostic's* beliefs and desires is just what is in question. If the only access we have to the agnostic's mental states are her avowals of ignorance about the agent's actions, then of course we have no access at all to her beliefs and desires. But let us suppose that these avowals of ignorance are part of a larger discourse in which various beliefs and desires are also avowed, and that the various parts of this discourse cohere in such a way as to make it reasonable to conclude that there is a single subject responsible for all of it. Then, perhaps, we could get enough information about the agnostic's beliefs and desires to know that they rationalize the agent's actions to such an extent that it is reasonable to conclude that those actions stem from those beliefs and desires and, therefore, that the agnostic and the agent are one.

Now if we, as observers, are in a position to conclude this, so is the agnostic. For it is the agnostic's introspective knowledge of her own beliefs and desires, as manifested in her utterances, that provides the basis of our reasoning; so, necessarily, the agnostic knows at least as much about her beliefs and desires as we do. On the other hand, if she didn't have this introspective knowledge, neither we nor she could even begin the enterprise of finding out whether the agent's actions are hers. The question of whether there can be self-blindness with respect to beliefs and desires will be discussed shortly. But what we have seen here indicates that whether or not it is necessary *simpliciter* that one have introspective access to one's beliefs and desires, it is necessary that one have such access if one is to have any access *at all*, even an inferential access, to one's intentions, volitions, and actions.

So it is a necessary condition of one's having knowledge of one's own agency, even inferential knowledge of it, that one *not* be self-blind with respect to one's beliefs and desires. It is a further question, which is too complex for me to take up here, whether introspective access to one's own beliefs and desires is sufficient, as well as necessary, for knowledge of one's own agency. If it is, self-blindness with respect to agency is impossible. I am inclined to think that this is so; but I will content myself here with the conclusion that knowledge of one's own agency is incompatible with self-blindness with respect to one's beliefs and desires.

V

What I have just argued could be turned into an argument against the possibility of a creature that is self-blind with regard to its own beliefs and desires by being supplemented with an argument against the possibility of a creature, suffering from no cognitive deficiency, that is incapable of having even inferential knowledge of its own agency. But instead of pursuing this line, I will argue directly against the possibility of self-blindness with respect to beliefs and desires. Here I shall be developing arguments I have presented elsewhere (see Essay 2 and my 1991).

Remember that as I have defined self-blindness, it is supposed to be like ordinary blindness in not entailing any *cognitive* deficiency. The person who lacks sight can in principle be equal in intelligence, rationality, and conceptual capacity to any sighted person. Likewise, the person who lacks access by inner sense to some kind of mental state, and so is self-blind with respect to that kind of mental state, can in principle be equal in intelligence, rationality, and conceptual capacity to someone who is not self blind.[3] What I shall be arguing, in the first instance, is that if someone is equal in intelligence, rationality, and conceptual capacity to a normal person, she will, in consequence of that, behave in ways that provide the best possible evidence that she is aware of her own beliefs and desires to the same extent that a normal person would be, and so is not self-blind.

I shall use the expression "rational agent" as short for "person with normal intelligence, rationality, and conceptual capacity," and I will use the expression "self-aware agent" as short for "person who has normal introspective awareness of his or her own beliefs and desires." Let us see why a rational agent will give every indication of being a self-aware agent.

First, consider what she will say. Rationality does not guarantee honesty, and it does not guarantee openness. But one thing that will be true

---

3 A qualification is needed here. It widely held that a person blind from birth would necessarily lack some concepts, namely color concepts, which normally sighted persons have. It does not seem obvious to me that this is right; but supposing it is, then it is not quite true that someone blind from birth could equal a normal sighted person in conceptual capacity. And, carrying the analogy along, perhaps there are some concepts that a self-blind person could not have. But notice that "blind" doesn't mean "blind from birth," and "self-blind" shouldn't be taken to mean "self-blind from birth." People who are blind but not blind from birth clearly can have concepts of particular colors; and presumably someone self-blind but not blind from birth can have whatever concepts any normal person has. Insofar as my argument depends on the possibility of the self-blind person being equivalent in conceptual capacity to a normal person, what the argument directly shows is the impossibility of a case in which someone has introspective access to the mental states in question long enough to acquire the relevant concepts, and then becomes self-blind. I think that if the impossibility of this is established, there will be little plausibility in the view that the corresponding sort of self-blindness from birth is possible.

of a rational agent, whether her intentions are honest or dishonest, is that she will answer affirmatively to the question "Do you believe that P?" if and only if she will answer affirmatively to the question "Is it true that P?" This is assuming, of course, that she has the relevant concepts and knows the meanings of the relevant words – in particular, the concept of belief, and the meaning of the word "believe." Mastery of those concepts and meanings, together with her rationality and intelligence, will be enough to make her appreciate the logical impropriety of affirming something while denying that one believes it, or denying something while affirming that one believes it, and so enough to make her give appropriate answers to questions about what she believes – true ones if her intentions are honest, false ones if she is out to deceive. But it will also make her realize that "I believe that P," said in a given context, necessarily has the truth value that an affirmative answer to the question "Do you believe that P?" would have in that context, and essentially the same effect on the audience; and this should dispose her to sometimes volunteer the statement "I believe that P" in circumstances in which she would respond affirmatively to the question "Do you believe that P?" if it were asked.

Similar remarks apply to desire. The rational agent who wants X and has normal mastery of language will, ceteris paribus, respond affirmatively to the question "Shall I give you X?" And given her mastery of the concept of desire, she will respond affirmatively to the question "Do you want X?" if she will respond affirmatively to the question "Shall I give you X?" So she will, unless she has devious motives, give correct answers to questions about what she wants. But since she knows, given her mastery of the relevant concepts, that it is true to say "I want X" just in case it is true to answer affirmatively to "Do you want X?", and that these are similar in their effects on others, whatever motivates her to answer affirmatively to the question of whether she has a certain want can be expected motivate her to volunteer the statement that she has that want in cases in which the question is not raised.

What these arguments establish, at least in the first instance, is only a connection between the ability to give verbal expression to beliefs and desires and the ability to self-ascribe them. But there is another pair of arguments that establishes a more direct connection between the having of beliefs and desires and the self-ascription of them – or at any rate the behavior we would take as evidence of such self-ascription.

Again let us begin with the case of belief. A rational agent who believes that P will be disposed to use the proposition that P as a premise in her reasonings. Moreover, she will know that for any proposition whatever, if that proposition is true then, other things being equal, it is in anyone's interest to act on the assumption that it is true – for one is most likely to achieve one's aims if one acts on assumptions that are true. She will also know that to act on the assumption that something is true is to act as if one believes the thing; and she will know that if it is in one's interest to act in this way it will normally be in one's interest to make manifest to others that one is so acting – this will increase the likelihood that other believers in the truth of the proposition will cooperate with her in endeavors whose success depends on the truth of the proposition, and it will tend to promote belief in that proposition within her community and so to promote the success of endeavors whose success depends both on the proposition being true and on its being believed to be true by participants in the endeavors. Knowing that it is in anyone's interest to act in these ways if a proposition is true, she will know that it is in her own interest to so act. So she can reason as follows: "P is true. So it is in my interest to act as if I believed that P and, in normal circumstances, to act in ways that would make others believe that I believe that P. Since the circumstances are normal, I should so act." Assuming that she is rational enough to act in conformity with the conclusions of her own practical reasoning, and to know what will make others believe that she believes something, this should lead her to behave in the ways characteristic of someone trying to manifest to others that she believes that P, including saying "I believe that P."

Similar considerations apply to wanting. Wanting that P be the case, unlike believing that P is the case, does not of course involve a disposition to use the proposition that P as a premise in one's reasonings. But it does involve, in a rational agent, conforming one's practical reasoning to the injunction "In the absence of reasons for not doing this, so act as to promote the likelihood of P's being the case." And the rational agent will know that in certain circumstances, namely when one is in the company of people who are cooperative and obliging, or willing to trade favors, presenting evidence that one wants something to be the case will increase the likelihood of its becoming the case. So when she is in such circumstances, the rational agent who wants it to be the case that P will be disposed to present evidence that she wants this, presumably including saying things like "I want it to be the case that P."

There is a worry about this pair of arguments. Consider the argument about belief. I said there that the rational agent who believes that P would be disposed to use the proposition that P as a premise in her rea-

238

sonings, and would have available an argument from this premise to the conclusion that she should act as if she believed that P, including saying things like "I believe that P," and I took this to show that such a rational agent could not be self-blind. But it is natural to reply to this that while such an argument is available, it is not by the use of such an argument that *we*, who have introspective access to our beliefs, come to make statements about our own beliefs. And, it seems natural to add, if it is *only* by the use of such arguments that a person could rationally come to such putative belief reports, then that person *would* be self-blind, even if nothing in her behavior could give away her self-blindness.

But this worry rests on a misunderstanding. The reason for pointing out that such reasoning is available is not to suggest that it regularly goes on in us – obviously it doesn't – but rather to point out that in order to explain the behavior we take as showing that people have certain higher order beliefs, beliefs about their first order beliefs, we do not need to attribute to them anything beyond what is needed in order to give them first-order beliefs plus normal intelligence, rationality, and conceptual capacity. What the availability of the reasoning shows is that the first-order states rationalize the behavior. And in supposing that a creature is rational, what one is supposing is that it is such that its being in certain states tends to result in effects, behavior or other internal states, that are rationalized by those states. Sometimes this requires actually going through a process of reasoning in which one gets from one proposition to another by a series of steps, and where special reasoning skills are involved. But usually it does not require this. I see an apple and I reach for it. It is rational for me to do so, and this can be shown by presenting an argument, a bit of practical reasoning that is available to me, in terms of my desires and my beliefs about the nutritional and other properties of apples. But I needn't actually go through any process of sequential reasoning in order for the beliefs and desires in question to explain and make rational my reaching for the apple. And no more does the rational agent need to go through a process of sequential reasoning in order for her first-order belief that P, plus her other first-order beliefs and desires, to explain and rationalize the behavior that manifests the second-order belief that she believes that P. (A different worry is discussed in Essay 2, §VI.)

This argument strikes at the heart of the perceptual model of self knowledge. From an evolutionary perspective it would certainly be bizarre to suppose that, having endowed creatures with everything necessary to give them a certain very useful behavioral repertoire – namely that of creatures with normal human intelligence, rationality, and conceptual capacity, plus the ability to acquire first order beliefs about the environment from sense-perception – Mother Nature went to the trouble of installing in them an *additional* mechanism, a faculty of Inner Sense, whose impact on behavior is completely redundant, since its behavioral effects are ones that would occur anyhow as the result of the initial endowment.

There is an additional argument against the possibility of self-blindness, which I can sketch only very briefly here.[4] Briefly, the idea is that it is essential to being a rational being that one be sensitive to the contents of one's belief-desire system in such a way as to enable its contents to be revised and updated in the light of new experience, and enable inconsistencies and incoherences in its content to be eliminated. In some cases, no doubt, the sensitivity responsible for belief and desire revision consists in the operation of automatic mechanisms that do not involve anything as cognitively sophisticated as introspective awareness. Perhaps this is always true in the case of lower animals. But in an important class of cases the rational revision or adjustment of the belief-desire system requires that we undertake investigations aimed at determining what revisions or readjustments to make – either "external" activities of conducting tests or experiments, or "internal" activities of constructing and evaluating arguments. Testing and argument construction are voluntary activities, which are the results of beliefs and desires that "rationalize" them. And here the beliefs will include higher-order beliefs, beliefs about the contents of one's belief-desire system. One does not test propositions at random, or evaluate arguments for arbitrarily chosen propositions. Where it makes sense to engage in such activities is where, for example, the outcome of the investigation will decide which of several ways of rendering one's belief system consistent is the best way; and to know this one must know a good deal about what the contents of that system are. It is because one believes certain things, and has apparent reason to believe certain other things, and because not all these things can be rationally believed together, that one initiates the particular course of investigation one does. What rationalizes the investigation are one's higher-order beliefs about what one believes and has reason to believe. Creatures without introspective access to their beliefs and desires would lack this resource for rational revision of these beliefs and desires, and would fall short of normal human rationality.

I want to make two final points in clarification of what I have said

4 See Essay 2 and Shoemaker 1991; also McGinn 1982.

about knowledge of one's beliefs. First, if we distinguish between "explicit" beliefs and "tacit" beliefs, all that I mean to commit myself to by my arguments is the view that a rational person who believes that P at least tacitly believes that she believes that she believes that P. An account of tacit belief I find very plausible is that of Mark Crimmins. He suggests that "A at-least-tacitly believes p just in case it is as if A has an explicit belief in p," where the right hand side of this can be paraphrased "A's cognitive dispositions are relevantly as if A has an explicit belief in p" (see Crimmins, 1992). My claim is that to the extent that a subject is rational, and possessed of the relevant concepts (most importantly, the concept of belief), believing that p brings with it the cognitive dispositions that an explicit belief that one has that belief would bring, and so brings with it the at least tacit belief that one has it.

My second point concerns my argument which starts from the point that a rational person who believes that P will be disposed to use the proposition that P as a premise in her reasonings. We should be clear that all of us regularly fall sort of the ideal of rationality here articulated. We do so, of course, when we repress beliefs, or are self-deceived about them. But we also do so in the more commonplace case in which we temporarily forget, or fail to access, something we perfectly well know – a good example of this is the case in which, having put one's watch in one's pocket so as to wash the dishes, one looks all over for it before remembering that one put it there.[5] In such cases one has a belief that is, perhaps only temporarily, not *available* for use as a premise, or as a guide to action. What my argument shows is that if a belief is available as a premise, then the subject will be disposed, insofar as she is rational, to act in ways that manifest the belief that she has it. But this is only part of what the "self-intimation" of beliefs, and its connection to rationality, amounts to. The other part consists in the fact that while one can have beliefs that are not available, the very having of a belief that P involves being disposed to have, under certain conditions, an available belief that P. It is a mark of rationality that one's beliefs will become available when there is occasion to use them, i.e., when one is faced with problems to which their contents are relevant. And here rationality differs in degree – some are more rational than others, and the same individual may be more rational about some matters than about others. But the minimal degree of rationality that is a necessarily condition of being a believer at all requires that there is at least a tendency of beliefs to become available

5 I take this example from Crimmins 1992.

under certain conditions. If states of a creature encoded information about the world, but did so in such a way that there was no tendency for this information to figure in the creature's reasoning or the guidance of its actions, those states would not count as beliefs. So an account of access to beliefs – and I think the same is true of desires and intentions – should have two parts. The first would be an account of how beliefs become available on appropriate occasions. I have said nothing about this, except that there must be a tendency for it to happen. The second would be an account of the relation between a belief's being available and the subject's believing that she has it. The latter is what my discussion here has mainly been about.

VI

If, as I have argued, it is of the essence of many kinds of mental states and phenomena to reveal themselves to introspection, what sort of account can we give of the relation of these to the introspective awareness of them? Take the case of belief, which I have just been discussing. A natural way of thinking is to say that the belief that P is one thing, the introspective belief that one believes that P is another, and that introspective awareness consists in the first giving rise to the second. Going with this is a way of thinking about how those mental states are realized in the brain. The belief that P is realized in one neural state, perhaps a highly distributed one, the belief that one believes that P is realized in another, and the brain is so wired that, under certain conditions, the first neural state gives rise to the second. This is what suggests that the existence of the belief should be logically independent of its being accessible to introspection, and that self-blindness with respect to belief ought to be a logical possibility. How are we to avoid this conclusion without denying, what seems obvious, that to believe something is not the same as to believe that one believes it? Here again we have the "distinct existences argument."

When we speak of the realization, or implementation, of a mental state, we should distinguish between what I call the *core realization* of it and what I call the *total realization* of it. The core realization will be a state that comes and goes as the mental state comes and goes, and which is such that, given relatively permanent features of the organism, it plays that "causal role" associated with that state – it is caused by the standard causes of the state, and causes its standard effects, usually in conjunction with other states. The total realization will be the core realization plus those relatively permanent features of the organism, features of the way its brain is "wired," which enable the core realization to play that causal role. So, for example, given the standard philosophical fiction about pain and C-fiber stimulation, C-fiber stimulation would be the, or at any rate a, core-realization of pain, while the (or a) total realization would be C-fiber stimulation plus those features of the way the brain is wired which make it the case that C-fiber stimulation is related as it is to bodily damage, to wincing and groaning, and to the desires and beliefs and distractions associated with pain.

This suggests a way, in fact two ways, in which a mental state and the belief that one is in that mental state could be different and yet such that it is of the essence of the mental state that under certain conditions it gives rise to that belief. One possibility is that while the two states have different core realizations, and so different total realizations, their total realizations overlap in a certain way. Suppose that the core realization of pain in us is C-fiber stimulation, and that the core realization of the belief that one is in pain is something we will call Z-fiber stimulation. While these are distinct states, it could be that the total realization of pain includes being such that under certain conditions C-fiber firing causes Z-fiber firing, and that the same thing is part of the total realization of the belief that one is in pain. If all of the possible total realizations of a state and of the belief that one is in that state were related in this way, it would be of the essence of that state that under certain circumstances it tends to give rise to that belief, and it might also be of the essence of that belief that in the absence of malfunctioning it is caused by that state. This would amount to the state's being self-intimating, and the belief's being, if not infallible, at least highly authoritative.

But this is not the only way in which we could get this result. Instead of the first-order state and the belief about it having different core-realizations but overlapping total realizations, it might be that they have the same core realization and that the total realization of the first-order state is a proper part of the total realization of the first-person belief that one has it. I suggest that this is how it might be when the two states are, respectively, an available first-order belief, say that the sun is shining, and the second-order belief that one has that first-order belief, say the belief that one believes that the sun is shining. What my earlier discussion suggested is that if one has an available first-order belief, *and* has a certain degree of rationality, intelligence, and conceptual capacity (here including having the concept of belief and the concept of oneself), then automatically one has the corresponding second-order belief. If it is possible to have the available first-order belief without having the second-order belief, this is because it is possible to have it without having that degree of rationality, intelligence, and conceptual capacity – which is perhaps the case with some lower animals. But on this conception, all you have to add to the available first-order belief, in order to get the second-order belief is the appropriate degree of intelligence, etc. It is not that adding this pushes the creature into a new state, distinct from any it was in before, which is the core realization of believing that it has this belief. It is rather that adding this enables the core realization of the first-order belief to play a more encompassing causal role, one that makes it the core-realization of the second-order belief as well as the core-realization of the first-order belief. The more encompassing role will include its contribution to the monitoring of person's belief-desire system, including the motivating of investigations aimed at revising the system in the direction of greater coherence. The more encompassing role will also include its contributing to the motivating of behavior, including speech behavior, aimed at intimating to others that the person has that belief.

If, as I have suggested, believing that one believes that *P* can be just believing that *P* plus having a certain level of rationality, intelligence, and so on, so that the first-order belief and the second-order belief have the same core realization, then it will be altogether wrong to think of the second-order belief in such cases as *caused* by the first-order belief it is about. Here the relation of an "introspective" belief to the state of affairs it is about is altogether different from the relation of a perceptual belief to the state of affairs it is about. In the other sort of case, where the first-order mental state and the belief about it have different core-realizations but overlapping total realizations, there is a sense in which the first-order state can cause the belief about it; it causes it in the sense that its core realization causes the core realization of that belief. And presumably that will be the standard way in which such a belief will be acquired. But this causal relationship is altogether different from the sort that holds between a perceived state of affairs and the perceptual belief about it. Thought of as a relation between the mental states, rather than between their core realizations, the relation is an internal one, whose relata are not "distinct existences." Either way, our introspective access to our own mental states differs markedly from our perceptual access to things in our environment.

But, to sum up, I think that the fundamental difference between perception and introspection is the failure of the latter to satisfy the "independence condition." Perception and introspection are of course alike in being modes of noninferential knowledge acquisition. But in the case of perception, the mechanisms involved are ones whose function it is to give us knowledge of an independent reality, one that was not made to be accessible to us and our faculties. In the case of introspection, on the other hand, the reality known and the faculty for knowing it are, as it were, made for each other – neither could be what it is without the other. The contrast is perhaps not *quite* as sharp as I have drawn it. From an evolutionary point of view, it may be that it is as much true that flowers developed the colors they have in order to be perceived by bees as that bees developed color vision in order to see the colors of flowers; flowers need bees for pollination as much as bees need flowers for nectar. And as my next lecture will emphasize, the features of things we perceive include ones that constitutively involve relations to perceiving creatures. Not everything we count as sense perception conforms even to the broad perceptual model. But the central cases of it do – and it is the assimilation of introspection to these that I have been campaigning against.

12

Self-knowledge and "inner sense"
Lecture III: The phenomenal character of experience

I

These lectures have been organized around the question of whether there is any good sense in which our introspective access to our own mental states is a kind of perception, something that can appropriately be called "inner sense." In my first lecture I distinguished two versions of the perception model of introspection, based on two different stereotypes of sense-perception. One of these, based primarily on the case of vision, is what I called the object-perceptual model – it takes perception to be in the first instance a relation to objects and only secondarily a relation to facts. I argued in my first lecture that introspection does not have nonfactual objects of the sort required to make this model applicable. The other, which does not require perception to have nonfactual objects, I called the broad perceptual model; its key tenet is that the existence of the objects of perception, whether they be factual or nonfactual, is independent both of their being perceived and of there being the possibility of their being perceived. The view that introspection conforms to this was my target in my second lecture, where I argued that it is of the essence of various kinds of mental states that they are introspectively accessible.

But one important issue was left dangling. If we had only such intentional states as beliefs and desires to deal with, the view that introspective awareness is awareness of facts unmediated by awareness of objects would seem phenomenologically apt. My awareness of a belief just comes down to my awareness that I believe such and such. This goes with the fact that the properties of beliefs that enter into the content of such awareness seem to be primarily intentional or representational properties, and include few if any of the "intrinsic" properties which, on the object-perception model, objects of perception ought to be perceived as having. But in the case of sensations, feelings, and perceptual experiences, things seem to be different. While a few philosophers have recently maintained that the only introspectively accessible properties of these are intentional ones, I think that the majority view is still that these have a "phenomenal" or "qualitative" character that is not captured simply by saying what their representational content, if any, is.[1] There is, in the phrase Thomas Nagel has made current, "something it is like" to have them. It is commonly held, and has been held by me, that the introspectable features of these mental states or events include nonintentional properties, sometimes called "qualia," which constitute their phenomenal character and determine what it is like to have them. While these qualia are taken to be themselves nonintentional, or nonrepresentational, they are held to play a role in determining the representational content of experiences; *within* the experiences of a single person, sameness or difference of qualitative character will go with sameness or difference of representational contents. But it is held to be conceivable that in different persons, or the same person at different times, the same qualitative character might go with different representational contents. Then we would have a case of "inverted qualia." The classic case of this is John Locke's example of spectrum inversion, in which one person's experiences of red are phenomenally like another person's experiences of green, and vice versa, and likewise for other pairs of colors (see Locke, *Essay* II,xxxii,15).

Qualia are often taken as paradigms of *intrinsic* properties. And insofar as our introspective awareness of sensations and sense experiences involves awareness of qualia, it may seem to satisfy one of the requirements of the object-perception model of introspection that is not satisfied by introspective awareness of beliefs and other intentional states, namely that it is in the first instance awareness of intrinsic properties of objects of the awareness. And there is in fact one conception of qualia that presupposes the object-perception model. Philosophers sometimes give as examples of qualia properties they call by such names as "phenomenal redness." This suggests a view according to which for each "sensible quality" S that we can perceive an external thing to have, there is a property, phenomenal S-ness, such that perceiving an external thing to be S involves "immediately" perceiving, or in some way being directly aware of, an internal "phenomenal object" that is phenomenally S. This is the much re-

---

1 For the view that all introspectively accessible features of experience are intentional, see Gilbert Harman 1990. There are similar views in William Lycan 1987, and Michael Tye 1991. The view advanced in this lecture can be seen as an attempt to reconcile the intuitions behind this view with belief in "qualia."

viled sense-datum theory of perception. If we reject this, we are left with the question of what conception of qualia, and of introspective awareness of them, we can accept if we do not accept the version that goes with the sense-datum theory.

But this question is inextricably bound up with others. There are questions about the relationship between the phenomenal or qualitative character of experiences and their representational content. And, closely related to these, there are questions about the status of, and the nature of our awareness of, the so-called "secondary qualities" of external objects – for the identity of the latter seems in some way bound up with the phenomenal character of our perceptual experiences of them. These collectively make up what I shall call the problem of phenomenal character.

II

Wittgenstein speaks of the "feeling of an unbridgeable gulf between consciousness and brain process," which occurs when I "turn my attention in a particular way on to my own consciousness, and, astonished, say to myself: THIS is supposed to be produced by a process in the brain! – as it were clutching my forehead" (Wittgenstein 1953, I, 412). The sense of mystery is all the greater, I think, if we replace "produced by" in Wittgenstein's expostulation with "consist in," getting "THIS is supposed to consist in a process in the brain." Wittgenstein goes on to comment on how queer this alleged business of "turning my attention on to my own consciousness" is. But we can get much the same puzzle without any attempt to turn our attention inward. I look at a shiny red apple and say to myself "THIS is supposed to be a cloud of electrons, protons, etc., scattered through mostly empty space." And, focusing on its color, I say "THIS is supposed to be a reflectance property of the surface of such a cloud of fundamental particles." Here we have, of course, the seeming disparity between what Wilfrid Sellars called the "manifest image," the world as we experience it, and what he called the "scientific image," the world as science tells us it is (see Sellars 1963). How, one wonders, can the color one experiences be any part or aspect of what the best scientific theory tells us is out there?

And it is not only in the case of such properties as color that we can generate perplexity about this disparity without any problematic turning of attention onto one's own consciousness. For consider the case of pain. The pain of a stubbed toe is, after all, experienced as being in one's toe, a part of one's body. Attending to such a pain, one may well be inclined to say to oneself, incredulously, "THIS is supposed to be a neural process in the brain!" For many of us the perplexity this generates is not dissipated by Wittgenstein's attempt to show that such remarks are, in a philosophical context, a case of language gone on a holiday.

In the first instance, then, the problem of phenomenal character isn't really a problem about the objects of *introspective* awareness. At least in the case of color, taste, smell, etc., it is about the objects of *perceptual* awareness. The case of pains, itches, tickles, etc., is tricky. There is a well established tradition of regarding these as mental entities, and that may make it seem that the awareness of them must be introspective. Yet, as I observed, we experience these items as being in one place or another in our bodies. Since the seventeenth century, at least, a prominent subtheme in discussions of these matters has been that despite differences in the way they are treated in ordinary language, pain and the secondary qualities are metaphysically on a par. In a few philosophers this has led to attempts to objectify pains – to construe them as states of the body which we perceive in having pain experience (See Graham and Stephens 1985, and Newton 1989). More commonly it has led to attempts to subjectify the secondary qualities – to construe them as features of sensations.

I will assume here that colors are where the contents of our visual experiences and our ordinary ways of talking place them – on the surfaces of physical objects, or in expanses of sky or water. Grass is green, the sky is blue, ripe tomatoes are red. But reflection on the disparity between the manifest and the scientific image makes inescapable the conclusion that, to put it vaguely at first, the phenomenal character we are confronted with in color experience is due not simply to what there is in our environment but also, in part, to *our* nature, namely the nature of our sensory apparatus and constitution. The intuition that this is so finds expression in the inverted spectrum hypothesis – it seems intelligible to suppose that there are creatures who make all the color discriminations we make, and are capable of using color language just as we do, but who, in any given objective situation, are confronted with a very different phenomenal character than we would be in that same situation, and it is not credible that such creatures would be misperceiving the world. But I think that the intuition is plausible independently of that. How *could* the phenomenal character we are confronted with be solely determined by what is in the environment, if what there is in the environment is anything like what science tells us is there? At the very least, the way things appear to us is determined in part by limitations on the powers of resolution of our sensory organs. And it seems obvious that it depends on the nature of our sensory constitution in other ways as well. There is good reason to think, for example, that the phenomenological distinction between "unique" hues such as red and "binary" hues such as orange is grounded in a feature of our visual system, and has no basis in the intrinsic physical properties of the objects we see as colored (see Hardin 1988).

I have deliberately used the vague phrase "the phenomenal character we are confronted with," which leaves it unspecified what is supposed to *have* this phenomenal character – the external objects perceived, or our subjective experiences of them. And the problem is, in part, about how to eliminate this vagueness. Looking at the matter one way, the obvious solution is to put the phenomenal character in the experiences. This gets us off the hook with respect to the problem of reconciling the manifest image with the scientific image, as the latter applies to the external objects – although it still leaves us, if we are materialists, with the problem of reconciling the manifest image, i.e., the phenomenal character, with what we think about the real nature of the mind itself. But, putting this latter problem on the side for now, locating the phenomenal character in the experiences seems to fly in the face of the phenomenology. For what seemed to pose the problem was the experienced character of redness, sweetness, the sound of a flute, and the smell of a skunk. And *these* are not experienced as features of sensations or sense-experiences; they are experienced as features of things in our environment.

If we insist on saying that the phenomenal character really belongs to experiences or sensations, it is hard to avoid the conclusion that our sense-experience systematically misrepresents its objects in the environment – that it represents them as having features that in fact belong to the experiences themselves. This is the view I have called "literal projectivism" – that we somehow project onto external objects features that in fact belong to our experiences of them.[2] But this seems, on reflection, to be unintelligible. I am looking at a book with a shiny red cover. The property I experience its surface as having, when I see it to be red, is one that I can only conceive of as belonging to things that are spatially extended. How could *that* property belong to an experience or sensation? Remember that an experience is an experienc*ing*, an entity that is "adjectival on" a subject of experience. It seems no more intelligible to suppose that a property of such an entity is experienced as a property of extended material objects than it is to suppose that a property of a number,

2 See Essay 5, The view I call literal projectivism has recently been advocated in Perkins 1983, and Boghossian and Velleman 1989.

such as being prime or being even, is experienced as a property of material things. The literal projectivist view may seem more palatable if the projected properties are said to be properties of portions of the visual field (see Boghossian and Velleman 1989). But that, if taken literally, amounts to a resurrection of the sense-datum theory, with all of its difficulties.

A different view is what I have called "figurative projectivism." This concedes that qualia, understood as properties of experiences, are not properties that could even seem to us to be instantiated in the world in the way in which colors, for example, are perceived as being. But it says that associated with each quale is a property that can seem to us to be instantiated in the world in this way – and that when an experience instantiates a quale, the subject perceives something in the world as instantiating, not that quale itself, but the associated property. The property is in fact not instantiated in the external object perceived, nor in any other object – its seeming to be instantiated there is a result of how the perceiver is constituted. That is what makes the view projectivist. But the property also is not instantiated in the experiences of the perceiver – that is what makes the projectivism figurative. In fact, on this view, the "secondary qualities" that enter into the intentional content of our experiences are never instantiated anywhere. They live only in intentional contents; in Descartes' terminology, they have only "objective" reality, never "formal" reality.[3]

This view has its own set of unattractive consequences. Like literal projectivism, it implies that our perceptual experience is incurably infected with illusion – that we cannot help but perceive things as having properties that they do not and could not have. In addition, while we can make sense of the idea of there being properties that are in some way

3 Such a view is suggested by Barry Stroud's formulation of the "theory of secondary qualities" in Stroud 1977, pp. 86–87. It also seems to be the view of John Mackie in Mackie 1976. Although in some passages the view Mackie attributes to Locke, with approval, seems to be literal projectivism, in the end it seems closer to figurative projectivism. For, on Mackie's reading, the resemblance thesis Locke affirms for primary qualities and denies for secondary qualities says, not that our ideas resemble things in the world with respect to their intrinsic natures (this is held to be false for the ideas of *both* sorts of qualities), but that the way external things are represented in our ideas resembles the way they actually are. Given that the rejection of this thesis as applied to secondary qualities and their ideas does not reduce to the rejection of the first resemblance thesis (that which is rejected for secondary and primary qualities alike), it amounts to figurative projectivism. There is a more recent expression of figurative projectivism in Averill 1992 – the "sensuous colors" that he says our experiences attribute to objects are not, he says (p. 569), instantiated "in any physically possible world."

represented in our experience but never instantiated in anything – e.g., the property of being a ghost – it is difficult, to say the least, to make sense of the idea that experienced color could be such a property. Granted that there are in fact no ghosts, we at least have some idea of what would *count* as someone veridically perceiving an instantiation of the property of being a ghost. But if we ourselves do not count as veridially perceiving the instantiation of redness-as-we-experience-it, I think we have no notion of what would count as veridically perceiving this.

Although it seems to me clearly unacceptable, figurative projectivism has some of the features that I think an acceptable account ought to have. It holds that the phenomenal character we are presented with in perceptual experience is constituted by some aspect of the representational content of our experience, thereby acknowledging the fact that we focus on the phenomenal character by focusing on what the experience is *of*. It holds that the properties that enter into this representational content, and in that way (i.e., by being represented) fix this phenomenal character, are not themselves features of our experiences – are not themselves qualia. But it holds that the qualia instantiated in an experience do determine the representational content that fixes the phenomenal character. Indeed, it holds that it is of the essence of any given quale that its instantiation by an experience makes a certain determinate contribution to that experience's representational content. But this is not to say that all aspects of the representational content of an experience are among the features that determine its qualitative character. For suppose Jack and Jill are spectrum inverted relative to each other. When both are looking at a ripe tomato, their experiences will be markedly different in phenomenal character, and so in one sense different in representational content – given that phenomenal character is determined by representational content. Yet I would want to say, and a figurative projectivist could agree, that the experiences of both represent the tomato, and represent it correctly, as being red. So the figurative projectivist need not say, and I think should not say, that redness is among those properties represented in our experience but not instantiated anywhere in the world, although he may want to say this of "redness-as-we-experience-it," on some understanding of that phrase. Further, the figurative projectivist would say, and I would agree, that despite the differences in phenomenal character, and representational content, between the experiences of Jack and Jill, there is no sense in which the experience of one of them is more or less true to the objective nature of what is experienced, namely the tomato, than the experience of the other. They experience the tomato differently, but not in

252

a way that makes the experience of one of them more or less veridical than the experience of the other. All of this I agree with. The question is how one can hold all this without going all the way with figurative projectivism and holding that the experiences of *both* Jack and Jill, each in a different way, misrepresent the tomato by representing it as having a property it does not have, and that, more generally, every visual experience represents its object as having properties that *nothing* in this world has?

Once these desiderata for a solution to the problem have been made clear, it begins to be clear what sort of solution it must have. How can the experiences of Jack and Jill represent the tomato differently and yet neither of them misrepresent it, given that the same information about its intrinsic nature is getting to both? This can only be because the different properties their experiences attribute to the tomato are *relational* properties. So the bare bones of the solution is this. Let Q1 be the quale associated with redness in Jack and let Q2 be the quale associated with redness in Jill. There is a relational property constituted by a relation to experiences with Q1. And there is one that is constituted by a relation to experiences with Q2. Jack's experience represents the tomato as having the first of these relational properties, and Jill's experience represents it has having the second of them. And in fact it has both. Neither property is the property of being red, which is also attributed to the tomato by the experiences of Jack and Jill. So while the contents of their experiences have something in common (both represent the tomato as being red), they also differ in a way that does not involve either of them misrepresenting the tomato.

Let us call these relational properties "phenomenal properties." What, more specifically, are they? They ought to be of a kind such that where, intuitively, the color experiences of two subjects are phenomenally the same, the subjects are perceiving (or seeming to perceive) the same property of this kind, and that where the color experiences of two subjects are phenomenally different, they are perceiving (or seeming to perceive) different properties of that kind. Assuming the possibility of spectrum inversion, this would mean that the properties should be of a kind such that different perceivers can, under the same objective conditions, perceive the same objective thing, or things of exactly the same color, to have different properties of that kind, and perceive things having different colors to have the same properties of this kind, this because of differences in their subjective constitutions. This rules out dispositional properties defined with respect to particular creatures or creatures with particular sorts of subjective constitutions. And as best I can see, the only properties that satisfy this requirement are the relational properties things have in virtue of actually causing experiences of certain sorts. E.g., if R is the quale that characterizes my experiences of red things, the phenomenal properties would include the property something has just in case it is currently producing an R-experience in someone related to it in a certain way, namely someone viewing it under normal lighting conditions. This, unfortunately, is a property nothing has when it is not being perceived.[4] But it satisfies, as I think no other actually instantiated property does, the prime requirement for being a phenomenal property. Subjects who are perceiving, or seem to be perceiving, the same property of this kind will necessarily be having color experiences that are phenomenally alike, and subjects who are having experiences that are phenomenally alike will be perceiving, or seeming to perceive, the same property of this kind.

But it is bound to be objected that it cannot possibly be the representing of such *relational* properties as these that constitutes the phenomenal character of perceptual experiences. We do not, at least ordinarily, experience things *as* affecting our experience in certain ways. The content of our experience is not relational in this way. Insofar as the difference between the experiences of Jack and Jill lies in what properties they ascribe to the tomato, it surely consists in what *monadic* properties they ascribe to the tomato.

But the way properties are represented in our experience is not an infallible guide to what the status – as monadic, dyadic, etc. – of these properties is. Reflection shows that the relation *to the right of* is, at least, triadic, but do we experience it as such? And consider *being heavy*. What feels heavy to a child does not feel heavy to me. Reflection shows that instead of there being a single property of being heavy there are a number of relational properties, and that one and the same thing may be heavy for a person of such and such build and strength, and not heavy for a person with a different build and strength. But when something feels heavy to me, no explicit reference to myself, or to my build and strength, enters into the content of my experience. Indeed, just because one is not oneself among the objects of one's perception, it is not surprising that where

---

4 I say "unfortunately" for two reasons. First, it is prima facie counterintuitive that properties we perceive to be instantiated in external things are properties whose *esse* is *percipi*. Second, if what I claim here is right, then there are cases of sense-perception, namely perception of phenomenal properties, that do not conform to what I have called the broad perceptual model.

one is perceiving what is in fact the instantiation of a relational property involving a relation to oneself, one does not, prereflectively, represent the property as involving such a relation. Thus it is that one naturally thinks of *to the right of* as dyadic.

Just as one's self is not among the objects one perceives, so the qualia of one's experiences are not among the objects, or properties, one perceives. And so these too are not explicitly represented in the content of one's experience. Does this mean that we are not introspectively aware of the qualia? Well, if I am right in my rejection of the perceptual model of introspection, we don't in any sense *perceive* them. But neither do we in any sense *perceive* the representational content, and the phenomenal character, of the experience. Introspective awareness is awareness *that*. One is introspectively aware that one has an experience with a certain representational content, and with the phenomenal character this involves. And if one reflects on the matter, and has the concept of a quale, this brings with it the awareness that one's experience has the qualia necessary to bestow that content and that character. But it would be wrong to say either that one is aware of what the qualia are like or that one is not aware of what the qualia are like. In the sense in which there is something seeing red is like, there is nothing qualia are like (just as, in that sense, there is nothing electricity is like, and nothing apples are like). What is "like" something in this sense is an experience, sensation, or whatever, or perhaps the having of an experience or sensory state, and being like something in this sense is a matter of having phenomenal character, which in turn is a matter of having a certain sort of representational content. The relation of qualia to this phenomenal character is not that of *being* it, and not that of *having* it, but rather that of being constitutive determiners of it. The qualia are determiners of it in two ways. It is partly in virtue of having the qualia it does that the experience represents what it does. And part of what it represents is the instantiation of a property, a "phenomenal property," which is in fact, although it is not explicitly represented as, the relational property of producing experiences having these qualia.

This account needs qualia because it needs a way of typing experiences that does not consist in typing them by their representational contents. It needs this because only so can there be properties whose identity conditions are given by saying that things share a certain property of this type just in case they are producing experiences of a certain type. Such types can be called phenomenal types. Sameness of phenomenal type, and likewise phenomenal similarity, is a functionally definable relation (see Shoemaker 1975a, 1975b, and 1982 and Essay 6). I shall say more about this later on; for now I will say only that qualia will be the features of experiences in virtue of which they stand in relations of phenomenal similarity and difference, and belong to phenomenal types. It is usual to characterize qualia as being, among other things, nonintentional features of experiences. But if, as I have suggested, the properties represented by our experiences include ones that are constituted by their relations to the qualitative character of the experiences, qualia will be very intimately related to a kind of intentional property. If, for example, an experience having quale R represents its object as having a phenomenal property, call it $R^\star$, which something has just in case it is producing R-experiences, then R will be necessarily coextensive with the intentional property an experience has just in case it represents something as having $R^\star$ in a way that involves having R.[5]

It is an important part of this view that what in the first instance we re introspectively aware of, in the case of experience, is it representational content. In this respect my view is similar to that of Gilbert Harman,

---

5 Suppose that someone has a remarkable perceptual sensitivity such that just by looking at someone viewing a red object she can see whether that object is producing in that person an R-experience, or just by looking at an object she can see whether it is apt to produce R-experiences in persons with a certain sort of perceptual system, even though she herself does not have that sort of perceptual system and is incapable of having R-experiences. It would seem that that person could have an experience with the intentional property *represents something as having $R^\star$*, but lacking the quale R. If this case is possible, it will hardly do to say that it is the possession of this intentional property that confers on the experience its phenomenal character. (I owe this objection to Michael Tye.) What this example shows is the need to distinguish between intentional properties that are "reference-individuated" and ones that are "sense-individuated." (I make this distinction in Essay 5.) If Jack is someone whose experience represents something as being $R^\star$ in virtue of having quale R, and Jill is someone with the remarkable perceptual sensitivity just imagined, then when both perceive something to be $R^\star$, their experiences will share the reference-individuated property *represents something as having $R^\star$*. But the senses, or modes of presentation, by means of which $R^\star$ is represented will be different, and Jill's experience will not have the sense-individuated intentional property that Jack's experience has. It is those sense-individuated intentional properties whose possession essentially involves having certain qualia that confer phenomenal character.

To at least one reader there has seemed to be a "whiff of circularity" here. But while $R^\star$ is defined in terms of R, there is no sense in which R is defined in terms of $R^\star$. And while it is true that in virtue of having R, an experience represents a property, $R^\star$, which is in fact a relational property that is defined in terms of R, this property is not represented *as* a relational property, and no reference to R enters into the content of the experience. Compare literal projectivism. According to it, an experience having R thereby represents an external object as having R; but although R is in fact a property of experiences, and is the very property whose possession by the experience gives it its representational content, it is not represented as being such. If, as I think, there is no circularity here (just implausibility), there is certainly none in my account.

who claims that the only introspectable features of experiences are their intentional or representational ones (See Harman 1990). Harman does not recognize the special class of intentional features that according to me determine the phenomenal character of experiences, namely those that represent relational properties that an object has in virtue of producing experiences with certain qualia. But let me focus for a moment on the point of agreement between him and me, namely that in the first instance introspective awareness is of representational content, or what comes to the same thing, of intentional features. What are the reasons for saying this?

One reason is phenomenological. As I have said already, if asked to focus on "what it is like" to have this or that sort of experience, there seems to be nothing for one's attention to focus on except the content of the experience. Indeed, it may seem at first that there is nothing to focus on except the external object of perception – e.g., the tomato one sees. Initially it may seem as though the question of what seeing the tomato is like can be none other than the question of what the visually detectable aspects of the tomato are. But then reflection makes one realize that one could be having the experience one does even if there were no tomato, and that there could be creatures whose experience of the tomato is different but who don't misperceive it. Even after this realization, however, one's attention remains fixed on the tomato – although now with the awareness that it doesn't matter, to the "what is it like" question, whether the tomato one sees is really there or is merely an intentional object. If one is asked to focus on the experience without focusing on its intentional object, or its representational content, one simply has no idea of what to do.

But this phenomenological fact goes with a fact about what our representational faculties are *for*, and what they presumably evolved to enable us to do. The most central fact about minded creatures is that they are able to represent aspects of their environment, both as they take it to be and as they want it to be, and to be guided by these representations of their environment in their interactions with it. In intellectually more sophisticated creatures the control over the world that is bestowed by this representational capacity is enhanced by a second-order representational capacity – a capacity to represent their own first-order representational states. But what this is in aid of is still effective representation of the environment (including the subject's own body). So it is not surprising that introspective awareness is keyed to representational states, and to the contents of these states.

257

Although I have focused on the example of visual experience, and in particular our experience of color, I think that what I have said can be applied to other sorts of perceptual experience – smell, touch, taste, and hearing. In all of these cases the phenomenal character of the experiences consists in a certain aspect of its representational character, i.e., in its representing a certain sort of property of objects, namely "phenomenal properties" that are constitutively defined by relations to our experience.

I think that the same account can also be extended to the case of pains, itches, and the like. When, for example, I have the experience I describe as a pain in my foot, my experience represents my foot as having a certain property. What property? The best available name for it is "hurting." This really is a property of my foot. But what it is for my foot to have this property is for its condition to cause me to have an experience having certain qualia. It is therefore a relational property. But I am not aware of it *as* a relational property, just as in my visual experience I am not aware of a red object *as* having a relational property defined in terms of a color quale. And my awareness of the quale of the pain experience, insofar as I am aware of it at all, is of the same sort as my awareness of the color quale; if you like, it is knowledge by description. What is primary here is a case of *perceptual* awareness – awareness of my foot as having a certain phenomenal property, namely hurting. Normally this goes with perceptual awareness of the foot that goes beyond awareness of it as having this property – e.g., feeling that it is bruised or cut. Going with this perceptual awareness of the foot hurting is introspective awareness *that* one is having an experience of one's foot hurting. And this should not be thought of as an inspection by inner sense of the quale that gives the experience this introspective character. There is no such inspection. The kinds of awareness there are here are, first, perceptual awareness of the foot, second introspective awareness (which is awareness *that*) to the effect that one is having an experience which, if veridical, constitutes such a perceptual awareness, and, third, the theoretically informed awareness that the experience has qualia that enable it to have the representational content it has.

I maintain that there is a sense in which our color experiences, our tactual, gustatory, etc. experiences, and our bodily sensation experiences have the same structure. This should not be taken to mean that color words, words for odors and tastes, and words like "pain" and "itch" all have the same sort of semantics, or express the same kinds of concepts. I doubt, for example, that "red" and "bitter" have the same sort of semantics. Consider Jonathan Bennett's example of phenol-thio-uria, which tastes bitter to three-quarters of the population and is tasteless to the rest (see Bennett 1968). If as the result of selective breeding, or surgical tampering, it becomes tasteless to everyone, I say it has become tasteless. And if more drastic surgical tampering makes it taste sweet to everyone, I say it has become sweet. But I don't think that if overnight massive surgery produces intrasubjective spectrum inversion in everyone, grass will have become red and daffodils will have become blue; instead, it will have become the case that green things look the way red things used to, yellow things look the way blue things used to, and so on. I think that our color concepts are, for good reasons, more "objective" than our concepts of flavors. Here the semantics of our terms reflects our interests. Our dominant interest in classifying things by flavor is our interest in having certain taste experiences and avoiding others, and not our interest in what such experiences tell us about other matters. With color it is the other way around; the evidential role of color dominates such interest as we have in the having or avoiding of certain color experiences.

Despite the differences between "red" and "bitter," both name properties of objects of perception, properties things can have when no relevant experiencing is going on. "Pain" does not name such a property. And probably "hurts" does not. If someone reports that there is a pain in his foot, we do not say that he is mistaken if there is nothing wrong with his foot and his feeling of pain is induced by direct intervention in his brain. And probably we do not say he is wrong in this case if he says that his foot hurts – although someone who said this would not seem wildly out of line. We could have had a usage in which the truth-value of a pain ascription depends on what is going on in the part of the subject's body in which she reports feeling pain; and there are recessive tendencies in that direction in our actual usage, as is shown by our uncertainty about how to describe cases of "phantom limb pain." But here again, the actual semantics reflects our interests. We have a strong interest in pain experiences, namely in avoiding them and getting rid of them, which is independent of our interest (which of course is not negligible) in what they reveal about the condition of our bodies. And this interest provides a reason for having an economical way of reporting and expressing these experiences – a way more economical than saying "I *seem* to feel a pain in my foot." But the phenomenology of pain experience, and the aspects of our usage of "pain" that reflect it (i.e., our speaking of pains as located in parts of our bodies), does not go comfortably with our truth conditions for pain ascriptions. The experience we report by saying that we feel a pain in the foot or the tooth does represent something about the foot or tooth; but we make the condition of the foot or tooth logically irrelevant to the truth of the pain ascription. In any case, what is important for my present purposes is that the differences in the semantics of "red," "bitter," and "pain" should not hide the similarities there are between the structure of our experiences of color, taste, and pain. The seventeenth century writers who were fond of comparing the status of the "secondary qualities" to that of pain were on to something right.

IV

What I have said so far goes only part of the way toward resolving the seeming disparity between the phenomenal character we are presented with in our experience of the world and our scientifically informed beliefs about what the true nature of the world is – or, in Sellarsian terms, between the manifest image and the scientific image. Placing the phenomenal character in the representational content, and pointing out that the representational content includes the ascription of properties things have in virtue of their relations to experiences, goes *some* way towards resolving this seeming disparity – it removes the appearance of disparity between the phenomenal character we are presented with and our beliefs about the objective nature of our external environment. But, as is often observed, it does not remove the seeming disparity between the phenomenal character we are presented with and our beliefs about the nature of the world as a whole, including our own minds – not if our minds themselves are physically constituted, and part of nature. It does not remove the "giddiness" Wittgenstein says accompanies the thought "THIS is supposed to be produced by a process in the brain."

The sense of a disparity here is related to several prominent themes in recent philosophy of mind. There is Frank Jackson's "knowledge argument." Jackson makes the plausible claim that no amount of physical information, either about states of affairs outside our heads or states of affairs inside them, would tell one what it is like to see red, or, in David Lewis's version, to taste vegemite.[6] And Jackson uses this to argue that physicalism must be false. There is also Joe Levine's "explanatory gap" argument (see Levine 1984). One has, Levine argues, no notion of what an

6 See Frank Jackson 1982. See also David Lewis 1990.

260

explanation would look like of why a given arrangement of the physical substrate of the world should give rise to experiences having a particular phenomenal character, rather than ones having a different phenomenal character structurally like that one. For example, one has no notion of what an explanation would look like of why, given that our physical constitution and that of the rest of the world is as it is, red things look to us the way they do rather than the way they would look if our spectrum were inverted. This, like Jackson's argument, seems to call into question whether the physical facts can be all of the facts, or can fix all of the facts.

I think that the best response to these worries is to show that the existence of these apparent disparities between manifest and scientific image is just what an acceptable physicalist theory should lead us to expect. What I shall argue is that a broadly functionalist view, combined with physicalism, predicts that we will be presented in experiences with a phenomenal character that is in a certain sense irreducible to its functional and physical underpinnings.

A good place to start is with the truism that, on any view, creatures with the capacity for perceiving their environments will have "quality spaces," in Quine's sense of that term (see Quine 1960 and 1969). For any given kind of such creatures, there will be physically different stimuli that are indistinguishable by creatures of that kind, in that they lack the capacity to respond differentially to such stimuli. And among the stimuli they can discriminate, some will be easier to discriminate than others. This imposes a similarity ordering on possible stimuli. The ordering will be relative to that kind of creature; the same stimuli may be ordered differently in the quality spaces of different kinds of perceivers. And, what goes with this, the similarity ordering for a given sort of creature is unlikely to "carve nature at its joints" to any significant extent – i.e., it is unlikely to coincide with the similarity ordering that a classification in terms of the principles of physics or chemistry would impose on the same stimuli. The quality space of a creature presumably evolves together with its dietary needs and tastes, its reproductive system and mating behaviors, its having a physical structure subject to certain kinds of damage from things in its environment, and countless other aspects of it that influence its interaction with its environment – and the structure of the quality space is more answerable to these than it is to the structure of the environment as represented in the "scientific image." Physically very different stimuli may be very close to one another in the similarity ordering, and physically very similar ones may be very far apart; this because of what the significance of these various stimuli is for the organism in the environment in which it lives. Among other things, the structure of the quality space will determine what sorts of conditioning the creature is subject to, and what sorts of inductions it is prone to make.

Corresponding to the multidimensional similarity ordering on stimuli that constitutes a creature's quality space will be a similarity ordering on internal states of the creature produced by these stimuli, internal states that have the function of being perceptual representations of the external objects or states of affairs which, in the creature's environment, are the standard causes of the various sorts of stimuli. The similarities and differences amongst these states that enter into this similarity ordering are what I call "phenomenal" similarities and differences. These are functionally definable relationships. Roughly speaking, perceptual states have the phenomenal similarities and differences they do in virtue of the roles they play in producing the behaviors that exhibit the quality space of the creature – the discriminations it makes, the kinds of conditioning it is capable of, the kinds of inductions it makes, and so forth. These roles will be more or less rich depending on the overall complexity and conceptual sophistication of the sensory and cognitive system of the creature in question. In relatively primitive creatures, the phenomenal difference between two sensory states may consist primarily in the fact that there are stimuli that produce one and not the other, and circumstances in which the presence of one of them elicits a bit of behavior, while the presence of the other does not. In more sophisticated creatures the existence of a phenomenal difference between sensory states may involve much more, including the formation of beliefs about objective differences in the environment, and beliefs about differences in how things appear.

Qualia I take to be the features of experiences in virtue of which they stand in these relations of phenomenal similarity and difference. They will stand to one another in relations of phenomenal similarity and difference in virtue of the roles they play in contributing to the phenomenal similarity or difference of the experiences that have them. The same experience may have many different qualia, and the overall similarity and difference relationships between two experiences will be a function of the similarity and difference relationships between the qualia instantiated in them. If, as I have said, the relations of phenomenal similarity and difference are functionally definable, then we should also be able to define in functional terms what the identity conditions of qualia are, and what it is to be a quale. That will be enough to allow qualia to be physically realized – and, moreover, to be physically realized in any of a variety of different ways. Letting R be the quale that characterizes my experiences of red things, it may well be that the physical property that is the realization or implementation of R on one occasion is different from that which is the realization or implementation of it on another occasion; all that is necessary is that these different properties stand in the right functional relationship of phenomenal similarity. So not only should we not expect similarities and differences in the qualitative character of our experience to line up with intrinsic similarities and differences between things in our environment, as these would be described by the "objective" sciences of physics and chemistry; we also should not expect them to line up with neurophysiological similarities and differences between the states of our brains and nervous system that are their realizations.

So the seeming disparity between the phenomenal character we are presented with in our experience of the world and our scientifically in-formed beliefs about the true nature of the world is due in part of the fact that, like any other biological species, we have a quality space that is to some extent idiosyncratic and tailored to our particular biological sit-uation and needs, and in part to the fact that qualia, like other mental properties, are "multiply realizable."

As I have argued elsewhere, the claim that the similarity relationships and identify conditions of qualia are functionally definable is compatible with the claim, first argued some years ago by Ned Block and Jerry Fodor, that individual qualia are not functionally definable.[7] If behav-iorly undetectable spectrum inversion is a possibility, then different col-or qualia may be in a certain sense functionally indistinguishable. They will occupy different locations in a "space" of qualia, but because of the symmetrical nature of that space it will be impossible to give a function-al description that applies to the one but not to the other − rather in the way that if one is describing in spatial terms a spatially symmetrical array of objects, then any description one gives of an object will apply as well to its symmetrical counterpart. If this is so, then color qualia will be "in-effable" in a way that goes beyond the irreducibility to particular physical properties that goes with multiple realizability.

Whether behaviorally undetectable spectrum inversion is possible, or more generally whether behaviorally undetectable "qualia inversion" is a possibility, is a hotly contested issue. And here different issues need to be sorted out. One issue is empirical. Is the structure of our color quality space symmetrical in such a way that two creatures having a quality space with that structure could differ in the way their qualia are linked with

7 See Block and Fodor 1972, and Shoemaker 1975 and 1982.

objective stimuli? Reasons have been given for saying that it is not: e.g., that there are fewer discriminable shades between certain of the "pure" colors (the "unique hues") than between others, and that colors that have been thought to be candidates for inversion, e.g., red and green, have phenomenological "polarity" features (e.g., red is experiences as a "warm" color and green as a "cool" one) that make them functionally discriminable.[8] To the best of my knowledge, the question of whether the quality spaces associated with other senses have the required sort of symmetrical structure has not been much investigated.

A different question, which seems to be more conceptual than empirical, is whether there could be creatures, psychologically pretty much like us, some of whose quality spaces are symmetrical. If there can be, then there can be qualia that are not functionally definable. There is not time for me to pursue this question in any detail here. I will simply say, without argument, what I think about it. First, I think that the answer is yes – it is possible that there should be such creatures. Probably we are not such creatures, but even that doesn't seem to me obvious. Second, I think that if the phenomenal character of our experiences can be realized physically, as I believe it is, the same could be true of the phenomenal character of the experiences of such creatures. Finally, and most controversially, I think that if it is so much as possible that there should be creatures that have symmetrical quality spaces, and so are subject to behaviorally undetectable qualia inversion, then it is also possible that there be creatures who share the same *a*symmetrical quality space and yet differ systematically in the phenomenal character of their experiences in the same objective circumstances – because the qualia instantiated in the experiences of one of the creatures are altogether different from those instantiated in the experiences of the other. And if this last claim is true, then individual qualia of ours are not functionally definable, whether or not our quality spaces are all asymmetrical in a way that precludes qualia inversion. (On these matters, see Essay 7.)

If this last is right, we have an account, compatible with a materialist view of mind, which predicts that the phenomenal character of experience will be ineffable, and so irreducible, in a very strong sense. But that would be the frosting on the cake, and I do not think that we really need it in order to dissipate the mystery that may seem to arise from the disparity between the way we experience the world, perceptually and intro-

---

8 The issue is addressed in Harrison 1973, Shoemaker 1975, and Hardin 1988, Chapter III.

spectively, and what the best science available tells us the true nature of the world is.

It may seem that there is something none of the considerations I have raised explains. How can it be true, indeed necessarily true, that whatever has a state with certain physical properties has *this* quale – or a quale that bestows *this* phenomenal character? (To simplify the discussion, I will pretend in the remainder of this section that what we have epistemological access to, and can make demonstrative reference to, are qualia, rather than the phenomenal properties and phenomenal characters that are grounded in them.) If the relation between the physical properties and the quale were a causal one, then answering this question would seem to require positing causal laws that are "brute" and "unintelligible." But of course, that isn't how I think of it. I take the quale to be physically realized, which I take to mean that an instantiation of the quale is nothing over and above the instantiation of one of the physical properties that realizes it. So the question becomes: how can it be necessarily the case that an instantiation of a particular physical property is identical with an instantiation of *this* quale? Well, part of the answer is that the property is, by hypothesis, one that plays a certain functional role, one that I claim to be constitutive of qualia. Suppose, to simplify matters, that just one quale is currently instantiated in my experience. I have a state with a certain physical property, one functionally suited for being a qualia instantiation, and the quale instantiated in my experience is *this* one. And so it is necessary that if something has this physical property, it has *this* quale. If it is felt that this does not make it intelligible how it can be necessary that whatever has a certain property has a certain quale, it seems fair to ask whether this differs from any other case in which an explanation is demanded of how something indicated indexically is identical with something indicated in some other way. E.g., how can it be necessary that the person who originated in a certain sperm and egg is *me*? Couldn't it have just as well been someone else? (Compare: couldn't the quale associated with this physical property just as well have been a different one?) Here the only explanation available consists of a general modal claim, the essentiality of origins, together with the empirical claim that humans originate in the fertilization of eggs by sperm, together with the brute fact that if you trace back my history you get to that sperm and egg. The explanation I have given is parallel; it combines a modal claim (necessarily any instantiation of a property satisfying a certain functional characterization is a quale instantiation), a general empirical claim (certain physical properties satisfy that functional characterization), and a matter of brute fact (I have a state with a certain physical property, and the only quale instantiated in my experience is this one). Of course, part of what creates the air of mystery here is that my epistemic access to my quale, and my ability to refer to it, requires no knowledge of functional role or physical makeup. (It is, indeed, part of the functional role of qualia that their subjects have this sort of epistemic and referential access to them – or, more accurately, to the associated phenomenal properties and characters.) But this has its counterpart in the fact that my first-person epistemic and referential access to myself requires no knowledge of essentially of origins and facts about sperm and eggs.

<h1 style="text-align:center">V</h1>

Let me now conclude by saying something about the bearing of all this on the general theme of these lectures, the question of whether introspection should be conceived on a perceptual model. I think that where philosophers find it most natural to think of introspection as a kind of perception is in those cases where we are confronted with "phenomenal character." In part this is because it is in these cases that it is most natural to adopt an "act-object" account of the mental states in question, thus making the object-perception model of introspection seem applicable. But it is also because we seem to have introspective access in such cases to properties that on the one hand seem to be mental properties, but on the other hand seem so closely related to the perceived properties of objects that it is easy to fall into confusing them with those properties. It is these that are supposed to determine the phenomenal character of experience, something which prereflectively we are disposed to think of as the character of the external objects of perception. If one takes these to be qualia, thought of as nonrepresentational features of experiences, it is natural to think that our awareness of them is perceptual. To suggest that we are merely aware *that* certain features are instantiated in our experience, without being presented in a perceptual or quasi-perceptual way with the instantiation of these features, seems false to the phenomenology of the matter – for it is, precisely, in being presented *perceptually* with the instantiation of sensible properties that we are confronted with phenomenal character, and while we have reasons for thinking that this phenomenal character has to do with our subjective constitution rather than the objective nature of the external objects perceived, it goes against the grain to deny that our access to it is in some sense perceptual.

On the account I have offered, we can do justice to the intuition that our access to phenomenal character is perceptual in two related ways. First, we can allow that in one sense we do perceive external objects to have phenomenal character – we perceive them to have "phenomenal properties" of the sort I characterized earlier, relational properties that constitutively involve a relation to qualia. But this access is a mode of sense-perception, not introspection, so its perceptual character gives no support to any perceptual model of introspection. Second, if we move to an access to phenomenal character that is introspective, what this is an access *to* is the representational content of perceptual experiences. So such introspective awareness occurs precisely in cases where we have or seem to have perceptual awareness of something, and it is an awareness of what it is that we are ostensibly perceiving. If we confuse *being aware of what it is that we are ostensibly perceiving* and *being aware of what we are ostensibly perceiving*, it will seem that the awareness is itself perceptual. But of course we should not confuse these. The first, unlike the second, is not perceptual awareness; it is simply awareness *that* one's perceptual experience has a certain representational content. Although normally when this occurs there is an object of which one is perceptually aware, and although what one is introspectively aware of in such cases is that one's experience represents an object of the sort that object is, it is not *by* being aware of that object that one is introspectively aware of this fact. For example, it is not *by* being perceptually aware of the apple that I am aware that I am having an experience as of an apple. Nor it is by being aware of any other object that one is aware of it. This is awareness of facts unmediated by awareness of objects.

On the face of it, three different sets of properties enter into this introspective awareness. There are the properties that the introspected experience represents the external object of perception as having. These are of course "sensible qualities," properties of the kind we have access to by sense-perception. But of course, relative to this introspective awareness these are merely "intentional objects"; what we introspect is not that these are instantiated, but that they are perceptually represented as being instantiated. What we do know by introspection to be instantiated are what we can call representational or intentional properties of experiences – e.g., the property that an experience has just in case that experience represents there being something red in front of one. As we noted in Lecture I, such representational properties are not promising candidates for being "intrinsic" properties, and so are not promising candidates for being the perceived properties of any sort of objects.

The third set of properties are qualia. Assuming that these are distinct

267

from the intentional properties they bestow on experiences, and that our introspective access is in the first instance to the latter, it would seem that we know the qualia themselves only "by description." We know them as those properties of experiences whose position in our quality space determines the phenomenal similarities and differences amongst our experiences, and as those properties that experiences must have if external objects are to have phenomenal properties. So regarded, these too are unpromising as candidates for being the perceived properties of any sort of objects. I have toyed with the idea that qualia should be simply identified with the intentional properties that represent phenomenal properties. I have not the space here to discuss the pros and cons of such an identification. But if we do make such an identification, which at the moment I am inclined *not* to do, then again qualia will be unpromising as candidates for being the perceived properties of any objects, for just the reasons that intentional properties are. So they are unpromising as candidates for that whether or not we make the identification. And if qualia are not the perceived properties of mental entities, I think it is safe to conclude that there are none.

References

Armstrong, D. 1963: "Is Introspective Knowledge Incorrigible?" *Philosophical Review*, 72, 417–432.

Armstrong, D. 1968: *A Materialist Theory of the Mind*. London: Routledge & Kegan Paul.

Armstrong, D. 1981: "What is Consciousness?" In *The Nature of Mind and Other Essays*. Ithaca: Cornell University Press.

Armstrong, D. 1984: "Consciousness & Causality." In *Consciousness & Causality*, by D.M. Armstrong and Normal Malcolm. Oxford: Basil Blackwell.

Averill, E. 1992: "The Relational Nature of Color." *Philosophical Review*, 101, 3, 551–588.

Bennett, J. 1968: "Substance, Reality and Primary Qualities." In C.B. Martin and D.M. Armstrong (eds), *Locke and Berkeley, A Collection of Critical Essays*. New York: Anchor Books.

Black, M. 1954: "Saying and Disbelieving." In his *Problems of Analysis*. London: Routledge & Kegan Paul.

Block, N. 1990: "Inverted Earth," *Philosophical Perspectives, 4, Action Theory and Philosophy of Mind*, 53–79.

Block, N., and Fodor, J. 1972: "What Psychological States are Not." *The Philosophical Review*, 81, 2, 159–181.

Boghossian, P. 1989: "Content and Self-Knowledge." *Philosophical Topics*, 17, 1, 5–26.

Boghossian, P., and Velleman, D. 1989: "Color as a Secondary Quality." *Mind*, 98, 81–103.

Burge, T. 1979: "Individualism and the Mental." *Midwest Studies in Philosophy*, IV, 73–121.

Castaneda, H.N., 1968. "Indicators and Quasi-Indicators," *American Philosophical Quarterly*, 4.

CIBA, 1993. *Experimental and Theoretical Studies of Consciousness*, Ciba Foundation Symposium, 174.

Clark, A. 1987: "From Folk-Psychology to Naive Psychology," *Cognitive Science*, 11, 2, 139–154.

Cottingham, J., Stroothoff, R., and Murdoch, D. 1984: *The Philosophical Writings of Descartes*, 2 Vols, Cambridge: Cambridge University Press.

Crimmins, M. 1992a: "Tacitness and Virtual Beliefs." *Mind and Language*, 7, 3, 240–263.

Crimmins, M. 1992b. *Talk About Beliefs*. Cambridge: MIT Press.

Curley, E.M., 1972: "Locke, Boyle, and the Distinction between Primary and Secondary Qualities." *The Philosophical Review* 88, 438–464.

Dennett, D. 1988: "Quining Qualia," in *Consciousness in Contemporary Science*, A.J. Marcel and E. Bisiach, eds., Oxford Science Publications, Oxford: The Clarendon Press, 42–77.

Dennett, D. 1991: *Consciousness Explained*. Boston: Little Brown.

Dennett, D. 1993a: "The Message is: There is no *Medium.*" *Philosophy and Phenomentological Research*, 53, 4, 919–931.

Dennett, D. 1993b: Review of John Searle, *The Rediscovery of Mind. Journal of Philosophy*, 90, 4, 193–205.

Dretske, F. 1981: *Knowledge and the Flow of Information*. Cambridge, Mass.: Bradford-MIT.

Dretske, F. 1993: "Conscious Experience," *Mind*, 102, 263–281.

Evans, G. 1982: *The Varieties of Reference*. Oxford: Oxford University Press.

Fodor, J. 1987: *Psychosemantics: The Problem of Meaning in the Philosophy of Mind*, Cambridge, MA: Bradford Books.

Frankfurt, H. 1971: "Freedom of the Will and the Concept of a Person," *Journal of Philosophy*, 68, 5–20.

Goldman, A.I. 1993: "The Psychology of Folk Psychology." *Behavioral and Brain Sciences*, 16, 15–28.

Graham, G., and Stephens, L. 1985: "Are Qualia a Pain in the Neck for Functionalists?". *American Philosophical Quarterly*, 22, 2, 72–80.

Grice, H.P., 1941: "Personal Identity," *Mind*, 50, 330–350. Reprinted in Perry 1975.

Grice, H.P., 1957: "Meaning," *The Philosophical Review*, 66, 377–388.

Grice, H.P., 1969: "Utterer's Meaning and Intentions," *The Philosophical Review*. 78, 147–177.

Hardin, C.L., 1988: *Color for Philosophers: Unweaving the Rainbow*. Indianapolis, Indiana: Hackett Publishing Company.

Harman, G. 1990: "The Intrinsic Quality of Experience." In J. Tomberlin (ed.), *Philosophical Perspectives, 4, Action Theory and Philosophy of Mind*, 31–52. Ascadero, CA: Ridgeview Publishing Co..

Harrison, B., 1973: *Form and Content*. Oxford: Blackwell.

Horgan, T. 1984: "Jackson on Physical Information and Qualia," *Philosophical Quarterly*, 34, 147–151.

Hume, D. 1888: *Treatise of Human Nature*. Ed. by L.A. Selby Bigge. Oxford: Oxford University Press.

Jackson, F. 1982: "Epiphenomenal Qualia." *Philosophical Studies*, 32, 127–136. Reprinted in Lycan, 1990.

Kant, I., 1953: *Critique of Pure Reason*, trans. by Norman Kemp Smith. London: Macmillan.

Kaplan, D. 1989: "Demonstratives." In J. Almog, J. Perry & H. Wettstein, *Themes From Kaplan*, 481–563. New York: Oxford University Press.

Kitcher, P. 1982: "Kant's Paralogisms," *Philosophical Review* 91, 515–548.

Kripke, S. 1980: *Naming and Necessity*. Cambridge: Harvard University Press.

Kripke, S. 1982: "Postscript: Wittgenstein and Other Minds," in *Wittgenstein on Rules and Private Language*. Cambridge: Harvard University Press.

Levine, J. 1984: "Materialism and Qualia: The Explanatory Gap." *Pacific Philosophy Quarterly*, 64, 354–361.

Lewis, D. 1979: "Attitudes De Dicto and De Se," *Philosophical Review* 88, 513–544.

Lewis, D. 1983: "Postscript" to "Mad Pain and Martian Pain," in *Philosophical Papers, Volume I*. Oxford: Oxford University Press, 130–132.

Lewis, D. 1990: "What Experience Teaches." In Lycan, 1990.

Loar, B. 1990: "Phenomenal States," *Philosophical Perspectives, 4, Action Theory and Philosophy of Mind*, 81–107.

Locke, J. 1975: *An Essay Concerning Human Understanding*, ed. by Peter H. Nidditch. Oxford: Oxford University Press.

Lycan, W.G. 1987: *Consciousness*. Cambridge Mass.: Bradford-MIT.

Lycan, W.G. 1990: *Mind and Cognition, A Reader*. Oxford: Basil Blackwell.

Mackie, J.L. 1976: *Problems From Locke*. Oxford: Oxford U.P..

McGinn, C. 1982: *The Character of Mind*. Oxford: Oxford University Press.

Mellor, H., 1978: "Conscious Belief." *Proceedings of the Aristotelian Society*, 78, 87–101.

Moore, G.E. 1922: "The Refutation of Idealism," in *Philosophical Studies*, London: Routledge & Kegan Paul. Originally published in *Mind*, 7, 1903, 1–30.

Nagel, T. 1974: "What is it Like to be a Bat?", *Philosophical Review*, 81, 2, 127–136.

Nagel, T. 1977: "Brain Bisection and the Unity of Consciousness." *Synthese* 22.

Nagel, T. 1986: *The View From Nowhere*. Oxford: Oxford University Press.

Nemirow, L. 1980: "Review of Nagel's *Mortal Questions*," *Philosophical Review*, 87, 3, 473–477.

Newton, N. 1989: "On Viewing Pain as a Secondary Quality." *Nous*, 23, 5, 569–598.

Nisbett, R, and Wilson, T. DeC., 1977: "Telling More Than We Know: Verbal Reports on Mental Processes." *Psychological Review*, 231–259.

Parfit, D. 1984: *Reasons and Persons*. Oxford: Clarendon Press.

Peacocke, C. 1989: "Perceptual Content." In J. Almog, J. Perry, and H. Wettstein, eds., *Themes from Kaplan*. New York: Oxford University Press.

Peacocke, C. 1991: "Scenarios, Concepts, and Perception." In T. Crane, ed., *The Contents of Perception*. Cambridge: Cambridge University Press.

Perkins, M. 1983: *Sensing the World*. Indianapolis, Indiana: Hackett Publishing Company.

Perry, J. 1975: *Personal Identity*. Berkeley: University of California Press.

Perry, J. 1977: "Frege on Demonstratives." *Philosophical Review*, 86, 474–497.

Perry, J. 1979: "The Problem of the Essential Indexical." *Nous* 13, 3–21.

Pitcher, G. 1970: "Pain Perception." *Philosophical Review*, 79, 368–393.

Putnam, H. 1975a: "The Meaning of Meaning." In Putnam, *Mind, Language, and Reality; Philosophical Papers, Vol. II*. Cambridge: Cambridge University Press.

Putnam, H. 1975b: "The Nature of Mental States." In *Philosophical Papers, Vol. II*.

Putnam, H. 1981: *Reason, Truth and History*. Cambridge: Cambridge University Press.

Quine, W.V.O., 1960: *Word and Object*. Cambridge, Mass.: MIT Press.

Quine, W.V.O., 1969: "Natural Kinds," in Ontological Relativity and Other Essays. New York: Columbia University Press.

Reid, T. 1801: *An Inquiry Into the Human Mind*, 5th edition, Edinburgh: A.D. Neill & Co.

Rosenthal, D., 1986: "Two Concepts of Consciousness." *Philosophical Studies*, 49, 329–359.

Rosenthal, D., 1993: "Thinking that One Thinks." In M. Davies and G.W. Humphreys, ed., *Consciousness*. Oxford: Basil Blackwell, 197–223.

Russell, B. 1912: *The Problems of Philosophy*. London: Oxford University Press.

Searle, J. 1980: "Minds, Brains and Programs," *The Behavioral and Brain Sciences* III, 3, 417–424.

Searle, J. 1992: *The Rediscovery of Mind*. Cambridge: MIT Press.

Sellars, W. 1963: "Philosophy and the Scientific Image of Man," in *Science, Perception and Reality*, London: Routledge & Kegan Paul.

Shoemaker, S. 1963: *Self-Knowledge and Self-Identity*. Ithaca: Cornell University Press.

Shoemaker, S. 1968: "Self-Knowledge and Self-Awareness." *Journal of Philosophy*, 65, 19, 555–567.

Shoemaker, S. 1970: "Persons and Their Pasts." *American Philosophical Quarterly*, 7, 4, 269–285.

Shoemaker, S. 1975a: "Functionalism and Qualia." *Philosophical Studies*, 27, 291–315.

Shoemaker, S. 1975b: "Phenomenal Similarity." *Critica*, 7, 20, 3–34.

Shoemaker, S. 1976: "Embodiment and Behavior." In A. Rorty (ed.), *The Identities of Persons*. Berkeley: University of California Press.

Shoemaker, S. 1979: "Identity, Properties and Causality." *Midwest Studies in Philosophy*, 4, 321–342.

Shoemaker, S. 1980: "Causality and Properties." In Peter van Inwagen (ed.), *Time and Change. Dordrecht, Netherlands: D. Reidel Publishing Company.*

Shoemaker, S. 1981: "Absent Qualia Are Impossible: A Reply to Block," Philosophical Review, 90, 4, 581–599.

Shoemaker, S. 1982: "The Inverted Spectrum." *Journal of Philosophy*, 79, 7, 357–381.

Shoemaker, S. 1984a: *Identity, Cause, and Mind*. Cambridge: Cambridge University Press.

Shoemaker, S. 1984b: "Personal Identity: A Materialist's Account," in S. Shoemaker and R. Swinburne, *Personal Identity*. Oxford: Basil Blackwell.

Shoemaker, S. 1991: "Rationality and Self-Consciousness." In K. Lehrer and E. Sosa, eds., *The Opened Curtain, A U.S.-Soviet Philosophy Summit*. Boulder, Colorado: Westview Press.

Shoemaker, S. 1993a: "Lovely and Suspect Ideas." *Philosophy and Phenomenological Research*, LIII, 4, 905–910.

Shoemaker, S. 1993b: "Special access lies down with theory-theory." *Behavioral and Brain Sciences*, 16, 78–79.

Shoemaker, S. 1994a: "Phenomenal Content." *Nous*, 28, 21–38.

Shoemaker, 1995: "Moore's Paradox and Self-Knowledge." *Philosophical Studies* 77. 211–228.

Smart, J.J.C., 1962: "Sensations and Brain Processes." In *The Philosophy of Mind*, V.C. Chappell, ed.. Englewood Cliffs, N.J.: Prentice Hall. This is a slightly revised version of a paper first published in *The Philosophical Review*, 68, 1959, 141–156.

Stalnaker, R. 1984. *Inquiry*. Cambridge MA: MIT/Bradford.

Stich, S. 1978: "Autonomous psychology and the belief-desire thesis." *The Monist* 61, 573–591.

Strawson, P.F. 1966: *The Bounds of Sense*. London: Methuen.

Stroud, B. 1977: *Hume*. London: Routledge & Kegan Paul.

Tye, M. 1986: "The Subjective Qualities of Experience." *Mind*, 95, 1–17.

Tye, M. 1991: *The Imagery Debate*, Cambridge, Mass.: Bradford-MIT.

Wilkes, K. 1988: *Real People: Personal Identity Without Thought Experiments*. Oxford: Clarendon Press.

Wittgenstein, L. 1953: *Philosophical Investigations*. Translated by Elizabeth Anscombe. Oxford: Blackwell.

Wittgenstein, L. 1958: *The Blue and Brown Books*. Oxford: Blackwell.

Index

absent qualia, 121–2, 125, 128
act-object conception, 8, 20–22,
    24, 209, 214–217, 220, 211,
    266
adjectival on, 10
after-images, 214–7, 219–20.
Albritton, R., 81n
Alston, W., 10n, 14n
Armstrong, D., 6, 23, 67n, 101, 189,
    193–4, 203, 207, 216–7,
    222–3, 225
assent conditions, 77ff, 87
attention, 218–20
Averill, E., 251n

belief, 61–2, 64, 69–70
    availability of, 80–1, 83, 86, 91–3,
        241
    knowledge of, 27–45
    tacit, 83, 92, 241
Bennett, J., 259
Berkeley, G., 208
Black, M., 74
blindsight, 123, 225–6
Block, N., 121, 134, 151n, 263n
Boghossian, P., 115n, 139n, 212–3,
    219, 250n,
Boyle, R., 105
brain in a vat, 57
Burge, T., 212

Cartesian dualism, 3, 24, 50
Cartesianism/anti-Cartesianism, 25–7,
    30, 50, 157, 224–5
Casteneda, H.N., 180

Clark, A., 129
cogito argument, 52–3
color, 97, 105–7, 136
consciousness, 191–2
content, wide vs. narrow, 59–60
copersonality, see mental unity, and
    unity of consciousness
Crimmins, M., 80, 83, 133n, 241
Curley, E.M., 105

Davidson, D., 32, 41n, 56, 69, 72
deliberation, 28. 30–1
Dennett, D., 69, 100, 121, 129, 132,
    143n, 151, 168
Descartes, R., 3, 25, 50, 52, 56, 251
desire, 60
    knowledge of, 31–4, 45–8, 238
distinct existences argument, 68–9,
    225, 242–5
Dretske, F., 207

Evans, G., 15n, 196n, 207n
externalism (about content), 212–3,
    218

Field, H., 65n
first-person agnosticism, 51–2, 70
first-person authority, 51, 55–8, 63–4,
    69, 72, 167, 171
first-person perspective, 54–5 157–
    75
Fodor, J., 60n, 129, 151n, 263
folk psychology, 125, 129–31, 139
Frankfurt, H., 29, 30
Freud, S., 49, 50, 101, 191, 225

275

276